PRAISE FOR
THE SPIRITUALITY OF IMPERFECTION

"A brilliant anthology of wisdom stories from all the great traditions centered around a most compelling and discerning issue."

—M. Scott Peck

"Filled with the fruits of compassionate wisdom, this book is a heartfelt understanding of our humanity that awakens and heals."

—Jack Kornfield, author of *Stories of the Spirit,
Stories of the Heart* and *A Path with Heart*

"The stories you tell may save someone's life. . . . *The Spirituality of Imperfection* is aimed at . . . anyone interested in an age-old tradition of spiritual literature that asks the hard questions of the human condition."

—*Asheville Citizen-Times*

The Spirituality of Imperfection

STORYTELLING AND THE
JOURNEY TO WHOLENESS

❖

Ernest Kurtz
and Katherine Ketcham

BANTAM BOOKS
New York Toronto London Sydney Auckland

To all who have, over the years, told us stories . . . but most of all to Richard Quinn, Robert MacNamara, Marvin Becker, Loren Baritz, Frank Freidel, Oscar Handlin, and William R. Hutchison, who taught us that history is the greatest story.

THE SPIRITUALITY OF IMPERFECTION
A Bantam Book

PUBLISHING HISTORY
Bantam hardcover edition published May 1992
Bantam trade paperback edition/January 1994

For permissions, please see page 294.
All rights reserved.
Copyright © 1992 by Ernest Kurtz, Ph.D., and Katherine Ketcham.
Book design by Kathryn Parise.
Library of Congress Catalog Card Number: 91-41088
ISBN 0-553-37132-0

Published simultaneously in the United States and Canada

Bantam Books are published by Bantam Books, a division of Bantam Doubleday Dell Publishing Group, Inc. Its trademark, consisting of the words "Bantam Books" and the portrayal of a rooster, is Registered in U.S. Patent and Trademark Office and in other countries. Marca Registrada. Bantam Books, 1540 Broadway, New York, New York 10036.

PRINTED IN THE UNITED STATES OF AMERICA
BVG   0 9 8 7 6 5 4 3 2 1

CONTENTS

❖

Part Three
EXPERIENCING SPIRITUALITY
157

A NOTE TO THE READER

❖

This book retells over one hundred stories. These stories—the stories that tell spirituality's story—came to us first by hearing. Some stories we first heard in school, or in church; some were told by a loved grandparent or a favorite aunt or uncle; and others, as we grew older, were shared by friends or acquaintances. In the process of researching those stories—exploring sources, examining different versions, looking for ways of making them more available to our readers—we came across a few "new" anecdotes, but the majority of the tales we re-tell have their first source in memories . . . memories of hearing that awaken yet other memories of living.

Some readers, with different memories, will recall different renderings of some of these stories; there are many favorite tellings of any tale. But, in truth, there are no new stories. Stories become "new" to us when something in our own experience makes us ready to hear them. Story-listening requires a childlike wisdom that combines innocence and experience, and no one can be both innocent and experienced in the presence of every story. And so not every reader will "get" every story, at least not "right away." Story, like the spirituality that it conveys, cannot be commanded or forced; it must float loosely within its vehicle, the better to lodge in each hearer's individual spirit.

One spiritual teacher cautions: "If you respect your listeners enough to tell the story, respect them enough to let them draw their own conclusions." And another master began one of his books with a story that consoles anyone who must confront the impossibility of "explaining" story:

A disciple once complained, "You tell us stories, but you never reveal their meaning to us."

Said the master, "How would you like it if someone offered you fruit and chewed it up before giving it to you?"

No one can find your meaning for you.

Not even the master.*

<hr>

* The notes on sources and related comments generally appear in the back of the book, beginning on page 245. The first quotation here is from William R. White, *Speaking in Stories* (Minneapolis: Augsburg, 1982), p. 20; the final story in the Introduction is adapted from Anthony de Mello, *The Song of the Bird* (New York: Doubleday-Image, 1982), p. 1.

The
Spirituality
of
Imperfection

An Introduction

THE STORY OF SPIRITUALITY

❖

Baseball teaches us, or has taught most of us, how to deal with failure.
We learn at a very young age that failure is the norm in baseball and,
precisely because we have failed, we hold in high regard those who fail
less often—those who hit safely in one out of three chances and become
star players. I also find it fascinating that baseball, alone in sport,
considers errors to be part of the game, part of its rigorous truth.

Francis T. Vincent, Jr.,
Commissioner of Baseball[1]

Baseball, as its Commissioner points out, teaches that errors are part
of the game and perfection is an impossible goal. Because his thought
fits as perfectly as possible the theme of this book, we offer this revision of Mr. Vincent's insight:

> Spirituality teaches us, or has taught most of us, how to deal with
> failure. We learn at a very young age that failure is the norm in
> life . . . errors are part of the game, part of its rigorous truth.

Discovering spirituality in the game of baseball is not so strange as
it sounds. For literally thousands of years, sages and saints have explored the ordinary and everyday in the attempt to understand the
extraordinary and divine. The ritual of the Japanese tea ceremony—
simply carrying and serving tea—is a profound spiritual exercise. The
posture of kneeling in prayer conveys acceptance and mindfulness.
Standing up in a crowded room and saying, "My name is John, and
I'm an alcoholic," calls forth the spiritual realities of humility, gratitude, tolerance, and forgiveness.

Spirituality takes many forms, and all spiritualities do not look on failure and imperfection in the same way. But through the centuries a recurring spiritual theme has emerged, one that is more sensitive to earthly concerns than to heavenly hopes. This spirituality—the spirituality of imperfection—is thousands of years old. And yet it is timeless, eternal, and ongoing, for it is concerned with what in the human being is irrevocable and immutable: the essential imperfection, the basic and inherent flaws of being human. Errors, of course, are part of the game. They are part of our truth as human beings. To deny our errors is to deny ourself, for to be human is to be imperfect, somehow *error-prone*. To be human is to ask unanswerable questions, but to persist in asking them, to be broken and ache for wholeness, to hurt and to try to find a way to healing through the hurt. To be human is to embody a paradox, for according to that ancient vision, we are "less than the gods, more than the beasts, yet somehow also both."

We are not "everything," but neither are we "nothing." Spirituality is discovered in that space between paradox's extremes, for there we confront our helplessness and powerlessness, our *woundedness*. In seeking to understand our limitations, we seek not only an easing of our pain but an understanding of what it means to hurt *and* what it means to be healed. Spirituality begins with the acceptance that our fractured being, our imperfection, simply *is:* There is no one to "blame" for our errors—neither ourselves nor anyone nor anything else. Spirituality helps us first to *see,* and then to *understand,* and eventually to *accept* the imperfection that lies at the very core of our human *be*-ing. Spirituality accepts that "If a thing is worth doing, it is worth doing badly."

Rabbi Zusya said, "In the coming world, they will not ask me: 'Why were you not Moses?' They will ask me: 'Why were you not Zusya?' "[2]

The spirituality of imperfection speaks to those who seek meaning in the absurd, peace within the chaos, light within the darkness, joy within the suffering—without denying the reality and even the necessity of absurdity, chaos, darkness, and suffering. This is not a spirituality for the saints or the gods, but for people who suffer from what the philosopher-psychologist William James called *"torn-to-pieces-*

hood" (his trenchant translation of the German *Zerrissenheit*). We have all known that experience, for to be human *is* to feel at times divided, fractured, pulled in a dozen directions . . . and to yearn for serenity, for some healing of our "torn-to-pieces-hood."

The Spirituality of Imperfection relates the continuing story of a spirituality that speaks to both the inevitability of pain and the possibility of healing *within* the pain. This story can be traced back thousands of years to Egyptian pharaohs, Hebrew prophets, and Greek thinkers. Beginning in the ancients' anguished questions about the nature of human life, the spirituality of imperfection took on new meaning with the dawn of Christianity and the seemingly endless, often inspired questions posed by the early Christians as they discovered the implications of their new way of life.

From the Desert Fathers and Mothers to Saint Augustine and Saint Francis, into the Renaissance and Reformation, the spirituality of imperfection was continually created and re-created, adapted and modified, told and retold. In the eighteenth century, Hasidic reawakening to ancient insight inspired a renewal of Jewish inspiration; at the same time, on the new American continent, the Puritan theologian and pastor Jonathan Edwards began delineating the "sense of the heart" that signaled the beginning of a uniquely American contribution to this onflowing stream of spiritual insight.

Through the nineteenth and twentieth centuries, this self-consciously imperfect tradition continued to challenge the very different, generally perfectionistic, expressions of spirituality that were the main response of most religions to the modern age.[3] As contact with Oriental cultures increased, so, too, did an appreciation for the variety of spiritual sensitivities and expressions. Within the Western tradition itself, unconventional thinkers from Søren Kierkegaard and Abraham Lincoln to William James and Carl Jung enriched the story with their insights into the wrenching realities of modern life.

And yet profound as these insights were, they found little expression in the daily lives of ordinary people. Most men and women in the twentieth century were cut off from this spirituality. They had no vocabulary and few concepts in which to articulate it, and the emphasis on perfection common to most religious expressions of the time suggested a different approach. Then, in 1934, the year historian Sidney Ahlstrom named *annus mirabilis*—"that year to be wondered at"

—the tradition of a spirituality of imperfection found a thoroughly modern voice.[4]

> On a chill, rainy afternoon in November 1934, two men sat catercorner at the kitchen table of a brownstone house in Brooklyn, New York. On the white oilcloth-covered table stood a pitcher of pineapple juice, two glasses, and a bottle of gin recently retrieved from its hiding place in the overhead tank of the toilet in the adjacent bathroom.
>
> The visitor, neatly groomed and bright-eyed, smiled gently as his tall, craggy-faced host reached for the bottle and offered him a drink.
>
> "No, thanks," Ebby said. "I'm not drinking."
>
> "Not drinking! Why not?" Bill was so surprised that he stopped pouring to look with concern at his old friend. "What's the matter?"
>
> "I don't need it anymore," Ebby replied simply. "I've got religion."
>
> *Religion? Damn!* For a fleeting moment, Bill wondered about his friend's sanity. Ebby, after all, was a drinking buddy from way back. Now, apparently, he had gone off the deep end—his alcoholic insanity had become religious insanity!
>
> Bill gulped a slug of gin. Well, dammit, not him. Religion was for the weak, the old, the hopeless; *he'd* never "get religion."[5]

Bill Wilson never did "get religion," but he did get sober, and unlike Ebby, who would die destitute after thirty more years of sporadic drinking, Bill stayed sober. How? Through a spiritual program that grew precisely from his realization that religion, with its canons and commandments, wouldn't work for him and the seemingly contradictory understanding that without help from a power greater than himself, he was lost. *"We must find some spiritual basis for living,"* Bill later said about himself and other alcoholics, *"else we die."*

Alcoholics Anonymous has been called the most significant phenomenon in the history of ideas in the twentieth century.[6] In the half century since William Griffith Wilson, Dr. Robert Holbrook Smith, and their first followers gave the new fellowship a name, A.A. has helped millions of alcoholics to get and to stay sober. More important for our story—the story of the spirituality of imperfection—many other individuals have found in the twelve-step program pioneered by Alcoholics Anonymous healings they were unable to find in either psychology or religion.

Why is this so? How does this happen? The answer is extraordinarily simple: A.A. taps into an ancient source of spiritual awareness, making available to modern men and women the long and rich tradition of the spirituality of imperfection. True to one hallmark of this tradition, it is the *unconventionality* of A.A.'s spirituality—its wariness of the dogma and directives of organized religion—that has appealed to so many men and women who, like Bill Wilson, could not find the answer to their despair in conventional religion. For although it insists on the necessity of "the spiritual" for recovery, A.A. has always presented its program as "spiritual rather than religious." The problem with organized religions, Bill Wilson once complained, "is their claim how confoundedly right all of them are."[7] The spirituality of imperfection that forms the heart and soul of Alcoholics Anonymous makes no claim to be "right." It is a spirituality more interested in questions than in answers, more a journey toward humility than a struggle for perfection.

The spirituality of imperfection begins with the recognition that trying to be perfect is the most tragic human mistake. In direct contradiction of the serpent's promise in Eden's garden, the book *Alcoholics Anonymous* suggests, "First of all, we had to quit playing God." According to the way of life that flows from this insight, it is only by ceasing to play God, by coming to terms with errors and shortcomings, and by accepting the inability to control every aspect of their lives that alcoholics (or any human beings) can find the peace and serenity that alcohol (or other drugs, or sex, money, material possessions, power, or privilege) promise but never deliver.

❖

Where and how did the earliest members of Alcoholics Anonymous discover this ancient "spirituality of imperfection" that would offer so much to the modern world? They were not, after all, great thinkers, at least not in the usual sense. They were everyday people who struggled, as we all do, with the ordinary tasks of daily living. Yet their experiences, drinking and newly sober, allowed them to assemble a patch-work quilt of spirituality, weaving threads borrowed directly and indirectly from the traditions of Greek, Jewish, and Christian thought that shaped the culture in which they lived, piecing together the thoughts and experiences of more than twenty-five centuries of spiritual thinkers.

So it is that in the spirituality of Alcoholics Anonymous, we can recognize the contributions of such spiritual geniuses as the Hebrew prophet Jeremiah and the Greek philosopher Socrates, of Church Fathers such as Ignatius of Antioch, of the Desert Fathers and Mothers, of the monks Basil and Gregory, of the saints Augustine and Benedict and Francis of Assisi, of mystics such as Julian of Norwich, of reformers as diverse as Calvin and Luther and Caussade, of the rabbinic commentators and the Baal Shem Tov, of William James and Carl Jung, of the brothers Niebuhr and D. T. Suzuki—to name but some of the most obvious influences. A.A.'s earliest members "tried on" the ideas and insights of these brilliant, often eccentric thinkers, and whatever matched their own experience became part of the patch-work.

"*Matched their own experience.*" The spirituality of imperfection is based in the lived acceptance of human limitations and powerlessness. In keeping with this tradition, Alcoholics Anonymous tested ideas not on the basis of some revelation or dogma but against the reality of everyday living. If a thought or idea didn't fit their own experience, it was rejected. More than anything else, then, A.A.'s Twelve Steps came to embody a spirituality that *works*, offering not just theory or technique but a way of life and a way of thinking with a language, traditions, and insights uniquely oriented to the realities of twentieth-century living.

The Spirituality of Imperfection tells the story of the ancient traditions of spirituality coming into contact with the modern world and its unique problems. In that collision between the old and the new, a spirituality many thousands of years old was both rediscovered and re-created. Who were the ancient architects of this spirituality, which reflects Greek, Jewish, Christian, and Eastern influences? What significance do their insights have for modern times? How did it happen that a bunch of twentieth-century drunks found their experience verified by (and verifying of) ancient wisdom? What are the changes that the twelve-step program brings about in the lives of so many and so varied inhabitants of the modern world? Why do alcoholics seem to need a spiritual program in order to stay sober? Why do so many people find a need for spirituality in their lives?

The Spirituality of Imperfection examines these questions, looking beyond A.A.'s Twelve Steps to the origins and significance of their inherent, abiding message. Following the tradition that we explore, we will attempt to tell our story of spirituality—both the ancient tale and its modern-day detailing in Alcoholics Anonymous—through myths, parables, and especially stories. For once upon a time, people told stories. In the midst of sorrow and in the presence of joy, both mourners and celebrants told stories. But especially in times of trouble, when "a miracle" was needed and the limits of human ability were reached, people turned to storytelling as a way of exploring the fundamental mysteries: *Who are we? Why are we? How are we to live?*

These most basic questions are spiritual questions, and so the stories that people told concerned spirituality. They also concerned imperfection—the limits experienced by those subject to failures of knowing and to other "unables" and "cannots." Without imperfection's "gap between intentions and results," there would be no *story*.

When the founder of Hasidic Judaism, the great Rabbi Israel Shem Tov, saw misfortune threatening the Jews, it was his custom to go into a certain part of the forest to meditate. There he would light a fire, say a special prayer, and the miracle would be accomplished and the misfortune averted.

Later, when his disciple, the celebrated Maggid of Mezritch, had occasion, for the same reason, to intercede with heaven, he would go to the same place in the forest and say: "Master of the Universe, listen! I do not know how to light the fire, but I am still able to say the prayer," and again the miracle would be accomplished.

Still later, Rabbi Moshe-leib of Sasov, in order to save his people once more, would go into the forest and say, "I do not know how to light the fire. I do not know the prayer, but I know the place and this must be sufficient." It was sufficient, and the miracle was accomplished.

Then it fell to Rabbi Israel of Rizhin to overcome misfortune. Sitting in his armchair, his head in his hands, he spoke to God: "I am unable to light the fire, and I do not know the prayer, and I cannot even find the place in the forest. All I can do is to tell the story, and this must be sufficient."

And it was sufficient.

For God made man because he loves stories.[8]

Listening to stories and telling them helped our ancestors to live humanly—to *be* human. But somewhere along the way our ability to tell (and to listen to) stories was lost. As life speeded up, as the possibility of both communication and annihilation became ever more instantaneous, people came to have less tolerance for that which comes only over time. The demand for perfection and the craving for ever more control over a world that paradoxically seemed ever more out of control eventually bred impatience with story. As time went by, the art of storytelling fell by the wayside, and those who went before us gradually lost part of what had been the human heritage—the ability to ask the most basic questions, the *spiritual* questions.

"One of our problems today is that we are not well acquainted with the literature of the spirit," the mythologist Joseph Campbell observed. "We're interested in the news of the day and the problems of the hour." Thus distracted, we no longer listen to those "who speak of the eternal values that have to do with the centering of our lives."[9]

"The news of the day and the problems of the hour." We have inherited a world that has lost all real sense of *time.* Our most common complaint is that we "have no time." We modern people are problem-solvers, but the demand for answers crowds out patience—and perhaps, especially, patience with mystery, with that which we cannot control. Intolerant of ambiguity, we deny our own ambivalences, searching for answers to our most anguished questions in technique, hoping to find an ultimate healing in technology. But feelings of dislocation, isolation, and off-centeredness persist, as they always have. What do we do with this confusion, this pain? How do we understand that inevitable part of life captured in the term *Angst*—the *anxiety* and *anguish* that seem an essential part of being alive today?

Spirituality hears and understands the pain in these questions, but its wisdom knows better than to attempt an "answer." Some answers we can only find: they are never "given." And so the tradition suggests: Listen! Listen to stories! For spirituality itself is conveyed by stories, which use words in ways that go beyond words to speak the language of the heart. Especially in a spirituality of imperfection, a spirituality of not having all the answers, stories convey the mystery and the miracle—the adventure—of being alive.

Two stories, one from the Far East and another from the Middle East, help to mark the boundaries of where—and how—we hope to go with "our" story:

The great master Mat-su, as a youth, was a fanatic about sitting in meditation for many hours at a time. One day, his patriarch's disciple Huai-jang asked him what on earth he hoped to attain by this compulsive cross-legged sitting.

"Buddhahood," said Mat-su.

Thereupon Huai-jang sat down, took a brick, and started to polish it assiduously. Mat-su looked at him, perplexed, and asked what he was doing.

"Oh," said Huai-jang, "I am making a mirror out of my brick."

"You can polish it till doomsday," scoffed Mat-su, "you'll never make a mirror out of a brick!"

"Aha!" smiled Huai-jang. "Maybe you are beginning to understand that you can sit until doomsday, it won't make you into a Buddha."[10]

If that story speaks to the limits of our endeavor, this story suggests the hope and, ultimately, the promise of our shared journey:

Time before time, when the world was young, two brothers shared a field and a mill. Each night they divided evenly the grain they had ground together during the day. Now as it happened, one of the brothers lived alone; the other had a wife and a large family. One day, the single brother thought to himself: "It isn't really fair that we divide the grain evenly. I have only myself to care for, but my brother has children to feed." So each night he secretly took some of his grain to his brother's granary to see that he was never without.

But the married brother said to himself one day, "It isn't

really fair that we divide the grain evenly, because I have children to provide for me in my old age, but my brother has no one. What will he do when he is old?" So every night he secretly took some of *his* grain to his brother's granary. As a result, both of them always found their supply of grain mysteriously replenished each morning.

Then one night the brothers met each other halfway between their two houses, suddenly realized what had been happening, and embraced each other in love. The story is that God witnessed their meeting and proclaimed, "This is a holy place—a place of love—and here it is that my temple shall be built." And so it was. The holy place, where God is made known, is the place where human beings discover each other in love.[11]

The spirituality of imperfection is such a place.

Part One

THE ROOTS OF
WISDOM

❖

*Wisdom is knowledge plus: knowledge—and the knowledge of its
own limits.*

Viktor E. Frankl[1]

We must find some spiritual basis for living, else we die.

BILL WILSON
PERSONAL CORRESPONDENCE

❖

Discovering an ancient spirituality in a roomful of drunks may seem strange, even paradoxical. Who would expect, walking into a smoke-filled room in a church basement, to encounter wisdom carved out by ancient Greeks, early Christians, Zen teachers, and Jewish scholars? Who would have thought that in the fellowship and program of Alcoholics Anonymous one would hear the voices of Aeschylus, Buddha, Saint Augustine, the Baal Shem Tov, William James, and Carl Jung? But then who would ever have believed, before A.A. came into being, that the two words *sober* and *alcoholic* could be spoken together with a straight face?

The spirituality of imperfection has always been characterized by the eccentric and unexpected, the unconventional and iconoclastic. In Part One, we will go back through time, seeking to mine the rich vein of wisdom that runs through all the centuries and culminates in modern times with the fellowship and program of Alcoholics Anonymous.

Be forewarned, however, that this will not be a systematic, straight-line pathway, beginning some thirty-three hundred years ago and progressing steadily into the twentieth century. This particular story is more of a *pilgrimage,* a wandering, digressing sort of journey that loops, spins, backtracks, sidesteps, repeats, and often contradicts itself. In one paragraph we may leap from the fourth to the twentieth century and back again, quote in the same breath Jean-Paul Sartre and Saint Augustine or Saint Francis of Assisi and Bill Wilson, and offer a Sufi story followed by a Hasidic tale or a Christian parable. In the end, few answers will be found—simply many, many more questions. But that is okay. Pablo Picasso offered a modern formulation of ancient thought about the importance of focusing on questions when he complained, "Computers are useless; they can only give you answers."[2]

The spirituality of imperfection is a spirituality of "not having all the answers." For those who have come to expect an answer to every question, a solution to every problem, and an end to every beginning, such an approach may be disconcerting at first. As we travel around in the past, rummaging through the different traditions, pulling out a thought here, relating a story there, revealing a way of seeing the world from over there, the reader may experience a sense of dislocation and disorientation. But continue on, for this seemingly disjointed wandering *is* the way of imperfection. By the end of this journey, the jarring notes, spatial dissonances, and cultural cacophonies will blend together into a sort of symphony, a chorus of separate, distinct, and sometimes off-key voices harmonizing into a whole . . . not *perfect* harmony, but harmony nonetheless.

Chapter 1

THE FRAGRANCE OF A ROSE

✧

Religion is for people who are afraid of going to hell; spirituality is for those who have been there.

Ross V.,
Member of Alcoholics Anonymous[1]

The disciples were absorbed in a discussion of Lao-tzu's dictum:

Those who know do not say;
those who say do not know.

When the Master entered, they asked him what the words meant.

Said the Master, "Which of you knows the fragrance of a rose?"

All of them knew.

Then he said, "Put it into words."

All of them were silent.[2]

What is spirituality? To have the answer is to have misunderstood the question. Truth, wisdom, goodness, beauty, the fragrance of a rose —all resemble spirituality in that they are intangible, ineffable realities. We may know them, but we can never grasp them with our hands or with our words. These entities have neither color nor texture; they cannot be gauged in inches or ounces or degrees; they do not make a noise to be measured in decibels; they have no distinct feel as do silk, wood, or cement; they give no odor, they have no taste, they occupy no space.

And yet they exist; they *are*. Love exists, evil exists, beauty exists, spirituality exists. These are the realities that have always been recognized as defining human existence. We do not define them, they define us. When we attempt to "define" spirituality, we discover not its limits, but our own. Similarly, we cannot *prove* such realities—it is truer to say that they "prove" us, in the sense that it is against them that we measure our human be-ing: the act and the process by which we exist. Life is not what we "have," or even what we do, connected as these may be: we are what and how and who we *are*, and *be*-ing is a real activity. Like "love," *spirituality* is a *way* that we "be."

This *way of be-ing* defies definition and delineation; we cannot tie it up, in any way package it or enclose it. Elusive in the sense that it cannot be "pinned down," spirituality slips under and soars over efforts to capture it, to fence it in with words. Centuries of thought confirm that mere words can never induce the experience of spirituality.

When the disciples of the Baal Shem Tov asked him how to know whether a celebrated scholar whom they proposed to visit was a true *zaddik*,* he answered:

"Ask him to advise you what to do to keep unholy thoughts from disturbing you in your prayers and studies. If he gives you advice, then you will know that he belongs to those who are of no account."[3]

"Words, as is well known, are the great foes of reality," wrote Joseph Conrad. But when words fail, where can we turn? In order to understand spirituality, in order to live a spiritual life, we must first be able to imagine ("image-in") such a life, to form a mental picture (a "re-presentation") of what it might look and feel like. But to do that, to *see* and *feel* spirituality, we need a deeper level of language to help us fathom our experience. And so, as people have done throughout the ages, we turn to metaphors, images, and stories.

---

* The *zaddik* is a teacher who lives an exemplary life, further described by one commentator as "an imperfect holy man."

"Metaphors govern understanding by suggesting that an unknown and ineffable entity, life, can best be understood as an activity one knows something about—pilgrimage, for example."[4] While *pilgrimage* is, perhaps, the most frequently used metaphor for the spiritual life, a modern spiritual writer uses another ancient example, that of *health:*

> Spirituality is a lot like health. We all have health; we may have good health or poor health, but it's something we can't avoid having. The same is true of spirituality: every human being is a spiritual being. The question is not whether we "have spirituality" but whether the spirituality we have is a negative one that leads to isolation and self-destruction or one that is more positive and life-giving.[5]

Images—detailed portraits or panoramic pictures stored in the mind's memory drawers—also have their role in moving our understanding toward the "standing-under" that is *experience,* a term that conveys a kind of "seeing" that both "thinks" and "feels." If we try to call forth spirituality in our imagination, do we envision a picture of some saint—Francis of Assisi, Albert Schweitzer, or Mother Teresa of Calcutta? Or perhaps a religious ceremony comes to mind—the echoes of ancient ritual in the Catholic Mass, the free-spirited enthusiasm of a revival meeting, the quiet serenity of a Quaker gathering. But still, something is missing. For while such images may help bring the concept of spirituality into finer focus, they fall far short of capturing the harmony of seeing, thinking, feeling that is spirituality.

But stories! Stories are the vehicle that moves metaphor and image into experience. Like metaphors and images, stories communicate what is generally invisible and ultimately inexpressible. In seeking to understand these realities through time, stories provide a perspective that touches on the divine, allowing us to see reality in full context, as part of its larger whole. Stories invite a kind of vision that gives shape and form even to the invisible, making the images move, clothing the metaphors, throwing color into the shadows. Of all the devices available to us, stories are the surest way of touching the human spirit.

In the third and fourth centuries, there lived in the wastelands of Egypt a group of individuals later named "the Desert Fathers," a rather ornery, unorthodox group of ascetics who committed themselves to a life of renunciation in an attempt to discover what it means to be human. Such curious practices as tying themselves to rocks for days on end, eating grass, or fasting for weeks at a time, were intended to extract information about the meaning—the *experience*—of life.

One of these individuals, the abba Poemen, was visited one day by a dignitary, who was most anxious to discuss his troubled soul and receive the monk's advice. But as soon as the visitor started talking, the abba averted his gaze and refused to speak to him.

Confused and distraught, the visitor left the room and asked one of the holy man's followers what was going on—why did the abba ignore him? The disciple spoke to abba Poemen, who explained, "He is from above and speaks of heavenly things, but I am of the earth and speak about earthly things. If he had spoken to me about the passions of his soul, then I should have answered him. But if he speaks about spiritual things, I know nothing of them."

Fortified with this knowledge, the dignitary tried again, beginning with the question, "What shall I do, abba, I am dominated by the passions of my soul?" And abba Poemen replied, "Now you are speaking rightly."[6]

In order to speak—and hear—"rightly," false assumptions about spirituality must be shattered. As the Poemen story suggests, the first supposition that requires revision is the belief that spirituality involves perfection. Spirituality has to do with the reality of the here and now, with living humanly as one is, with the very real, very agonizing, "passions of the soul." Spirituality involves learning how to live with imperfection.

"If you see someone going up to heaven by his own will," counseled John Kolobos, another of the Desert Fathers, "grab his leg and pull him down again." The search for spirituality brings down to earth, plants the feet firmly on the ground, and allows a vision of self as it is, as we are—imperfect and ambiguous. "Earthly spirituality" may sound like a contradiction, but it is instead paradox, and paradox is the nature of spirituality, for paradox is the nature of human beings.

Paradox has been defined as "an apparent contradiction": it combines two realities that don't seem to belong together, thus calling into question our assumptions about "seeming." In terms that would appeal to the boundary-stretching practices of the desert monks, the English essayist Gilbert Keith Chesterton described paradox as "Truth standing on her head to attract attention."[7]

❖

The core paradox that underlies spirituality is the haunting sense of incompleteness, of being somehow *unfinished*, that comes from the reality of living on this earth as part and yet also not-part of it. For to be human is to be incomplete, yet yearn for completion; it is to be uncertain, yet long for certainty; to be imperfect, yet long for perfection; to be broken, yet crave wholeness. All these yearnings remain necessarily unsatisfied, for perfection, completion, certainty, and wholeness are impossible precisely because we *are* imperfectly human —or better, because we are perfectly human, which is to say humanly imperfect.

This is the essential paradox of human life: We are always and inevitably incomplete, on the way, slipping and sliding, making mistakes. But the ancient voices insist that this is not failure; it is rather the necessary reflection of the paradox that we are. Paradox is the nature of *be-ing* human, of human being; paradox is the way it is meant to be, the way it *should* be, for it is the way we are made.

> Said the Lizensker Rebbe: "Only God is perfect. Man's actions must be basically defective in part. If one believes his good deed or holy study to be thoroughly pure and perfect, this is a sure sign that they are thoroughly bad."[8]

The lessons of the ancients are wise and continue to hold meaning for modern men and women. The search for spirituality is, first of all, a search for reality, for honesty, for true speaking and true thinking. At least from the time of the Delphic oracle's first admonition, *Know thyself*, the arch-foe of spirituality has been recognized to be "denial" —the *self-deception* that rejects self by attempting to repudiate the essential paradox that *is* our human be-ing. The philosopher Jean-Paul

Sartre termed such self-deception *mauvaise foi,* the "bad faith" of "the attempt to flee what one cannot flee—to flee what one is."[9]

A spirituality of imperfection suggests that spirituality's first step involves facing self squarely, seeing one's *self* as one is: mixed-up, paradoxical, incomplete, and imperfect. Flawedness is the first fact about human beings. And paradoxically, in that imperfect foundation we find not despair but joy. For it is only within the reality of our imperfection that we can find the peace and serenity we crave.

> Rabbi Elimelech Lizensker said: "I am sure of my share in the World-to-Come. When I stand to plead before the bar of the Heavenly Tribunal, I will be asked: 'Did you learn, as in duty bound?' To this I will make answer: 'No.' Again, I will be asked: 'Did you pray, as in duty bound?' Again my answer will be: 'No.' The third question will be: 'Did you do good, as in duty bound?' And for the third time, I will answer: 'No.' Then judgment will be awarded in my favor, for I will have spoken the truth."[10]

To speak the truth: spiritual writers such as Thomas à Kempis and August Hermann Francke found in that phrase one definition of prayer, for from flawedness flows the need for help. A spirituality of imperfection suggests that the first prayer *is* a scream, a cry for help. "O God, come to my assistance / O Lord, make haste to help me," reads Psalm 70, sung for over a millennium and a half at the beginning of each monastic hour. During the Reformation, John Calvin and others renewed this emphasis on the insight that humans could do nothing without God's help. And at the beginning of the modern age, the nineteenth-century nun Saint Thérèse of Lisieux rediscovered the original sense of prayer as a cry for help. From total darkness, in utter desolation, she cried out, echoing the call of the crucified Christ: *"J'ai soif!"* ("I thirst!"[11])

The insight is constant: Our darkness—our sins, our doubts—is a *thirst* . . . for "God," for "the spiritual," for *whatever* might alleviate this painful side of the human condition, for *whatever* might somehow fill the empty hole in our human be-ing. We seek help for what we cannot face or accomplish alone; in seeking help, we accept and admit our own powerlessness. And in that acceptance and admission, in the acknowledgment that we are *not* in control, spirituality is born. Spirituality begins in suffering because *to suffer* means first "to undergo," and the essence of suffering lies in the reality that it is *undergone,* that it has to do with *not* being in control, that it must be *endured.* We may endure patiently or impatiently, but because we are human beings, because we are not at each and every moment in ultimate control, we will suffer.[12]

A spirituality of imperfection is always mindful of the inevitability of suffering. As Simon Tugwell noted in his analysis of the *Ways of Imperfection:* "The first work of grace is simply to enable us to begin to understand what is wrong." And one of the first things that is "wrong" is that we are not "in control"; we do not have all the answers. The reality of that lack of control, the sheer truth of our powerlessness in the face of it, makes available the fundamental spiritual insight that insists on the necessity of *kenosis*—the ancient Greek term that signifies an "emptying out." Expressed in modern vocabulary, *kenosis* points to the need for "surrender," or, in the language of Alcoholics Anonymous, "hitting bottom." In the process of *kenosis*—emptying out, surrendering, hitting bottom—comes the realization that by ourselves, we are lost.[13]

The spirituality of imperfection begins in the recognition and rejection of human claims to be "God." The Hasidic tradition offers numerous stories intended to remind human beings that we are not in ultimate control, that we are not all-powerful, that we are not God. From the ancient Hebrew *shema* ("Hear, O Israel, I am the Lord, your God") to A.A.'s "First of all we had to quit playing God" is not a large leap.[14]

> When Rabbi Bunam was asked why the first of the Ten Commandments speaks of God bringing us out of the land of Egypt, rather than of God creating heaven and earth, he expounded: "Heaven and earth! Then man might have said: 'Heaven—that is too much for me.' So God said to man: 'I am the one who fished you out of the mud. Now you come here and listen to me.' "[15]

❖

"What is spirituality?" Our pursuit of the question has unearthed more questions than answers, more things that spirituality is not than features of what it is. Timeless wisdom suggests that spirituality can't be proven; it can't be defined; it is elusive, ineffable, unbounded; it does not involve demands for perfection; it is rooted in paradox; it is a cry for help.

Have we encountered an impenetrable roadblock in our pilgrimage, an unbridgeable chasm that mocks our need to know? If we can't define, prove, or somehow pin down spirituality, how can we ever hope to understand it? Rather than abandoning the quest, however, perhaps this very frustration signals that we should try a different route.

Traditions as diverse as the Buddhist, the Christian, and the Muslim agree that we speak most truly of the divine and therefore of "the spiritual" by recognizing what it is *not*. Somehow this process of the *via negativa,* the "negative way," in which we wander down divergent paths exploring what something is not, brings us closest to the place where we want to go. For there is a kind of spirituality in the recognition that in our effort to understand spirituality, we have encountered something bigger than our efforts to capture it. We discover a helplessness before the very word, the powerlessness that is the necessary beginning of spirituality itself.

T. S. Eliot described this spiritual path of the *via negativa* in "East Coker":

> In order to arrive at what you do not know
> You must go by a way which is the way of ignorance.
> In order to possess what you do not possess
> You must go by the way of dispossession.
> In order to arrive at what you are not
> You must go through the way in which you are not.
> And what you do not know is the only thing you know
> And what you own is what you do not own
> And where you are is where you are not.[16]

One word of necessary caution before setting out on this particular pathway. The *via negativa* or "route of negation," in which we come to know something by observing what it is not, has its own pitfalls—the dangers of comparison and judgment. When examining how one thing differs from another, there can arise a tendency to assign value and priority, to proclaim one reality better or more important than another. In what follows, then, we need to remember that this particular journey aims not to compare in order to put down, but only to identify the differences between distinct realities, *each* of which is valuable and useful. If we remain mindful of the risks, however, much can be learned by distinguishing *spirituality* from both *religion* and *therapy*.

Spirituality is not religion.

Distinguishing spirituality from religion is a slippery task. Some people equate the two, assuming that only religious people can lay claim to the title "spiritual." And yet those who try to live a spirituality of imperfection consistently present themselves as "spiritual rather than religious." What does this mean? Those who consider themselves "spiritual" and those who consider themselves "religious" seem to agree that there are differences between them, but those differences are only broadly delineated. Viewing religion, "the spiritual" see rigidity; viewing spirituality, "the religious" see sloppiness. Religion connotes boundaries, while spirituality's borders seem haphazard and ill-defined. The vocabulary of religion emphasizes the *solid;* the language of spirituality suggests the *fluid.*

Another image is offered by Walter Houston Clark, a modern student of religion and historian of the Oxford Group. Alcoholics Anonymous came into being within the Oxford Group, and A.A.'s earliest members left those auspices precisely because the non-alcoholic Oxford Group members seemed to them to be too "religious"— too insistent on fixed practices, too committed to perfection, as their demand for the effort to be "really maximum" attested. A lifelong observer of religious psychology, Clark suggested that religion often acts like vaccination: "One goes to church and gets a little something that then protects him or her against the real thing." Late in his life, Dr. Carl Gustav Jung expressed a similar view, remarking that "one of the main functions of formalized religion is to protect people against a direct experience of God."[17]

Those who think of themselves as "spiritual rather than religious" tend to equate religion with belief, and therefore with doctrine and authority; with worship, and therefore with the organization of community and its boundaries; with rewards and punishments, and therefore with greed and fear. Such negative consequences need not always follow from the religious impulse: they are indeed perversions of it. But as historian of theology Jaroslav Pelikan confessed with more than a little pain: "Religious belief is notorious for encouraging a sense of 'us' against 'them.' . . . The words of the hypocrite in the New Testament, 'God I thank thee that I am not as other men are,' are, unfortunately, a prayer that has been uttered, or at any rate felt, everywhere."[18]

How does spirituality differ from this? In the first place, spirituality has nothing to do with boundaries: Only the material can be bounded, and the first thing that "the spiritual" is not is material. The term *spirituality* was first used in ancient times as a contrast to materialism and signified attention to spiritual as opposed to material realities. "Spiritual realities" were understood quite simply as those that, like the wind or the fragrance of a rose, one experienced but could not literally see, touch, or especially, possess in the sense of *command*.

The word *spirituality* then fell out of usage for almost sixteen hundred years, when the postmodern age resurrected it, again as a contrast—but now less to "materialism" than to religion. The vocabulary of punishments and rewards, the motives of fear and greed, the sense of "us" against "them": Many modern people found religion more interested in closing boundaries than in opening them, more concerned with sanctions than with release, more an attempt to occupy space than to find it. Religion, in short, seemed to some to have sold out to the "material" world, to have adopted the same profane values that its rhetoric rebuked. As a contrast, then, to *both* "materialism" and religion—and perhaps especially to materialism *in* religion —spirituality came to be seen as the attempt to find a middle ground between religion and irreligion, a halfway house between total rejection and uncritical embrace of "the world" or "the culture" or whatever one names the context that both fascinates and threatens.[19]

Whether these be fair diagnoses or not, this is also the sense in which the fellowship of Alcoholics Anonymous presents itself as "spiritual rather than religious." For the simple truth is that, at least among most of the earliest A.A. members, bad connotations far outnumbered good when "religion" was mentioned. Many of them had tried to solve their "drinking problem" through religion, and because they had failed, they felt that "religion" had failed them. And because their experience and Bill Wilson's initial wariness of religion continue to abide at the very heart of the A.A. fellowship, Alcoholics Anonymous exemplifies the modern use of the word *spirituality*—a spirituality aware first of *its own* imperfection.[20]

Religion, of course, can also be aware of its own imperfections, as a delightful story conveys.

When the bishop's ship stopped at a remote island for a day, he determined to use the time as profitably as possible. He strolled along the seashore and came across three fishermen mending their nets. In pidgin English they explained to him that centuries before they had been Christianized by missionaries. "We Christians!" they said, proudly pointing to one another. The bishop was impressed. Did they know the Lord's Prayer? They had never heard of it. The bishop was shocked.

"What do you say, then, when you pray?"

"We lift eyes to heaven. We pray, 'We are three, you are three, have mercy on us.' "

The bishop was appalled at the primitive, the downright heretical nature of their prayer. So he spent the whole day teaching them the Lord's Prayer. The fishermen were poor learners, but they gave it all they had and before the bishop sailed away the next day he had the satisfaction of hearing them go through the whole formula without a fault.

Months later, the bishop's ship happened to pass by those islands again, and the bishop, as he paced the deck saying his evening prayers, recalled with pleasure the three men on that distant island who were now able to pray, thanks to his patient efforts. While he was lost in that thought, he happened to look up and noticed a spot of light in the east. The light kept approaching the ship, and as the bishop gazed in wonder, he saw three figures walking on the water. The captain stopped the ship, and everyone leaned over the rails to see this sight.

When they were within speaking distance, the bishop recognized his three friends, the fishermen. "Bishop!" they exclaimed. "We hear your boat go past island and come hurry hurry meet you."

"What is it you want?" asked the awe-stricken bishop.

"Bishop," they said, "we so, so sorry. We forget lovely prayer. We say, 'Our Father in heaven, holy be your name, your kingdom come . . .' then we forget. Please tell us prayer again."

The bishop felt humbled. "Go back to your homes, my friends," he said, "and each time you pray say, 'We are three, you are three, have mercy on us!' "[21]

Spirituality is not therapy.

Most people think of *therapy* as a modern concept, although the term originated in Homeric Greece, and its first connotation was of *spiritual* healing. In recent times, partially as a result of the practice of medicine being more and more transformed from art to science, most forms of therapy have also come to understand their "healing"—how they "make whole"—as other-than-spiritual. Therapy, in other words, has become *scientific:* attentive to measuring, demanding proof, relying on technique.

Although spirituality is not interested in measuring, proving, or manipulating, the boundaries between spirituality and therapy are often confused because both are concerned with *making whole.* We come to therapy and to spirituality when we are in pain, and therapy seeks what spirituality seeks: a mending to our brokenness, some soothing relief for our "torn-to-pieces-hood." Nevertheless, the paths of spirituality and therapy, while not in conflict, are divergent. A story told by an Episcopal priest relating her own experience may shed light on the difference.

Once, on her annual retreat, she sought out as confessor a Jesuit priest of long experience. In that context, she rehearsed with him the behaviors that troubled her, especially those prominent in the past year—a dawning area of insensitivity, a tendency to domination, and so forth. Then, drawing on what she had come to know of herself from recent reading and especially from her participation in groups, she began to detail how these behaviors seemed connected to her experience of being related to an alcoholic.

At that point, the grizzled veteran confessor reached out and, gently patting her hand, asked: "My dear, do you want forgiveness . . . or an explanation?"[22]

Therapy offers explanations; spirituality offers forgiveness. Both may be necessary, but one is not the other. The therapeutic approach looks to origins, to push forces that compel, as the psychological language of "drives" and the sociological focus on "the shaping environment" attest. Spirituality, in contrast, attends to directions, to the pull-force of motives, which attract or draw forward—the language of spirituality is the vocabulary of "ideals," of "hope." Therapy may release *from* addiction; spirituality releases *for* life.

Therapy relies, too, on the medical metaphor, using the lexicon of *illness:* Behavior is "symptomatic," situations are "dysfunctional," individuals are thought to be "sick" or "unhealthy." Spirituality prefers the language of *weakness* and *flaw;* choosing among various metaphors, it favors the ancient image of the archer's arrow falling short of its mark. Before the advent of Alcoholics Anonymous, alcoholics were taught to think of themselves as "orally fixated" or "latently perverted." One of A.A.'s great, freeing gifts to alcoholics can be found in its vocabulary of "defects of character" and "shortcomings."

Finally, therapy's goal is happiness, in the modern-day sense of "feeling good," while spirituality suggests that valid feeling follows be-ing, and that the more realistic goal is therefore the time-honored one of "being good," of finding a real fit between self and reality outside of self. As the root of the word *good* hints—*gê*, the same root as in the words *gather* and *together*—*goodness* involves fitting rightly, "fitting" not in the sense of some mere conformity but in the sense of discovering and embracing the whole of which one is part.[23]

❖

At least some forms of therapy—and of religion—tend to imply that we are either "all bad" ("total depravity") or "all good" ("I'm okay, you're okay"). A spirituality of imperfection suggests that there is *something* wrong—with me, with you, with the world—but *there is nothing wrong with that,* because that is the nature of our reality. That is the way it is, just because we are human, and therefore limited, flawed, and imperfect. The name of the game, according to this vision, is *I'm Not All-Right, and You're Not All-Right, But That's Okay— THAT'S All-Right.*

The ancient tradition that we are exploring, the tradition that finds its modern fulfillment in Alcoholics Anonymous, suggests that spirituality involves first seeing ourselves truly, as the paradoxical and imperfect beings that we are, and then discovering that it is only within our very imperfection that we can find the peace and serenity that is available to us. This is not an ideology claiming to have discovered immutable truths, but a vision celebrating experience and enabling choice; it is not a therapy interested in explanations and techniques, but a way of life; it is not exclusive, dogmatic, and authoritative, but open-minded, questioning, and capable of laughing at itself. The spirituality of imperfection is above all a *realistic* spirituality: It begins with acknowledgment and acceptance of the dark side, the down side, of human experience. Rather than seeking ways to explain away or ignore suffering and pain by focusing on sweetness and light, the spirituality of imperfection understands that tragedy and despair are inherent in the experience of essentially imperfect beings.[24]

"Man is the creature who wants to be God," Jean-Paul Sartre observed. The spirituality of imperfection wrestles directly with that quest, assuring that—although "first of all, we have to quit playing God"—whoever or whatever "God" is, He, She, or It does not scorn our quest or despise us for our defects and imperfections. Imperfection is rather the crack in the armor, the "wound" that lets "God" in. As Meister Eckhart wrote almost seven hundred years ago: "To get at the core of God at his greatest, one must first get into the core of himself at his least."[25]

In a modern expression of Eckhart's insight, Jungian analyst Marion Woodman identifies addiction as one of the "wounds" that lets "God" in:

Addiction keeps a person in touch with the god. . . . At the very point of the vulnerability is where the surrender takes place—that is where the god enters. The god comes through the wound.[26]

"God comes through the wound": Our very imperfections—what religion labels our "sins," what therapy calls our "sickness," what philosophy terms our "errors"—are precisely what bring us closer to the reality that no matter how hard we try to deny it, we are not the ones in control here. And this realization, inevitably and joyously, brings us closer to "God":

One of the disconcerting—and delightful—teachings of the master was: "God is closer to sinners than to saints."

This is how he explained it: "God in heaven holds each person by a string. When you sin, you cut the string. Then God ties it up again, making a knot—and thereby bringing you a little closer to him. Again and again your sins cut the string—and with each further knot God keeps drawing you closer and closer."[27]

Chapter 2

BEYOND THE ORDINARY

❖

What we call basic truths are simply the ones we discover after all the others.

Albert Camus

Concepts create idols; only wonder comprehends anything. People kill one another over idols. Wonder makes us fall to our knees.

Saint Gregory Of Nyssa[1]

One day Mohammed was offering morning prayer at the mosque. Among the people praying with the Prophet was an Arab aspirant.

Reading the Koran, Mohammed recited the verse in which Pharaoh makes the claim, "I am your true God." On hearing this the aspirant was so filled with spontaneous anger that he broke the silence and shouted, "The boastful son of a bitch!"

The Prophet said nothing, but after prayer was over the others began to scold the Arab. "Aren't you ashamed of yourself? You have surely displeased God because not only did you interrupt the holy silence of prayer but you used filthy language in the presence of God's Prophet."

The poor Arab trembled with fear, until Gabriel appeared to Mohammed and said, "God sends greetings to you and wishes you to get these people to stop scolding that simple Arab; indeed, his spontaneous profanity moved my heart more than the holy prayers of the others."[2]

Spirituality points, always, beyond: *beyond* the ordinary, *beyond* possession, *beyond* the narrow confines of the self, and—above all—*beyond* expectation. Because "the spiritual" is beyond our control, it is never exactly what we expect.

The word *spiritual* originally meant what the most obvious synonyms of *spirit*—breath, wind—signify: something that cannot be seen but that we nevertheless experience.

> Although the wind is very powerful and you can feel its presence, in and of itself it cannot be seen. You know it is there by its effect on others. The great trees, the grasses and waves on the sea bend with its force. If you are aware of your surroundings, you know it is there long before you feel it. So it is with the ineffable.[3]

In calling to mind a "picture" of the wind—an everyday reality that is *beyond* our visual grasp and control—we come closer to an understanding of the spiritual. Spirituality involves, first, an awareness —"if you are aware of your surroundings"—that comes not through the eyes, the ears, the hands, or any specific sense but through a larger openness, a general opening-up to life's experiences. And that awareness implies a sensitivity to others: We first discover that spirituality is there, in the world, because we notice its effects not in ourselves but on others. As the trees and the grasses bend with the force of the wind, so do human beings move within the force and power of the spirit, "in-spired" by it no matter how hard we try to take charge, no matter how adamantly we claim to be in control.

For spirituality is, always, *beyond control.* We can't hold it in our hands and touch it, manipulate it, or destroy it. Because it is *beyond* control, it is also *beyond possession:* We can't own it, lock it up, divide it among ourselves, or take it away from others.

Beyond all else, *spiritual* means "other-than-material." To those who first used the word *spirituality,* it signified "led by or lived by the Spirit." Such a life is lived in contrast to a life centered in material reality. It involves a different way of seeing, one wary of "appearances." Proverbs that capture the wisdom-sayings of the Hebrew and Christian scriptures remind that "charm is deceptive and beauty fleeting," advising that we "praise not a man for his looks and despise not a man for his appearance." For appearances tend to be illusory. "Least is the bee among winged things, but she reaps the choicest of harvests," as the biblical wisdom-writer illustrates.[4]

Appearances tend also to be irrelevant.

> The daughter of Caesar said to Rabbi Y'hoshu'a ben Hananya: "Why is glorious wisdom contained in an ugly vessel like you?"
>
> He said to her: "Does your father keep his wine in earthen vessels?"
>
> She said to him: "In what else should he keep it?"
>
> He said to her: "You people of importance should keep it in gold and silver!"
>
> She immediately went and told her father, who put the wine into golden and silver vessels. When it soured, Caesar confronted his daughter: "Who told you to do this?"
>
> She said to him: "Rabbi Y'hoshu'a ben Hananya."
>
> Caesar called the rabbi to him and asked: "Why did you tell that to my daughter?"
>
> "What she told me," the rabbi replied, "I told her."
>
> Caesar said: "But there are also beautiful people who are scholars?"
>
> "If they were ugly, they would be even greater scholars."[5]

Spirituality is discovered *beyond* immediate perceptions. Thus founded in a contrast with immediate perceptions, spirituality always involves both an affirmation—"Yes, there is something here"—and a rejection—"But there is more to it than meets the eye."

> Socrates believed that the wise person would instinctively lead a frugal life, and he even went so far as to refuse to wear shoes. Yet he constantly fell under the spell of the marketplace and would go there often to look at the great variety and magnificence of the wares on display.
>
> A friend once asked him why he was so intrigued with the allures of the market. "I love to go there," Socrates replied, "to discover how many things I am perfectly happy without."[6]

Material possessions are not "bad" in and of themselves, but as Socrates knew, the material realities that we possess tend also to possess us. The more we have, the more we want; and the more we want, the more we are possessed by our possessions. Spiritual reality, however, cannot be "possessed," any more than it can be said that we possess the wind or that we possess love, or wisdom. Spiritual and material realities differ in another fundamental way. Unlike material reality, spirituality is not inherently limited; one person having more spirituality does not mean that others will necessarily have less. Spirituality is instead the kind of reality that multiplies even as it is divided. "Virtue is as limitless as God himself," observed the Cappadocian monk Gregory of Nyssa:

> The possession of virtue . . . is always abundant for those who desire it, not like the possession of the earthly, in which those who divide it off into pieces for themselves must take their share from that of the other, and the gain of the one is the neighbor's loss. From this, because of hatred of loss, arise fights concerning wealth. But the wealth of [virtue] is unenvied, and he who [gains] more brings no penalty to him who is worthy of also participating equally in it.[7]

Spiritual realities are never commodities; they cannot be bought or sold. But while "spirituality" is other-than-material, it would be an error to think of spiritual realities as involving only such things as "virtue" or "goodness" or "love." We speak of *spirit* in many senses: School spirit, team spirit, and "morale" are all spiritual realities that do not decrease as more participate in them. Indeed, in some sense it is true that the more who participate, the greater the enjoyment of each participant. Who would want to be the only person in the stands for the homecoming game? Do parents love one child less after another is born?

The words *spirit* and *morale* help to convey the inherent attractiveness of spirituality: When we experience it, we want to take part in it. "If . . . you want what we have . . ." begins the key phrase that introduces the Twelve Steps in the chapter "How It Works" in the book *Alcoholics Anonymous*. What recovering alcoholics "have" is not a stake on ultimate wisdom or a lock on virtue, but a *way of life* that accepts imperfection as imperfection, permitting such spiritual qualities as "serenity" and "the joy of living" to coexist with such earthly realities as "defects" and "shortcomings." What hurting newcomers want when they first come to A.A. is not "sobriety," the reality of which they cannot even imagine, but *to be like that.* When we experience spirituality—when we *know it is there by its effects on others; when we know it is there long before we feel it*—we want to participate in it. But the crucial word here is *participate,* not *possess,* for only material realities can be possessed.

Around the end of the nineteenth century, a tourist from the United States visited the famous Polish rabbi Hafez Hayyim.

He was astonished to see that the rabbi's home was just a simple room filled with books. The only furniture was a table and a bench.

"Rabbi, where is your furniture?" asked the tourist.

"Where is yours?" replied Hafez.

"Mine? But I'm only a visitor here."

"So am I," said the rabbi.[8]

Greek thinkers, Hebrew prophets, Eastern sages, and Christian saints agree that the "problem" is not material realities but our attachment to material possessions—the attachment that hinders us from seeing and seeking our *own* good, the "goods" *proper* to us because they *fit* the spiritual reality into which *we* "fit." Material realities tend to stunt spirituality because as we possess them, they possess us. Possessions can lead to obsessions; consumers become consumed with getting things, keeping them, safeguarding them, adding to their hoard. Obsession with possessions crowds out the spiritual.[9]

The philosopher Diogenes was sitting on a curbstone, eating bread and lentils for his supper. He was seen by the philosopher Aristippus, who lived comfortably by flattering the king.

Said Aristippus, "If you would learn to be subservient to the king, you would not have to live on lentils."

Said Diogenes, "Learn to live on lentils, and you will not have to cultivate the king."[10]

The overwhelming attractiveness of Saint Francis of Assisi stems in large part from how well he epitomizes this understanding of spirituality. The son of a reasonably prosperous merchant, Francis was a happy, well-liked young man who enjoyed spending his father's money. His parents were concerned about Francis's extravagance, not so much because he liked to buy expensive clothing but because he then turned around and gave his new possessions to the poor. After a series of mystical experiences that moved him to take the admonitions of the Christian Gospel very literally, Francis embraced poverty with a completeness that may strike the modern mind as weird. It wasn't that the *Poverello* (Francis's nickname, which means "little poor man") believed material possessions to be "evil"; he loved the whole of creation too much to reject any part of it. Francis asked his followers to live in poverty because he believed that such a life-style would release them from self-centered demands for control. "Living without property," Francis once explained, "means never getting upset by anything that anybody does."[11]

In Saint Francis's understanding, material poverty creates an emptiness that may then be filled by spiritual reality. In renouncing our claim to possessions, we open ourselves to spirituality because we are also (and this is the more significant act) renouncing our self-will. Francis honored "Lady Poverty" because he believed that being without possessions makes it much less likely that we will insist on our own will . . . the willfulness that becomes the claim to be "God." Completely unprotected, we discover a new way of seeing: Rather than looking for what we don't have, we truly see what we do have. We learn to discern God's gift in everything that happens to us.

❖

"Beyond the ordinary"—*beyond* material, *beyond* possession, *beyond* the confines of the self. Spirituality transcends the ordinary; and yet, paradoxically, it can be found only in the ordinary. Spirituality is *beyond* us, and yet it is in everything we do. It is extraordinary and yet it is extraordinarily simple.[12]

Simple. The word is important, for "beyond the ordinary" is not meant to suggest something complicated, difficult, or self-consciously "special." Nothing is so simple (or so out of the ordinary for most of us) than "attending to the present," the focus on this day suggested by all spiritual approaches. Attending to the present—to the sacredness present in the ordinary if we can get *beyond* the ordinary—is, of course, a theme that pervades Eastern expressions of spirituality.

A Zen teacher saw five of his students returning from the market, riding their bicycles. When they arrived at the monastery and had dismounted, the teacher asked the students, "Why are you riding your bicycles?"

The first student replied, "The bicycle is carrying this sack of potatoes. I am glad that I do not have to carry them on my back!" The teacher praised the first student. "You are a smart boy! When you grow old, you will not walk hunched over like I do."

The second student replied, "I love to watch the trees and fields pass by as I roll down the path!" The teacher commended the second student, "Your eyes are open, and you see the world."

The third student replied, "When I ride my bicycle, I am content to chant *nam myoho renge kyo*." The teacher gave his praise to the third student, "Your mind will roll with the ease of a newly trued wheel."

The fourth student replied, "Riding my bicycle, I live in harmony with all sentient beings." The teacher was pleased and said to the fourth student, "You are riding on the golden path of non-harming."

The fifth student replied, "I ride my bicycle to ride my bicycle." The teacher sat at the feet of the fifth student and said, "I am your student."[13]

Agi quod agis. "Do what you are doing," urges a traditional admonition of classic Western spirituality. Eastern wisdom often interweaves with Western spirituality in the writings of the Trappist monk Thomas Merton. A friend of Merton recounts a story that the monk loved to tell on himself.

Once he met a Zen novice who had just finished his first year of living in a monastery. Merton asked the novice what he

had learned during the course of his novitiate, half expecting
to hear of encounters with enlightenment, discoveries of the
spirit, perhaps even altered states of consciousness. But the
novice replied that during his first year in the contemplative
life he had simply learned to open and close doors.

"*Learned to open and close doors.*" The quiet discipline of
not acting impetuously, of not running around slamming
doors, of not hurrying from one place to another was where
this novice had to begin (and perhaps end) in the process of
spiritual growth. "*Learned to open and close doors.*" Merton
loved the answer and often retold the story, for it exemplified
for him "play" at its very best—doing the ordinary, while
being absorbed in it intensely and utterly.[14]

An earlier story, a favorite one in the Western tradition, gently
teaches another important aspect of "beyond the ordinary": Spirituality does not connote *spectacular*. Saint Nicholas, an inspiration for our
modern figure of Santa Claus, has the distinction in the history of
spirituality of being one of the first individuals to be venerated as a
saint without first being a martyr. Virtually every saint before Nicholas performed the "miracle" of great heroism in the face of torture,
imprisonment, and death. In the fourth century, with peace, finally,
between the Roman state and the community of Christians, believers
searched for new models for their saints. They found one in Nicholas,
who impressed them as someone ready to help others anonymously
and for no personal advantage. His "miracle" was that of *constant and
singularly unselfish kindness in everyday life.*[15]

Fourteen hundred years after the death of Nicholas, a Hasidic
rabbi reflected a similar insight:

> The Belzer said to his wife that an "ehrlicher Yud," a truly
> pious Jew, a Jew par excellence, was dead. "Who is it?" in-
> quired his wife.
>
> "The Rabbi of Dinov," answered the Belzer.
>
> "Was he then, only an 'ehrlicher Yud,' and not a famous
> Rebbe?" was his wife's question.
>
> "There are many Rebbes," replied the Belzer, "but few
> truly pious Jews."[16]

Spirituality is not spectacular, but spectacularly simple, and that is precisely why we find it so difficult to define or describe. The profoundly simple is simply ineffable: It literally *cannot* be spoken. The Hebrew Bible portrays Moses and Jeremiah as protesting, when called by God, that they "cannot speak," a claim that has been interpreted by some scholars as evidence that these prophets labored under some kind of speech defect. This interpretation suggests two ideas: First, God chooses the least likely individuals to be divine spokespersons, and second, through this choice, God signals the ineffability—the literal "un-speakability"—of spiritual wisdom. The spiritual is simply *beyond* words.[17]

❖

The paradox of "beyond the ordinary yet not spectacular" reflects a central spiritual truth: the importance of avoiding the dichotomizing, dividing-into-two approach that is the bane of all spirituality. We tend to like our reality divided into neat and distinct parts, seeing it as either one or the other: either black or white, good or bad, answer or question, problem or solution. But the vision offered by the spirituality of imperfection cautions against that tendency, pointing out that the demand for an absolutely certain truth—the quest for a single, unalterable answer to our spiritual questions—involves the kind of "playing God" that denies and ultimately destroys our human reality. Precisely because we are *not* either-or, *not* one-or-the-other, paradox and ambiguity reside at the heart of the human condition and therefore at the heart of all spirituality. For we are *both:* both saint and sinner, both "good" and "bad," both less and more than "merely" human. In some strange (and not-so-strange) ways, our failures are our successes, our suffering is our joy, and our imperfections prove to be the very source of our longing for perfection.

Because paradox is at our very core, the spirituality of imperfection suggests that only by embracing the "dark side" of our ambiguous natures can we ever come to know "the light." We find ourselves only by giving up our selves, we gain freedom by submitting to the will of others, we attain autonomy by not insisting on our own rights. Sages and saints throughout the centuries have maintained that it is in this willingness to give up the self and give in to others that the road to human wholeness can be found. And for those who would give up "self," the first step is to give up certainty.[18]

> A rabbi was asked to adjudicate a case. The first man presented his argument, and the rabbi, after hearing his evidence, said to him, "You are right!"
>
> Then the second man presented his argument and the rabbi, after hearing his evidence, said, "You are right!"
>
> At this point, the rabbi's wife turned to her husband and asked, "How can both of these men be right?"
>
> The rabbi thought for a moment and then said, "Darling, you are right!"[19]

A more modern anecdote conveys the same insight. Donald Nicholl tells this story about the popular Austrian biographer Ida Friederike Görres and her husband Carl Josef.

> Ida told me that at the time when she and Carl Josef were preparing to marry she was an ardent teetotaller—and she could be fierce in her convictions. On the other hand Carl Josef, true Rhinelander that he was, enjoyed his wine. That was why Ida one day raised with Carl Josef the difficulties in their marriage which that difference might cause. "No difficulty," said Carl Josef quite calmly. "We shall not have wine in our home."
>
> Then, after they had been married some 20 years, Ida woke up one morning and said to herself, "Ida Görres, you are an awful prig! For 20 years you have deprived this good man of his wine." She immediately shared this revelation with Carl Josef who received the news with a smile and said, "Good! On my way home this evening I shall buy a bottle of wine, and we shall celebrate."[20]

❖

"Beyond the ordinary" . . . spirituality is that which allows us to get *beyond* the narrow confines of *self*. But another paradox lurks here, for our human task, as countless sages have suggested, is to get beyond

our selves without trying to escape ourselves. To get beyond the self to a place of interior peace where we are not obsessed with thoughts of material possessions, to get beyond the immediate concerns that dissipate us, we must first learn to put up with—to accept—our selfish, impatient, often recalcitrant human nature.

How grapple with this anomaly? How come to terms with our own paradox? "Rejoice every time you discover a new imperfection," suggested the eighteenth-century Jesuit spiritual director Jean-Pierre Caussade. If we find ourselves getting impatient, Caussade counseled, we can try to bear our impatience patiently. If we lose our tranquillity, we can endure that loss tranquilly. If we get angry, we ought not get angry with ourselves for getting angry. If we are not content, we can try to be content with our discontent. Caussade, the great Western apostle of an almost Zen-like "detachment," insisted above all that we must be detached from everything, even from detachment. The caution "Don't fuss too much about yourself" sums up Caussade's ultimate spiritual counsel.

And above all, don't fight the truth of yourself. The self "comes clean" when it is most exposed, most vulnerable to its own imperfection. In words written two hundred years before the founding of Alcoholics Anonymous, Caussade offered this paradoxically consoling vision of the experience that would come to be called "hitting bottom."

> The time will come when the sight of this wretchedness, which horrifies you now, will fill you with joy and keep you in a delightful peace. It is only when we have reached the bottom of the abyss of our nothingness and are firmly established there that we can "walk before God in justice and truth." . . . The fruit of grace must, for the moment, remain hidden, buried as it were in the abyss of your wretchedness underneath the most lively awareness of your weakness.[21]

In weakness, strength is discovered; in wretchedness, joy; in the "abyss of nothingness," "the fruit of grace." And so we need not escape ourselves to find peace or joy, for while spirituality is always *beyond*, it is discovered first within.

A man of piety complained to the Baal Shem Tov, saying: "I have labored hard and long in the service of the Lord, and yet I have received no improvement. I am still an ordinary and ignorant person."

The Besht answered: "You have gained the realization that you are ordinary and ignorant, and this in itself is a worthy accomplishment."[22]

Chapter 3

THE REALITY OF LIMITATION

❖

There is a crack in everything God has made.

Ralph Waldo Emerson[1]

It seems absolutely necessary for most of us to get over the idea that man is God.

Bill Wilson
Correspondence

A priest of the Greek Orthodox Church, Father Thomas Hopko, tells of a monk he met on Mount Athos.

> He was in a very bad state, very dark, very bitter, very angry. When asked what was the matter, he said, "Look at me; I've been here for thirty-eight years, and I have not yet attained pure prayer." And this other fellow on the pilgrimage was saying how sad he thought this was.
>
> Another man present said, "It's a sad story all right, but the sadness consists in the fact that after thirty-eight years in a monastery he's still interested in pure prayer."[2]

The image both troubles and consoles: the befuddled, bitter monk, unable to see that his futile quest for "pure prayer" is precisely the cause of his deepest anguish, and the observer recognizing not only the reality of the sadness but its source—the impossible ideal of perfection.

To deny imperfection is to disown oneself, for to be human *is* to be imperfect. *Spirituality,* which is rooted in and revealed by uncertainties, inadequacies, helplessness, the lack and the failure of control, supplies a context and suggests a way of living in which our imperfections can be endured. Spiritual sensibilities begin to flower when the soil is fertilized with the understanding that "something is awry." There *is*, after all, something "wrong" with us.

Throughout the centuries, spiritual writers and thinkers have expressed this experience of "awry-ness" as a sense of being off balance, out of kilter, ungrounded, fractured, broken, twisted, or torn apart. Almost twenty-five hundred years ago, Siddhartha Gautama, the Buddha, declared the first of his Four Noble Truths in three words: *Life is suffering*. To describe this suffering Buddha used the word *dukkha,* which means a bone or axle out of its socket, broken and torn apart from itself.

But perhaps the clearest exploration of this paradox can be found in the Desert Fathers. These ascetics went out into the desert in search of a setting that would allow them to explore the nature of the human be-ing that their faith told them had been "redeemed"; the desert became a laboratory for studying what it means to be human. The wastelands of Egypt and the hillsides of the Near East may seem distant from modern times and concerns, but these ancient spiritual teachers shaped the themes that would be analyzed and reformulated through the centuries, into modern times.

Their explorations depicted our human sense of alienation in terms of an inner tension or struggle. As early as the middle of the second century, the apostolic father Hermas described the conflict between the good and the bad angels within each of us. Because these spiritual forces can exert a powerful influence over us, we must take care, he warned, not to put our trust in "the wrong angel." Hermas offers no hope that we can entirely rid ourselves of the "bad angel" within us; he suggests not a plan for perfection but a program of survival . . . surviving our imperfections. We all sin, we all fall short, from time to time. The important question is: will we survive those fallings-short, our sins?[3]

To "survive our sins," they must be acknowledged *as sins:* accepting our imperfection, means accepting it *as* imperfection. For the Desert Fathers, such acceptance was the foundation of healing.

A brother said to the abba Poemen, "If I fall into shameful sin, my conscience devours and accuses me saying: 'Why have you fallen?' " The old man said to him, "At the moment when a man goes astray, if he says, 'I have sinned,' immediately the sin ceases."[4]

A more recent spiritual writer illustrates the necessity of accepting imperfection *as* imperfection with a modern story.

The chief executive of a large company was greatly admired for his energy and drive. But he suffered from one embarrassing weakness: each time he entered the president's office to make his weekly report, he would wet his pants!

The kindly president advised him to see a urologist, at company expense. But when he appeared before the president the following week, his pants were again wet! "Didn't you see the urologist?" asked the president.

"No, he was out. I saw a psychiatrist instead, and I'm cured," the executive replied. "I no longer feel embarrassed!"[5]

In our quest for spirituality, a chief danger is the temptation to change the rules. We attempt to escape our imperfection by redefining or lowering the standards necessary for "perfection" or by blaming our flaws and errors on someone else. The tradition of a spirituality of imperfection reveals such attempts for what they are—unnecessary. True healing follows the example of the early Christian church, which, rather than redefining the rules to allow anyone to declare himself perfect, sought to provide "a vision of life in which imperfections could be endured."[6]

Following the heyday of the desert hermits, who so strikingly explored the implications of this insight, the revered fourth-century Cappadocian Father, Gregory of Nyssa, described the only perfection that human beings can achieve as a "progress" that is never-ending, for the goal is ever-receding. Gregory's imagery paralleled that of the monk Macarius, who vividly portrayed the *journey* that had become the main monastic metaphor for the spiritual life as a process of falling and getting up again, building something up only to have it knocked down again.

According to Macarius, our imperfection—the weakness within us that allows sin—is beneficial, for it assures that we must "toil and struggle and sweat." The struggle itself proves our virtue, a synonym for *strength*, demonstrating that we are spiritually alive. "Unspeakable perfection" is unattainable because of the tension of the "two spirits" at work in us, but we can set a more realistic goal in which we refuse to lose heart when things are going badly and refuse to become complacent when things are going well. Neither extreme, Macarius assures us (and experience affirms), will last for long.

In the fifth century, Saint Augustine explored the tension between the flesh and the spirit, detailing how in this life everyone is to some extent defective and using this point to emphasize that no one is exempt from the need to seek forgiveness.[7]

Julian of Norwich set down in the fourteenth century an insight that T. S. Eliot would borrow from her in the twentieth: Sin is "behoovely"—*necessary* because without it there would be no sensuality. For Julian, "sensuality" involves the whole of human life, lived as it is within the confines of our bodies and our world; it is within our sensuality, she assures us, that God *wants to* dwell. "Sensuality" here, of course, signifies not its modern connotation of prurient sexuality but the reality of human life-as-a-whole, in all its earthy bodiliness.[8]

Midway in time between Julian and Eliot, the seventeenth-century philosopher Blaise Pascal wrote to his sister, Madame Perrier: "Christianity [is essentially] a confession of irreparable human infirmity. . . . Sickness is the natural state of a Christian." And we have already noted Caussade's suggestion, at the eighteenth-century dawn of the modern age, that we "rejoice" whenever we discover a new imperfection, for only when we learn how to put up with ourselves can we arrive at a place of interior peace.

In the nineteenth century Thérèse of Lisieux cried out from the depth of her loneliness and sorrow, "I have my faults, but I also have courage." And Leszek Kolakowski, a contemporary philosopher who began his own journey toward spirituality from within Marxism, suggests that "the Sacred is revealed to us in the experience of our failure," finding in all expressions of spirituality "the awareness of human insufficiency . . . the lived admission of failure."[9]

In this consistent vision, spirituality begins as an expression of what in human be-ing is incurable by human efforts. And it is an *expression:* not a philosophical or psychological description, not a theory, belief, opinion, or judgment, not dogma or doctrine or creed but *expression*—a howl of pain, a cry for help squeezed out of one's human core. "Lord, save me, whether I like it or not," one of the desert denizens prayed. "Dust and ashes that I am, I love sin."[10]

But if spirituality begins as a cry for help, it becomes a way of living with—of putting up with—our human imperfection. The saints and sages insist that imperfections be accepted as imperfections because such acceptance is necessary if we are to develop a vision of life and a way of living in which those imperfections can be endured and lived with creatively. And so the "second step" along that way involves accepting the uncertainties of life, refraining from asking for absolute assurances, and abandoning demands for perfection.[11]

The ancients knew something that many moderns, in their pursuit of "the perfect life," have forgotten. A critical error in the history of Western spirituality arises from the out-of-context quotation of the words of Jesus of Nazareth as recorded in the Gospel according to Matthew, Chapter Five, Verse 48: "Therefore be ye perfect as your Heavenly Father is perfect." The term *perfect* is translated from the Greek *teleios,* which means more accurately "fully complete." Verses 43 to 48 form a unit, the theme of which is the breadth of the love of the Father, who "lets His rain fall on the just and the unjust alike." When taken in context, then, the point of the admonition to "be perfect" is to be compassionate in a way that treats *all* others fairly, equally.

> You have learnt how it was said: *You must love your neighbor and hate your enemy.* But I say this to you: love your enemies and pray for those who persecute you; in this way you will be sons of your Father in heaven, for he causes his sun to rise on bad men as well as good, and his rain to fall on honest and dishonest men alike. For if you love those who love you, what right have you to claim any credit? Even the tax collectors do as much, do they not? And if you save your greetings for your brothers, are you doing anything exceptional? Even the pagans do as much, do they not? You must therefore be *teleios* as your heavenly Father is *teleios.*[12]

As the very concept of a "Heavenly Father" or any kind of "Higher Power" implies, spirituality is founded in the recognition and acceptance of one's creatureliness and finitude. There is, of course, "something wrong" with us: Finite beings, we thirst for the infinite. "Man is the creature who wants to be God," as Sartre sadly observed. But we are not God, and given our human nature, spirituality suggests not "I'm okay, you're okay," but "I'm not okay, and you're not okay, but that's all right."

This presents a difficult challenge for the modern mind, which tends to view problems from the perspective: "If it's wrong, it can be fixed." The corollary runs: "If we cannot fix it, then there must be nothing wrong." But if "nothing is wrong," then there is no need for spirituality. In a perfect world, there would be no spirituality at all. The *perfected* is the completed, that which is finished, ended. But because we are human, we are not and *cannot* be finished or ended while we are still alive. Imperfection is related to limits. As humans, we do not "have" limits; we *are limited*. Something *is* wrong and it *cannot* be "fixed." Whenever that reality of limitation is denied or rejected, spirituality suffers.

In 1937 in New York, and in 1939 in its other center, Akron, Ohio, the members of Alcoholics Anonymous departed Oxford Group auspices. Many factors weighed, but among the heaviest loomed the Group insistence on their "Four Absolutes": Absolute Honesty, Absolute Purity, Absolute Unselfishness, and Absolute Love.

These ideals are still mentioned in some A.A. groups, but co-founder Bill W. spoke for the fellowship as a whole in a 1940 letter in which he responded to a critic of A.A.'s abandonment of the "Four Absolutes":

> The ideals of purity, honesty, unselfishness, and love are as adhered to by members of Alcoholics Anonymous as by any other group of people, but we found that when you put the word "absolute" before them, alcoholics just couldn't stand the pace, and too many went out and got drunk again. . . .
>
> As you so well understand, we drunks are all-or-nothing people. In the old days of the Oxford Groups, they

> **were forever talking about the Four Absolutes. . . . There we saw people going broke on this sort of perfection— trying to get too good by Thursday.**[13]

Finite beings who thirst for the infinite, desperate creatures who "want to be God," all-or-nothing people who go broke on perfection . . . given our limitations, and our tendency to strain against them, how do we learn to put up with ourselves? The sages and saints have not left us without some thoughts on the subject. The Desert Fathers, that marvelous group of imperfect human beings who struggled tirelessly with their own imperfections, discovered quite a bit about learning how to "put up with ourselves." The secret, they determined, lies in *compassion,* which begins with "putting up with" others.

> **A monk was brought up before the brotherhood for having committed a grievous sin, and it was decided that he would be excommunicated. As the monk left the sanctuary, his head bent in shame, the esteemed Abba Bessarian stood up, fell into step behind his fellow monk and in a clear voice announced, "I, too, am a sinner."**[14]

The very solitude of their lives as hermits led the Desert Fathers to discover that we are like others not in our virtues and strengths, but precisely in our faults, our failings, our flaws. As Evagrius Ponticus, one of the most influential of the desert monks, put it: The nearer we draw to God, the more we should see ourselves as being one with every sinner.[15]

Many favorite stories of desert spirituality dwell lovingly on just this theme, for it was perhaps the most important discovery of an era infatuated with its discoveries—an era in this way not unlike our own.

> **Isaac of Thebes was visiting a monastic community when he saw a brother sin. Isaac condemned him in his heart. Later, when he returned to his cell for the night, he discovered an angel barring the doorway. "God has sent me to ask you where he is to put the fallen brother whom you have con-**

demned." Isaac was immediately contrite: If God did not judge the sinner, how could he?[16]

Among the oft-quoted "Sayings of the Old Men," as the Desert Fathers were called and as the word *abba* means, we find the following reminder:

> The old men used to say, "There is nothing worse than pass-ing judgement." And Abba Theodotos said, "If you live conti-nently, do not judge one who lusts, for just like him you disobey the law. For the one who said, 'Do not lust,' also said, 'Do not judge.' "[17]

In their solitude in the desert, the monks confronted their own weakness and developed a deep sense of their own sinfulness. *But their spirituality did not stop there—it only began there.* For out of that awareness of their own weakness, they developed a compassion for the weaknesses of others, the outstanding virtue that all of their sayings highlight. One of the most respected of the Desert Fathers was Moses the Black. A story suggests the foundation of his greatness.

> A brother at Scetis committed a fault. A council was called to which Abba Moses was invited, but he refused to go. Then the priest sent someone to say to him, "Come, for everyone is waiting for you." So he got up and went, taking a leaking jug filled with water and carrying it with him. The other monks came out to meet him and said, "What is this, Father?" The old man replied: "My sins run out behind me and I do not see them, and today I am coming to judge the faults of an-other." When they heard that, they said no more to the brother but forgave him.[18]

A similar story is told about Abba Ammonas, who was called upon by some monks to punish a local hermit who was thought to have a mistress living with him. Infuriated at their neighbor's casual immo-rality, the monks asked Ammonas to accompany them to the monk's cell, where they would confront the culprit and extract punishment for his sins.

When the hermit in question heard this, he hid the woman in a large barrel. The crowd of monks came to the place. As soon as he entered the monk's cell, Ammonas realized that the woman was hiding in the cask. Strolling over to it, he sat down on the barrel and then instructed the other monks to search the cell carefully. When the monks had searched everywhere without finding the woman, they retreated, abashed and apologetic. On his way out, Ammonas took his fellow monk's hand and said, "Brother, be on your guard; pay attention to yourself."[19]

"Pay attention to yourself!" Abba Ammonas was not primarily concerned with his fellow monk's actions—even the most venerated of the desert monks tended to be rather casual about what would excite later generations as matters of morality. But Ammonas was deeply concerned by the monk's apparent attitude of carelessness, of not facing up to what he was doing, of not being truthful with himself. What we do is important, but what we *are* is more important. Most important, of course, is that we understand the difference.

A favorite story of the Hasidim captures it.

Three youths hid themselves on a Sabbath in a barn in order to smoke. Hasidim discovered them and wished to flog the offenders. One youth exclaimed: "I deserve no punishment, for I forgot that today is the Sabbath." The second youth said: "And I forgot that smoking on the Sabbath is forbidden." The third youth raised his voice and cried out: "I, too, forgot." "What did you forget?" he was asked. The lad replied: "I forgot to lock the door of the barn."[20]

But how do we attain this understanding, this deep honesty concerning ourselves and our failures? The correspondence of two spiritual fathers who lived in the sixth century at Thavatha, a little south of Gaza, provides practical and realistic suggestions for learning from our imperfections. Barsanuphius and John, known respectively as "The Great Old Man" and "The Other Old Man," wrote replies to many who petitioned their guidance. More than eight hundred and fifty of their letters survive. One of Barsanuphius's correspondents was another Abba John, of Beersheba, and their exchange is particularly memorable.

> John had asked a friend to do something, and it had not been done quickly enough to satisfy him. He duly reprimanded the friend, who then became upset at the rebuke. So, John wrote to Barsanuphius, that was it—he would never say anything to anybody again!
>
> In his first response to John, Barsanuphius was gentle and indirect: "This generation is soft and delicate; you will find it hard to discover a man with a tough heart."
>
> John caught the quiet rebuke and moved to blunt it by readily admitting that he was the architect of most of his troubles: "I know, father," he wrote back to Barsanuphius, "that these things happen to me because of my sins and that I am a fool and that all my troubles are my own fault."
>
> But Barsanuphius saw right through him. "You call yourself a sinner and yet you do not believe this, judging from what you do," he fired back. "A man who holds that he is a sinner and the cause of his own troubles does not go round contradicting people and fighting them and getting angry with them." He concluded his letter with the classic monastic admonition: "Pay attention to yourself, brother: this is not the truth."[21]

"Pay attention to yourself!" The emphasis is always and continually on self-knowledge, knowing oneself and honestly accepting—"owning"—one's *own* imperfections. For *honesty* is first and foremost honesty *with self*, and true honesty concerns acknowledging and accepting our own imperfection. Pay attention to yourself and allow others to do the same, for other people can deal with their own imperfections. They don't need someone else to point out their problems.

Spirituality's constant emphasis on self-knowledge and the acceptance of one's own imperfection has not changed in the modern age. We find a recent expression of the insight in the novel *Lonesome Dove*, as author Larry McMurtry tells the story of two aging cowboys who could be considered the modern counterparts of Barsanuphius and John. Arguing about the merits of an occasional failure, Augustus accuses his friend Call of being too stubborn to admit he is ever wrong.

> "You're so sure you're right it doesn't matter to you whether people talk to you at all. I'm glad I've been wrong enough to keep in practice."
>
> "Why would you want to keep in practice being wrong?" Call asked. "I'd think it would be something you'd try to avoid."
>
> "You can't avoid it, you've got to learn to handle it," Augustus said. "If you come face to face with your own mistakes once or twice in your life it's bound to be extra painful. I face mine every day—that way they ain't usually much worse than a dry shave."[22]

The vocabulary is modern, but the insight is ancient: The main benefit of struggle and failure is that it helps protect against the ultimate bane of all spirituality, conceit—the self-centeredness that claims absolute self-sufficiency, the pride that denies all need. A key passage of the book *Alcoholics Anonymous* reads: "Selfishness—self-centeredness! That, we think, is the root of our troubles." A more classic expression of this spiritual perspective makes the same point in greater detail.

> God can exercise his mercy when we avow our defects. Our defects acknowledged, instead of repelling God, draw him to us, satisfying his longing to be merciful. As this is understood through meditation, the person realizes that those things by which he feels unlovable are exactly what he has to offer God to attract him.[23]

The ways of conceit can be treacherous, trapping not "even" the holy but *especially* those who would be holy.

> Said the Koretzer rebbe: "A wise man was asked by his Disciples for instruction how to avoid sin. He replied: 'Were you able to avoid offenses, I fear you would fall into a still greater sin—that of pride.' "[24]

And from the same tradition, another story.

> Once some disciples of Rabbi Pinchas ceased talking in embarrassment when he entered the House of Study. When he asked them what they were talking about, they said: "Rabbi, we were saying how afraid we are that the Evil Urge will pursue us."
>
> "Don't worry," he replied. "You have not gotten high enough for it to pursue you. For the time being, you are still pursuing it."[25]

The central theme of *honesty with self* pervades not only the Hasidic and desert sources but all spiritual visions. Those ancient hermit-monks settled in the desert in the first place because they understood the dangers of self-deceit; they sought in the wilderness a kind of laboratory, a setting devoid of distraction in which they hoped to discover the practices most favorable to the development of spirituality. It is sometimes suggested that the Desert Fathers and Mothers retreated to the desert in an effort to escape temptation, but as the numerous stories in this chapter illustrate, they knew full well the impossibility of such escape. Instead, they sought to confront temptation in a setting where they could recognize it for what it is. They viewed temptation as their most valuable tool, for by observing their desires, they came to know themselves. Far from longing for freedom from their passions, these hermits used—even courted—temptation as a source of essential energy. The ascetic's gravest danger was always recognized to be *acedia*—the boredom and self-pity that flourished when temptation disappeared.[26]

"What is 'failure' in the desert?" asks scholar Benedicta Ward. She goes on to detail the answer in her study *Harlots of the Desert*, tellingly subtitled: *A Study of Repentance in Early Monastic Sources.*

> What really lies outside the ascetic life is not lust itself but despair, the proud attitude which denies the possibility of forgiveness. . . . It is not judgement or discussion of sins, excuses, or understanding of alleviating circumstances that break the heart, but mercy and love. Fundamental to the life of the desert fathers was the insight not to judge but to love.[27]

From the central act of confronting the truth of one's own weakness began the development of that characteristic most admired by these earliest saints—the sense of *compassion,* the recognition that others' weaknesses render them not different from but like to oneself. Because the desert ascetics combined those deep awarenesses of their own sinfulness and of the weakness of *all* humanity, an almost exaggerated sense of compassion for the weakness of others comes through many of their sayings. When their stories are taken out of context, we tend to be shocked by their "weird" behavior, forgetting that their weirdness was their way of calling attention to the need for compassion.

The desert saints were not, of course, either the first or the last to recognize that spirituality begins in the acceptance of our limitations and in the compassion that emerges from such self-knowledge. Some seventeen centuries later, Bill Wilson drew on the same insight in formulating a response to a member troubled by some of the "goings-on" within Alcoholics Anonymous.

> Alcoholics Anonymous is a terribly imperfect society because it is made up of very imperfect people. We are all dedicated to an . . . ideal of which, because we are very human and very sick, we often fall short. I know because I constantly fall short myself.[28]

And from the eighteenth century we have this Hasidic story, which draws on an aspect of the Jewish experience that, after the Holocaust, Christianity has also begun to tap.

The Rabbi of Lelov said to his Hasidim:
"A man cannot be redeemed until he recognizes the flaws in his soul and tries to mend them. A nation cannot be redeemed until it recognizes the flaws in its soul and tries to mend them. Whoever permits no recognition of his flaws, be it man or nation, permits no redemption. We can be redeemed to the extent to which we recognize ourselves.

"When Jacob's sons said to Joseph: 'We are upright men,' he answered: 'That is why I spoke to you saying: Ye are spies.' But later, when they confessed the truth with their lips and with their hearts, and said to one another, 'We are verily

THE ROOTS OF WISDOM

guilty concerning our brother,' the first gleam of their redemption dawned. Overcome with compassion, Joseph
turned aside and wept."[29]

There is both good and evil in the world, but the line separating
them runs not *between* nations or institutions or groups or even individuals; the line that separates good and evil runs *through* the core of
each nation, each institution, each group, and, most tellingly, *through*
the core of each human being, *through* each one of us. Cutting
through each one of us is the reality of our own limitation. "There is a
crack in everything God has made," Emerson observed, and—not
least of all—in each one of us.[30]

Chapter 4

A SENSE OF BALANCE

❖

Somewhere in each of us we're a mixture of light and of darkness, of love and of hate, of trust and of fear.

Jean Vanier[1]

A preacher put this question to a class of children: "If all the good people in the world were red and all the bad people were green, what color would you be?"

Little Linda Jean thought mightily for a moment. Then her face brightened and she replied: "Reverend, I'd be streaky!"[2]

The most ancient wisdom of the human race is the vision of "the human" as essentially *mixed,* somehow *in the middle.* To-be-human is to be fundamentally finite, essentially limited, "not God." And yet, at the same time, to-be-human is to be capable of "more"—to be capable of both wisdom and love that transcend the limitations of time. In a very real sense, then, to be human is to be caught in an impossible situation: We crave that which is essentially beyond us.

This paradoxical insight has been stated variously throughout the ages. The ancient Egyptians and Greeks portrayed human beings as *less than the gods, more than the beasts, yet somehow also both.* Among the earliest classic myths we find the tale of how the human race sprang from the remains of the terrible Titans who, because they had eaten an infant god, contained a tiny portion of divine soul-stuff, which was passed on to humans. This Titan myth neatly explained to the ancient Greek why he felt himself to be at once a god and a criminal, why he experienced both the "Apolline" awareness of remoteness from the divine and the "Dionysian" inkling of identity with it.[3]

This paradox of dissonance and incompleteness was embodied by the ancient Greeks in the figure of Dionysus, the god of wine: paunchy, unsteady of gait, a foolishly lewd grin on his sagging face. Most pictorial representations of Dionysus are sufficiently detailed that modern clinicians readily recognize the mythic god as a classic alcoholic. His reported behavior, which ranged unpredictably from sentimental to savage, confirms the diagnosis. Yet because Dionysus represented not only the destructive power of alcohol but also its social and salutary influences, he was viewed as the promoter of civilization and a lover of peace. Like his compatriot Demeter, goddess of the harvest, Dionysus was both a "joy-god" and a suffering god.[4]

The ancient Greeks explored these paradoxes in stories about their gods: later generations would utilize different images, different vocabularies, different stories. Two thousand years after Dionysus's downfall, the French mathematician and mystic Blaise Pascal reflected in his famous *Pensées* (1654) on "the misery and grandeur of man," caught between "the two abysses of the infinite and nothing." Søren Kierkegaard observed in the nineteenth century that "the self is a union of the infinite possibility of the spirit with the finitude of the body and of everyday life." Twentieth-century philosopher-historian William Barrett suggests that postmodern thought begins with the rediscovery that

> . . . man occupies a middle position in the universe, between the infinitesimal and the infinite: he is an All in relation to Nothingness, a Nothingness in relation to the All. This middle position of man is the final and dominant fact of the human condition. . . . It is also a perfect image of the finitude of human existence. . . . Man *is* his finitude.[5]

And almost simultaneously with the flourishing of Alcoholics Anonymous, American theologian Reinhold Niebuhr pointed out that man, who "stands at the juncture of nature and spirit," is the subject of ". . . both freedom and necessity. On the one hand, he is involved in the order of nature and is therefore bound. On the other hand, as spirit he transcends nature and himself and is therefore free. Being both bound and free, both limited and unlimited, he invariably experiences anxiety."[6]

Caught between the infinite and the nothing, darkness and light, the end of things and their beginning, misery and grandeur, certain knowledge and absolute ignorance, the human being is in a decidedly disordered state. Classic imagery portrays this confused condition as being *both* "beast" and "angel." A more modern expression emphasizes that *both* "the best" and "the beast" reside within each of us. For it is when that both-ness is denied that problems arise. "He who would be an angel becomes a beast," observed Pascal. And at the beginning of the twentieth century, the Spanish-born American philosopher George Santayana developed the corollary to Pascal's image: "It is necessary to be a beast if one is ever to be a spirit." In our own times, the anthropologist Ernest Becker, aware that he was dying of cancer at age forty-nine, even as he was completing his Pulitzer Prize-winning book, *The Denial of Death*, captured his anguished thoughts on the subject of man's dual nature in a description both vulgar and vivid: "Man is a god who shits."[7]

The ultimate reflection of our two-sided nature is the uniquely human knowledge that we are going to die. "That is the unique gift that humans have above all other animals: they can share their death with each other," suggested William Barrett in *The Illusion of Technique*. And the Sufi tell an older story.

One day, the blessed Jesus caught a sheep from a pasturing flock and said something in its ear. The sheep stopped eating grass and would take no water.

A few days later, as the blessed Jesus was passing that same pasture, he pointed to the sheep and said to the shepherd: "Is that animal sick? Why is it not eating grass and taking water like the rest?"

Not recognizing him, the shepherd replied: "A person recently passed this way and said something in this sheep's ear. From that day to this the animal has been stupefied."

If you are curious to know what the venerable Jesus said in the sheep's ear, let me tell you. What the blessed Jesus said was: "Death exists!" Although it was only an animal, when it

heard of death that sheep stopped eating and drinking and
went into this state of stupor.[8]

The sages and saints leave no doubt that to be human is to be
caught between a rock and a hard place—or, perhaps more accurately,
between "heaven" and "hell." But then we moderns know that; all we
have to do is listen to ourselves talk.

"I'm so confused."
"I'm all torn up."
"I'm hopelessly muddled."
"I don't know who I am."

Titles of recent so-called "self-help" books confirm our inability to
accept the reality of our own paradox:

Afraid to Live, Afraid to Die
Killing Ourselves with Kindness
Am I Well Yet?
When Am I Going to Be Happy?

To think in such terms—to teeter at the extremes of self-love and
self-loathing, to pursue perfection because we despise our imperfections—is to find neither satisfaction in successes nor wisdom in failures. Life becomes a constant battle, a never-ending struggle to get
somewhere, to achieve something, to produce something. Having split
our world (and our selves) into either-or dualisms—god *or* beast,
angel *or* devil, right *or* wrong, left *or* right, good *or* evil, up *or* down—
we lack all sense of *balance*. We tend to sway precariously on the
teeter-totter of life, running from one extreme to the other, missing
the point that the only stable place to be is in the mixed-up middle. In
reality, that is the only place we *can* be.

However we come to understand that there are necessarily both
ups and downs *in life*, the same perspective reveals that *within ourselves* there is light within our darkness, good within our evil. In the
spirituality of imperfection, we learn to accept that we are *neither*
angel nor beast, for we are *both*.

> Rabbi Bunam said to his disciples: "Everyone must have two
> pockets, so that he can reach into the one or the other, ac-
> cording to his needs. In his right pocket are to be the words:
> 'For my sake was the world created,' and in his left: 'I am
> earth and ashes.' "[9]

Any spirituality of joy is also a spirituality of tragedy. Searches for
a constantly "happy spirituality" never work, for if genuine "feeling"
must be rooted in genuine *being*, the nature of our human be-ing
requires acceptance of ourselves, our lives, and our world as "both/
and" rather than "either-or." It is precisely our *twofold* nature that
spirituality embraces, and it is in embracing this spirituality that we
embrace the world—reality as it is—thus discovering who we are.[10]

In *The Varieties of Religious Experience*, a book that profoundly
influenced the earliest members of Alcoholics Anonymous, William
James distinguished between the "once-born" (the "healthy minded")
and the "twice-born," (the "sick souls"). The *once-born* know no
doubts. They seem, most of the time, to possess a serenity that does
not even recognize that it is serenity. Self-confident and self-possessed,
the healthy-minded assume that things will work out for the best,
even in the short run. On the rare occasions when they experience
tragedy, they do not think of it as tragedy; "bad luck" is the whole of
their vocabulary for frustration. Talk of "conversion" thus mystifies
them, for as open as they might be to changes in the world, they rarely
see the need for change in themselves. Such people simply *are,* and
they are never seduced by the temptation to ponder their be-ing. A
caricaturist would picture them smiling vacuously and label them
"Blah." They inhabit the more biting cartoons in *The New Yorker.*

Numbering himself among the "twice-born" *sick souls,* James vividly detailed how these very different individuals are haunted by a
deep sense of the risk, danger, and pervasive moral evil that runs
through the world. Conscious of possessing a self that is somehow
divided, these sick souls are examples par excellence of "the constitu-
tional disease" James calls *Zerrissenheit* ("torn-to-pieces-hood").
From the perspective of the "healthy-minded," these "sick souls"
seem to have no sense of unity or coherence to their lives. They appear
riddled by inner instability, torn by tension and conflict between the
various elements of their lives. The "twice-born" have known tragedy,

failure, and defeat, and they have named them such; but they also have a sense of the possibility of somehow rising above such experiences. A comic artist would nevertheless portray them anxiously insecure, identifying them with the label "Argh!" Sick souls also inhabit *New Yorker* cartoons, but they may be more familiar in the shape of Charles Schulz's Charlie Brown.[11]

Does such openness to suffering, to the dark side of human be-ing, signal some kind of denial or lack of spirituality? Are the recognition of darkness and the temptation to despair themselves failures? *NO!* The answer comes hurtling with all the force and wisdom of hundreds of voices echoing over thousands of years. These voices, the voices of the sages and saints, insist that it is the struggle itself that defines us. Our many failures give meaning to our few successes; only when we peer into the abyss can we appreciate the magnificence of heights that are more than mere "highs."

For to be human *is,* after all, to be other than "God." And so it is only in the embracing of our torn self, only in the acceptance that there is nothing "wrong" with feeling "torn," that one can hope for whatever healing is available and can thus become as "whole" as possible. Only those who know darkness can truly appreciate light; only those who acknowledge darkness can even *see* the light.

Our very brokenness allows us to become whole. "No one is as whole as he who has a broken heart," said Rabbi Moshe Leib of Sasov. "Wholeness," then, does not mean that the heart is not "broken," that the pain does not sear. To experience sadness, despair, tears, and howls of pain demonstrates not some violation or deficit of spirituality but rather the ultimate spirituality of acceptance.

For such acceptance is the beginning of spirituality: "The chiefest sanctity of a temple is that it is a place to which men can go to weep in common," wrote the Spanish philosopher Miguel de Unamuno. "Yes, we must learn to weep! Perhaps that is the supremest wisdom." But perhaps it was a Hasidic rebbe who best captured why this is so.

Said the Porissover: "Some Hasidim are so proud of their piety that they cannot believe the Lord sends them hardships in order to awaken in them penitence for their sins. They affirm: I am a perfect Jew, and I will accept these hardships as 'afflictions from love.' But afflictions from love are not sent in vain; they are intended as a means to arouse penitence. When the Riziner was imprisoned, he wept. He was asked: 'Why do you not accept this affliction as intended in love?' He answered: 'When God sends bitterness, we ought to feel it.' "[12]

❖

All spirituality—but especially a spirituality of imperfection—involves the perceiving, embracing, and living out of paradox. A "paradox" is an apparent contradiction: Two things seem to exclude each other, but in truth need not do so. "Square circle" is a contradiction; "saintly sinner" is a paradox, as is "holy fool," an incongruity especially cherished in the Russian Christian tradition. Openness to paradox allows both the understanding and the acceptance of our human condition as "both/and" (both a saint and a sinner) rather than "either-or" (either a saint or a sinner). The demand for "either-or," for one-or-the-other, signals the rejection of paradox and therefore the denial of spirituality.[13]

Within the long story of spirituality in the Western Christian world, failure to understand that to-be-human is to be both/and rather than either-or led to much confusion. The significance of Saint Augustine, for example, is not that he emphasized "sin," but that he sought to promote wholeness and balance by calling attention to "the other side." Faced with the destruction of the Roman Empire, Augustine sought to teach that *both* within each person *and* within the community as a whole, *both* good *and* evil, strength *and* weakness, co-existed.[14]

Both Augustine and the Augustinian monk Martin Luther a millennium after him understood the core truth of human be-ing: *everything* human is *limited*—inherently, because it comes conjoined with its opposite. Luther's description of the believer captures this well: *simul justus et peccator*—"righteous and a sinner at the same time." When we deny our both/and nature, the mixed-up-ed-ness that is part of our human be-ing, we refuse our very self—*deny* it in the sense of that lying to self that is *self-deception.* A central theme in all traditions of spirituality is the insistence that honesty—honesty with self about self—is essential to any spiritual quest. And the greatest, most treacherous *dis*honesty is the denial or refusal of our mixed human nature.

The Maggid of Koznitz said to a man who wore nothing but a sack and fasted from one Sabbath to the next, "The Evil Urge is tricking you into that sack. He who pretends to fast . . . but secretly eats a little something every day, is spiritually better off than you, for he is only deceiving others, while you are deceiving yourself."[15]

So deep is this essential need for self-knowledge, for honesty, for "paying attention" to oneself, that one of the most delightful tales told of Francis of Assisi deals with his recognition of the mutuality between honesty with self and honesty with others. Francis was concerned lest even an inadvertent deception of others might cause him to lapse into treacherous self-deceit and hypocrisy:

Once when Francis fell ill during his last years, his guardian and companion obtained a piece of soft fox-skin to sew into his tunic as protection against the winter cold. Francis would permit the fox-skin liner only if a piece of the fur was also sewn on the outside of his tunic so that no one would be fooled by the garment's coarse outer appearance into thinking Francis was being more ascetic than he actually was.[16]

Why all this concern over *hypocrisy* and *self-deception*, especially among those whom later generations honor as saints and sages? The reason is simple: These individuals *were* "sages and saints" *because* they knew the simple but essential truth that we human beings find it extremely difficult to know the truth about ourselves, for we cannot see directly our own incongruous mixedness. Just as the eye cannot reflect on itself—we cannot see our own face without some kind of mirror—the mind, the soul, cannot directly know its own nature. The Russians have a proverb: "You cannot kiss your own ear." We cannot directly know our own being.

Must we, then, forever grope blindly in the dark? What can we *do*, in order to *be*? Yet again, an ancient answer echoes across the centuries: *Listen! Listen to stories!* For what stories do, above all else, is hold up a mirror so that we can see ourselves. Stories are mirrors of human be-ing, reflecting back our very essence. In a story, we come to know precisely the both/and, mixed-up-ed-ness of our very being. In the mirror of another's story, we can discover *our* tragedy and *our* comedy —and therefore our very *human*-ness, the ambiguity and incongruity that lie at the core of the human condition.

The stories that sustain a spirituality of imperfection are wisdom-stories. They follow a temporal format, describing "what we used to be like, what happened, and what we are like now."[17] Such stories, however, can also do more: The sequential format makes it possible for other people's stories to become a part of "my" story. Sometimes, for example, hearing another's story can occasion profound change. Telling the story of that change then follows the format of telling *a* story within *my* story: *"Once upon a time, I did not understand this very well; but then I heard this story, and now I understand it very differently."*

Perhaps nowhere is this format clearer than in the tradition of Hasidic Judaism. Rarely do *zaddikim* answer questions. Sometimes the rebbe replies with another question; more often he tells a story. And the story, especially as it is told and retold, creates a community of those who are changed by those stories. One need not be Jewish to join that community or to be transformed by that wisdom.

Here is a story that reveals the power and the wisdom of that spirituality—a story that helps us to understand "how story works," how story makes whole.

On the day the Baal Shem Tov was dying, he called together his disciples and assigned each of them a task to carry on in his name, to continue his work. When he finished, he had still one more task. And so he called the last disciple and gave him this responsibility: to go all over Europe to retell stories about the Master. The disciple was very disappointed. This was hardly a prestigious job. But the Baal Shem Tov told him that he would not have to do this forever; he would receive a sign when he should stop and then he could live out the rest of his life in ease.

So after the Baal Shem Tov died, the disciple set off, and days and months turned into years and years of telling stories, until he felt he had told them in every part of the world. Then he heard of a man in Italy, a nobleman in fact, who would pay a gold ducat for each new story told. So the disciple made his way to Italy to the nobleman's castle. When he arrived, however, he discovered to his absolute horror that he had forgotten all the Baal Shem Tov stories! He couldn't remember a single one! He was mortified. But the nobleman was kind and urged him to stay on a few days anyway, in the hope that he would eventually remember something.

But the next day and again the next he remembered nothing. Finally, on the fourth day the disciple protested that he must go, out of sheer embarrassment. As he was about to leave, indeed as he was walking down the path leading from the nobleman's castle, suddenly he remembered one story. It wasn't much of a story, but at least it would prove that he was not a charlatan, that he indeed did know the great Baal Shem Tov, for he was the only disciple there when this story took place. Clinging to his memory of the story's thread, he made his way back to the castle, and as soon as he was shown into the nobleman's presence, this is the story the disciple began to pour out.

Once the Baal Shem Tov told him to harness the horses, so that they could take a trip to Turkey, where at this time of the year the streets were decorated for the Christians' Easter festival. The disciple was upset: It was well known that Jews were not safe in that part of Turkey during the Christian Holy Week and Easter. They were fair game for Christians shouting, "God-killer!" And, in fact, in the very region to which the Baal Shem Tov proposed to go, it was the custom during the Easter festival each year to kill one Jew in reparation.

Still, the Baal Shem Tov insisted and so they went. They went into the city and made their way into the Jewish quarter, where the Jews were all huddled indoors, behind closed shutters, out of fear. Thus secluded, they awaited the end of the festival, when they could go out on the streets again in safety. Imagine, then, how startled they were when the Baal Shem Tov, on being shown into the room where they were gathered, strode over to the shutters, threw them open, and stood there in full view, just as the procession was entering the town square!

Looking through the window, he saw the bishop leading

the procession. The bishop was arrayed like a prince with gold vestments, silver mitre, and a diamond-studded staff. Turning to the disciple, the Baal Shem Tov said: "Go tell the bishop I want to see him." Was he out of his mind? Did he want to die? Did he want me to die? the disciple remembered wondering. But nothing could deter this order, so the disciple went out into the square and, making his way through the crowd, came around behind the bishop just as he was about to mount the platform to begin his sermon. More gesturing than speaking the words, the disciple hoarsely whispered to the bishop that the Baal Shem Tov wanted to see him.

The bishop seemed agitated and hesitated for a moment. But after his sermon, he came, and he and the Baal Shem Tov went immediately into a back room, where they were secluded together for three hours. Then the Master came out and, without saying anything else, told his disciple that they were ready to go back home.

As the disciple finished the story, he was about to apologize to the nobleman for its insignificance, for its lack of point, when he suddenly noticed the enormous impact the story had had on the nobleman. He had dissolved into tears and, finally, when he could speak, he said, "Oh, disciple, your story has just saved my soul! You see, I was there that day. I was that bishop. I had descended from a long line of distinguished rabbis but one day during a period of great persecution, I had abandoned the faith and converted to Christianity. The Christians, of course, were so pleased that, in time, they even made me a bishop. And I had accepted everything, even went along with the killing of the Jews each year until that one year. The night before the festival I had a terrible dream of the Day of Judgment and the danger to my soul. So when you came the very next day with a message from the Baal Shem Tov, I knew that I had to go to him.

"For three hours he and I talked. He told me that there still might be hope for my soul. He told me to sell my goods and retire on what was left and live a life of good deeds and holiness. There might still be hope. And his last words to me were these: 'When a man comes to you and tells you your own story, you will know that your sins are forgiven.'

"So I have been asking everyone I knew for stories from the Baal Shem Tov. And I recognized you immediately when you came, and I was happy. But when I saw that all the stories had been taken from you, I recognized God's judgment. Yet now you have remembered one story, my story, and I know now that the Baal Shem Tov has interceded on my behalf and that God has forgiven me."

When a man comes to you and tells you your own story, you know that your sins are forgiven. And when you are forgiven, you are healed.[18]

Chapter 5

EXPERIENCING THE SPIRITUAL

❖

Unawareness is the root of all evil.

Anonymous Egyptian Monk

Spirituality is, above all, a way of life. We don't just think about it or feel it or sense it around us—we live it. Spirituality permeates to the very core of our human *be*-ing, affecting the way we perceive the world around us, the way we feel about that world, and the choices we make based on our perceptions and sensations. In the experience of spirituality, three essential elements are always at play: what we *see*; how we *feel*; and why we *choose*.

> Rabbi Levi Yitzchok of Berdichev once encountered a man eating on the fast day of Tishu B'Av. "Surely you have forgotten that this is a fast day," he said.
>
> "No," answered the man. "I know today is Tishu B'Av."
>
> "Aha! You are not well, and your doctor has instructed you not to fast," said the rabbi.
>
> "No, I am perfectly healthy," the man replied.
>
> Rabbi Levi Yitzchok lifted his eyes toward heaven. "Look how precious your children are, dear God. I have provided this man with ample excuse to explain away his behavior, but he refuses to deviate from the truth, even when it incriminates him."[1]

What a stubborn, rebellious man! someone else might have concluded. But Rabbi Levi Yitzchok saw the good, which enabled him to feel brotherhood with the man. Or was it his feeling of brotherhood with his fellow Jew that allowed the rabbi to see the good? Or were the seeing and the feeling both results of some prior choice?

The word *experience* speaks to the wholeness, the fitting-together of seeing, feeling, and willing. *Experience* is more than just feeling because it also involves knowing, and it is more than just seeing because it is knowledge of as well as knowledge about. *Experience* signifies a kind of "hands on" grasp that reaches out to taste the honey even as it tries to understand "sweetness." *Experience* "knows" life not as an object to observe but as a living, breathing reality that can be creatively embraced and that fully returns the embrace.[2]

People sometimes think of spirituality as if it were mainly "feeling" (an episode of rapture, a warm sensation of belonging) or primarily "willing" (the act of choosing). But of the three essential elements of the experience of spirituality, "seeing" holds a kind of necessary priority. Even if Rabbi Levi Yitzchok was able to see the good *because* he felt brotherhood with his fellow Jew, he first had to recognize that man's Jewishness for the story to begin. We must learn first "the proper way of viewing things,'" as the Jesuit priest Jean-Pierre Caussade insisted in introducing his eighteenth-century novices to spirituality's story.[3]

Caussade did not mean seeing with our physical eyes but with an inner vision that looks at the world in a way that sees "self" *in context*. This type of *vision* is often confused with "thinking," but the two are distinct—so distinct, in fact, that thinking too much about things can result in an inability to "see" them. "I begin to see an object when I cease to understand it," noted Thoreau. And Chinese Zen master Shen Hui suggested that: "The true seeing is when there is no seeing."[4]

Shen Hui's observation reminds that there can be a trap in the metaphor of *seeing*. The first "seeing" in his aphorism—"the true seeing"—signifies *experiencing*, which involves not just the eyes, but all the powers of sensation. The tradition of a spirituality of imperfection, with its emphasis on storytelling and storylistening, suggests that of all the senses, *hearing* enjoys a real claim to precedence. For one thing, as the philosopher Hans Georg Gadamer observed: "Unlike seeing, where one can look away, one cannot 'hear away' but must listen. . . . Hearing implies already belonging together in such a manner that one is claimed by what is being said."[5]

Hearing involves intimacies too frequently forgotten.

When a man whose marriage was in trouble sought his advice, the Master said, "You must learn to listen to your wife."

The man took this advice to heart and returned after a month to say that he had learned to listen to every word his wife was saying.

Said the Master with a smile, "Now go home and listen to every word she isn't saying."[6]

The sensations of taste and smell, which thrive in spiritual tradition, especially in the East, are also part of the "vision" that is spirituality. Recall the story of the master who asked his disciples if they could put into words the fragrance of a rose. "All of them were silent." Perhaps because the senses of smell and taste are simply ineffable—the experiences are impossible to put into words—efforts to capture the fullness of the experience of spirituality frequently appeal to the sense of "sweetness." Commenting on the Rosh Hashanah prayer for "a good and sweet year," Abraham Twerski, who is both a psychiatrist and an Orthodox rabbi, explains.

"Good" can be understood intellectually, but "sweet" is a sense experience which even a little child can appreciate. We ask G–d* for uncomplicated and unsophisticated goodness, the sweet kind of good that can be appreciated by all, rather than that which is understood only by people of profound faith. "Give us simple good, sweet as honey."[7]

The bitter herbs and the heavily sweet wine of the Passover supper convey as much of the story of the Exodus' beginnings as do the readings associated with that rite. The unleavened bread, the singing and standing and passing around the table: few rites can match the

* Out of respect for Rabbi Twerski and his tradition, we follow observant Orthodox practice in this direct quotation and refrain from writing out the divine name.

Jewish Passover in conveying an *experience*. It is not surprising, then, that Orthodox Jew Ari Goldman found especially meaningful this description explaining what the Koran means to a Muslim believer.

> **When a boy reaches the age of four years, four months and four days, [he] is dressed up like a little bridegroom and sent to school to recite his first verse of the Koran. The verse is written in honey on a slate and, after the boy masters it, the honey is dissolved in water. The boy drinks the sweet holy words as a spiritual and physical nourishment.[8]**

Similar sensitivity pervades the Greek and Russian Orthodox heritages of the Christian East, which employ ornate liturgical vestments, profuse incensings, and the eating of honeyed morsels as ways of communicating spirituality's riches. Even the language of this tradition lovingly relishes words such as *savor* and *flavor* as a way of conveying something of the undefinable yet somehow tangible essence of the spiritual. In all spiritual traditions, of course, the words *thirst* and *hunger* appear again and again.[9]

Smell, taste, sight, and hearing . . . the most fundamental spiritual experience involves all these senses, and more. In fact, the experience of spirituality perhaps comes closest to the final sense of touch, for it is ultimately a kind of kinesthetic experience: an awareness that flows from a sense of the *positioning* of our whole being. Most spiritual traditions suggest a posture—the Hasidic rocking, the Buddhist lotus-position, the Muslim prostration toward Mecca, the Christian kneeling. *Posture*, "an attitude of the body," both reflects and imparts attitudes of the mind, thus conveying as well as symbolizing an *experience*.

> **The Seventh Step of the Twelve Steps of Alcoholics Anonymous originally read: "Humbly on our knees asked Him to remove our shortcomings." Just before the publication of the A.A. "Big Book," out of the same concern that led to the addition of the phrase *"as we understood Him"* after the mention of "God" in Steps Three and Eleven, the phrase "on our knees" was dropped. Too redolent of Oxford Group practice, it also offended some lapsed Catholics.**

But although the phrase was dropped, and the practice of "kneeling to make surrender" was also abandoned after A.A.'s departure from the Oxford Group, the advising of the posture remains. "Get down on your knees in the morning and ask for help, and get down on your knees at night and say 'Thanks,' " runs a bit of frequently bestowed sponsorly wisdom.[10]

"Getting down on your knees" might signify the experience of submission, of openness, or of vulnerability. But whatever the experience—however represented, however phrased, however conceived, however "felt"—this positioning of one's whole being connects the core spiritual *act* of the cry for help that admits one's flawed imperfection with some sort of *experience* of fitting-in, of connectedness to others and to a greater whole, a higher power, a God.

This experience of connectedness and harmony is more than simply "feeling good": It involves *being* good. The word *good* derives from the same Indo-European root *gê* as the words *gather* and *together;* it thus signifies very simply the sense of "being joined or united in a *fitting* way." The experience of harmony and connectedness that is a part of spirituality—the "feeling good" that flows from the sense of *be*-ing "good"—derives from a vision of life that sees self in perspective, as somehow fitting into a larger whole . . . as somehow *linked.* This sense is, perhaps, the most important human experience. It is certainly the deepest human desire.

During the atrocities that accompanied the Bolshevik revolution in Russia, thousands of bewildered suspects were randomly arrested, rounded up, stripped naked, and shot one by one in the back of the head. One eyewitness account captures the depth as well as the poignancy of our need to feel *linked,* joined together: "Most of the victims usually requested a chance to say good-bye; and because there was no one else, they embraced and kissed their executioners."[11]

Fundamental to human be-ing is a root sense of *connectedness*—and specifically of that connectedness as somehow lost, missing, or wounded. The resultant yearning to be in some way united with reality beyond or larger than one's self underlies all art, religion, and love. When that connection is not present, we experience alienation and separation, a sense that "something is wrong" or, as the philosopher Alfred North Whitehead put it in locating the origins of spirituality, "Something is awry." We reach out to touch, we ache for contact, but something is missing. In the absence of that connection, we experience the sensation of being fractured, torn apart, pulled in a dozen different directions.

Putting the fractured pieces back together again—setting the bone back in its socket, bringing some wholeness to the sense of "torn-to-pieces-hood"—requires acknowledgment and acceptance of the essential connection between vision and feeling, between head and heart. Yet from the beginning of humankind's thoughtful presence on earth, human beings have been breaking themselves up into two—body-mind, thoughts-emotions, head-heart. Having made that division, philosophers for thousands of years and physicians and lawyers in more recent times hold lengthy debates about which bodily organ—the brain or the heart—is the more critical to being human.

Weaving in and out of this debate are the gentle voices of an august company of spiritual thinkers who resist these efforts to make the human being a one-sided conversation, a monologue, with either the head or the heart running the show. Our two-sidedness, our being both/and rather than either-or, means that we may be distinguishable, but we are not divisible. To be "mixed" is not to be *divided;* a stew is not a salad bar. The head and the heart are not only connected, but if we are to live a spiritual life, that essential connection must be nurtured and protected. How can we discover wholeness if we persist in dividing ourselves up into conflicting parts?

The American spiritual genius Jonathan Edwards is but one of many who steadfastly opposed all efforts "to divide human nature into separate compartments of mind, will, and emotion." Edwards loved to speak of "the sense of the heart": In rooting "the mind, will and emotion" in the heart, he was insisting that there *is* a center of human personality, so that "what we think is inevitably the product of the set of our wills, which in turn results from the basic direction of our hearts' desires."[12]

Edwards was perhaps the last representative of the ancient tradition that understood *heart* not in some sort of opposition to *head* but as a synonym for *the whole*—and as a word that carried with it the connotation of "affectivity." Affectivity, from the Latin *affectus*, describes not sheer "feeling" but that state of openness in which we leave ourselves vulnerable to the world outside us. *Affectivity* refers to that within us which is open to attraction from outside ourselves, that which can be moved, touched, even lured by another. Edwards's "sense of the heart" captures both aspects—the wholeness and the ready openness to attraction.

The Hasidic tradition offers this insight into wholeness in a saying and practice attributed to a rabbi who was a contemporary of Edwards.

Rabbi Mendel of Kotzk saw to it that his Hasidim wore nothing around the neck while praying. "For," he said, "when we speak to God, there must be no break between the heart and the brain."[13]

❖

A spirituality that can heal woundedness and pull fractured selves together into some kind of whole necessarily involves *both* brain *and* heart, thought *and* emotion, vision *and* feeling—but each in its proper role, each acting in a way that fits into that larger whole. Ancient wisdom and modern insight join in assigning priority to vision: the essential thing, the great spiritual teachers constantly remind, is to see oneself in the proper perspective. *"Pay attention to yourself!"*

This approach was imprinted irrevocably on the tradition by Evagrius Ponticus, one of the more influential of the Egyptian monks, who died near the end of their heyday, in the year 399. Evagrius, like his brother and sister contemplatives, emphasized honest self-knowledge. He set himself the task of detailing the different traps and temptations that can distort understanding by imposing on the mind some false perspective. Evagrius called these traps *logismos*—thoughts that bewilder and befog the mind so that slowly, bit by bit, we drift away into a world of self-destructive fantasy.[14]*

---

* The following fact may afford useful perspective on Evagrius: The greatest dangers to a monk, he was famed for saying, were women and bishops. He counseled avoiding both whenever possible.

The problem, Evagrius took care to point out, lay not in "bad thoughts" but in a process of *bad thinking* that is really *wrong vision*—seeing things from the perspective of our fears and fantasies (*un*realities) rather than seeing things truly. *Logismos* involves *choosing* to see the bad—*bad* in the sense of "unreal," not fitting reality. *Logismos* are the arch-enemies of the soul, the demons from within that destroy proper perspective on the world and thus prevent us from concentrating on the actual reality of our life, leading us further and further from our actual condition, making us try to solve problems that have not yet arisen and need never arise.

Evagrius' treatment of the *logismos* deftly outlines the "way of seeing" that sustains the way of life that is the spirituality of imperfection. It also underlies all later enumerations of the "fatal flaws" to which the human condition is subject, such as the listing of "the Seven Deadly Sins" offered by Alcoholics Anonymous co-founder Bill W. in describing A.A.'s Fourth Step inventory in the book *Twelve Steps and Twelve Traditions*.* Given that wide-ranging influence, Evagrius' *logismos* merit a bit of detailing.[15]

Despite the later penchant for finding *seven* such traps of thinking and seeing, Evagrius pointed out eight. First on his list came *gluttony*, defined as "anxiety about one's health, or about becoming ill." Be realistic in what you eat, he counseled; modify your diet when necessary, for example, and don't waste time and energy planning for something that has not yet happened and may never happen. As always, Evagrius spoke from experience. In typical desert monk fashion, he had experimented for a time with eating only uncooked foods, in an attempt to replicate Adam and Eve's experience in paradise. When he became seriously ill as a result, he solved the problem by immediately changing his diet. (*Well*, we can imagine him thinking as he lay in huddled misery, *there's another difference between Adam and Eve and me!*) This first *logismos* set the clear tone for Evagrius' whole list: "Don't waste time thinking about what thinking can't change."

Fornication came second on Evagrius' list. Real human relation-

---

* Wilson, in his exposition of A.A.'s Fourth Step ("[We] made a searching and fearless moral inventory of ourselves"), suggests: "let's take a universally recognized list of major human failings—the Seven Deadly Sins of pride, greed, lust, anger, gluttony, envy, and sloth" (*Twelve Steps and Twelve Traditions*, p. 50), thus following the classic list of "capital sins." More on this topic and its history may be found in the notes to this section.

ships with real human people are not the problem; Evagrius warns of imaginary entanglements, thoughts of "a variety of bodies," and a focusing on parts of bodies, all of which can lead to an obsession with the unreal rather than an attempt to cope with what is really there, in front of us.

Avarice, or the love of money, is the third type of *logismos.* Evagrius' concern is not "materialism" as we moderns usually think of it, but futile planning for an unreal future. He defines *avarice* not as pure material greed but as "the principle of thinking about what does not yet exist," a preoccupation with hopes and fears, with imaginary or future things. Hoarding money (or anything else) reveals lack of faith, Evagrius counsels; leave the future to God.

Envy, the fourth type of *logismos,* stands at a kind of opposite extreme from avarice: It involves obsession not with the future but with the past, a haunting remembrance of "the old days" as those "happy days" now gone and never to return. Evagrius expanded the Greek term *lype* [λυπη], which signified distress over deprivation, to include a kind of *depression,* a cultivated sorrow. Much of the pain of spiritual suffering, he suggests, comes from wallowing in wishes and fantasies of things being other than the way they are.[16]

Anger is number five, and by *anger* Evagrius means not the emotion but a *clinging to* its fervor—the resentment that refuses forgiveness. As an example, he offers the experience of *obsession* with someone who has wronged us, the situation of being "unable to think of anything else." Such fixations can ruin our health, give us nightmares, and eventually, Evagrius warns in images that even today can make the skin crawl, make us hallucinate poisonous snakes. As always, the trouble comes from failing to see the real issue. Anger, which is inevitable, is not to be squandered by focusing attention on the wrongs of others; rather, it should be directed at our own faults, and especially at how we have wronged others, thus moving us to make amends, to do something kind even for the people who have offended us.

After anger comes the classic trap, the "noonday devil," *acedia*—a kind of listlessness or boredom in which nothing engages our interest or appeals to us. We wander about in prickly tedium, picking up one thing after another, tossing it down, sighing, wishing for another's company but also dreading it, wondering how to get through a day that seems ninety hours long, nurturing bitter thoughts that trap us in the dark and tempt us to abandon our course. *What's the use? Nobody cares. Nothing matters, anyway.* The translation of *acedia* truest to Evagrius' thought is "self-pity," a far better term than "laziness" or "sloth," for it conveys both the utter melancholy of this condition and the self-centeredness on which it is founded.

The cure? "Be real!" Evagrius exhorts. Accept the reality that there is no exit from the human condition. Recognize that running away will not work, for we take these problems with us—they are where we are, and so we can escape them no more than we can escape ourselves.

Evagrius ends his catalog by dividing what later enumerators would put at the head of the list, *pride,* into the two most treacherous *logismos: vainglory* and *pride. Vainglory* he defines as daydreaming about one's own magnificence and imagined glory; *pride* consists in supposing that we can do anything without the help of God—it is, then, the claim to be God. Bill Wilson noted that pride "heads the procession" in his own list "not by accident," for it leads "to self-justification, and always spurred by . . . fears, is the basic breeder of most human difficulties."[17]

As in so many matters, Wilson here caught the essence of the tradition of the spirituality of imperfection: Each of these *logismos,* which from the medieval age onward would be termed the "capital sins" because so many difficulties flowed from them, involves an impoverished sense of self, a feeling of personal inadequacy. We try to fill the emptiness inside us with something external, but the craving self is a bottomless pit for which *addiction* is the perfect metaphor—"the equivalent, on a low level, of the spiritual thirst . . . for wholeness," as Carl Jung put it in his 1961 letter to Wilson.

All spiritual traditions agree that the core problem is insatiable desire. Buddhism locates the root of suffering in desire, while the Western tradition's *logismos* identify the everyday forms desire takes. The "deadly sins," then, are not evil acts we commit; they are the *roots* of evil deeds, the life patterns that flow from *viewing* things in ways that make us the sort of people who will then *do* such things. Bad vision leads to bad choices. The ultimate "evil" of the "capital sins" is that they make us excessively vulnerable to exploitation by those who revel in evil, the real "sinners" who view other human beings as mere instruments of their own greedy lusts.[18]

For *logismos*, the kinds of "bad" or foolish thinking that arise from preoccupation with self and self-love, trap us in a world wrongly structured—a world of which I imagine that *I* am the center. An A.A. axiom, periodically reprinted in *The A.A. Grapevine,* reminds: "The difference between a 'winner' and a 'whiner' is the sound of the 'I.'" In Evagrius' terms, the solution to the foolish thinking of the *logismos* is to be found in the simple monastic axiom: "Pay attention to yourself!" Only through vigilance aimed at seeing ourselves truly can we move toward the goal of being no longer at the mercy of inappropriate reactions—a state of harmony wherein passions, while accepted as a useful part of being human, do not sway us inappropriately, confusing and distorting our thinking, leading inevitably to actions that ultimately harm our selves.

❖

"Don't see the other human being angrily, see your own anger." "Live in a world of facts . . . attending to things as they are." They lived sixteen centuries apart, but Evagrius Ponticus and William James alike recognized and urged *willing*—choosing—as the key to spirituality's union of vision and feeling. Spirituality is experience, and as James so simply noted, *"My experience is what I agree to attend to."*[19]

James's own experience—his life, his story—richly illustrate the multifaceted interactions of seeing, feeling, and willing. A visionary as well as a thinker, William James influenced the modern course of both philosophy and psychology. In one of his notable contributions exploring the connections between seeing, feeling, and willing, the Harvard professor drew on a striking example from his practice as a mountain climber:

> Suppose, for example, that I am climbing in the Alps, and have had the ill-luck to work myself into a position from which the only escape is by a terrible leap. Being without similar experience, I have no evidence of my ability to perform it successfully; but hope and confidence in myself make me sure I shall not miss my aim, and nerve my feet to execute what without those subjective emotions would perhaps have been impossible.
>
> But suppose that, on the contrary, the emotions of fear

and mistrust preponderate; or suppose that, having just read [W. K. Clifford's] *Ethics of Belief*, I feel it would be sinful to act upon an assumption unverified by previous experience— why, then I shall hesitate so long that at last, exhausted and trembling, and launching myself in a moment of despair, I miss my foothold and roll into the abyss.

In this case (and it is one of an immense class) the part of wisdom clearly is to believe what one desires; for the belief is one of the indispensable preliminary conditions of the realization of its object. There are then cases where faith creates its own verification. Believe, and you shall be right, for you shall save yourself; doubt, and you shall again be right, for you shall perish. The only difference is that to believe is greatly to your advantage.[20]

"The mind does not just react to stimuli, it responds to meanings," James wrote later in his life. But to which meanings do we respond? Our problem, as Evagrius' *logismos* suggested, is that we are inundated by *too many* thoughts and ideas, an entangled mess of beliefs and opinions that fight it out with each other in the dark, eventually knocking each other out. *Choose* what you want to think about, both Evagrius and James counsel, and choose it carefully, because that choice determines the way you live your life. *"The essential achievement of the will, in short, when it is most 'voluntary,'"* James wrote, *"is to ATTEND to a difficult object and hold it fast before the mind."*[21]

Stories help us *attend*. And "attending," in a setting of storytelling and storylistening, helps us to *remember*, which means more than just to "recall." As Wendell Berry reminds in his novel *Remembering*, it also means to be re-membered (the opposite of being dis-membered); it means entering the "member"-ship of a community: "Memory is communal." Thus, although a spirituality of imperfection insists, "Pay attention to yourself," such attending is not a self-centered self-seeking but an awareness of oneself as related to others, as a member of a community.[22]

"Going it alone in spiritual matters is dangerous," the Oxford Group insisted, and Alcoholics Anonymous did not abandon that lesson. Spirituality's long-standing connection to story and storytelling ensures that we will never be alone in the spiritual way of life. For whenever and wherever there is a storyteller, there will also be a storyhearer. In the communal act of telling and listening, listening and telling, the sense of belonging begins. To recall Gadamer's insight: "Hearing implies already belonging together in such a manner that one is being claimed by what is being said."

As our vision of the world changes from a strictly self-centered viewpoint in which feelings are in control to an other-oriented perspective in which "feeling good" flows from "being good," we begin to see how we are connected with other realities and especially with other people. Most important, the tradition of spirituality suggests, we come to see that the criterion of spirituality is not subjective feeling but the reality of our relationships with others, the reality of community. For the "vision" that is spirituality involves

> . . . not a set of propositions but a way of life in which understand-
> ing, acceptance, and commitment emerge together in a single act.
> Since people enter upon such a way of life as a result of their actual
> participation in community, that way of life can be preserved and
> handed on only within a community that assumes the unity of un-
> derstanding, acceptance, and commitment.[23]

Understanding, acceptance, commitment . . . as a child learns to walk, first by crawling, then by standing, and finally by taking the first, tentative steps, so do all human beings learn the essential lessons in life not by reading about them or thinking about them but by *doing* them. We *act* ourselves into a new way of thinking. That insight underlies the "pragmatism" associated with the philosophy of William James, but it is older than James.

> A man once [approached Rabbi Israel of Rizhin and] said to
> him: "Rebbe, I so wish to repent, but I don't know what to
> do."
> "And to sin, you knew what to do?"
> "Yes, but that was easy. First I sinned, then I knew."
> "Exactly. Now do the same the other way around. Start by
> repenting; you'll know later."[24]

Understanding, acceptance, commitment . . . in community we learn that the experience of spirituality is more than seeing, more than feeling, more than willing—it is the essential interplay and interconnection of all three. The Sufi tell a story:

> Past the seeker, as he prayed, came the crippled and the beggar and the beaten. And seeing them, the holy one went down into deep prayer and cried, "Great God, how is it that a loving creator can see such things and yet do nothing about them?"
>
> And out of the long silence, God said: "I did do something about them. I made you."[25]

Chapter 6

SHARED VISION, SHARED HOPE

❖

To "feel less alone" is, without doubt, an ultimate quest of all life, yet perhaps never before has loneliness been so widespread as it is today.

Matina Horner[1]

Rabbi Hanokh loved to tell this story:

> For a whole year I felt a longing to go to my master Rabbi Bunam and talk with him. But every time I entered the house, I felt I wasn't man enough. Once though, when I was walking across a field and weeping, I knew that I must run to the rabbi without delay. He asked, "Why are you weeping?"
>
> I answered: "I am after all alive in this world, a being created with all the senses and all the limbs, but I do not know what it is I was created for and what I am good for in this world."
>
> "Little fool," he replied, "that's the same question I have carried around with me all my life. You will come and eat the evening meal with me today."[2]

Spirituality is nurtured in *community*, the oneness with others that springs from shared vision and shared goal, shared memory and shared hope. As Ignatius of Antioch advised first-century Christians, one cultivates the "way of life" that is spirituality by seeking out "the company of the saints": those seeking to live the same way of life. While spirituality can be discovered in solitude—by retreating to a cell of some kind, by reading, thinking, meditating, praying—it can be fulfilled only in community. The desert abba Poemen offered a telling observation: "It's possible to spend a hundred years in your cell without ever learning anything." Many hundreds of years later the Hasidic Rabbi Jacob Yitzhak clearly stated the reason: "The way cannot be learned out of a book, or from hearsay, but can only be communicated from person to person."[3]

Why do we need community? Saint Basil, criticizing a life lived "in service to the needs of the individual" as "plainly in conflict with the law of love," asked: "Whose feet wilt thou then wash? Whom wilt thou care for?" And Saint Augustine offered an interpretation of a familiar New Testament story that one popular modern speaker embellishes in explaining why, even though he is convinced that a "Higher Power" saved him from his alcoholism, he still needs Alcoholics Anonymous.

> It's sort of like the raising of Lazarus from the dead. After Jesus had called Lazarus forth from the tomb, he told the bystanders to free him from his burial bonds. My Higher Power raised me, called me forth, from my alcoholism, but I need the other drunks in Alcoholics Anonymous to unwrap me, to let me loose and keep me loose from it.[4]

Rather than asking *why* we need community, it may be more important to ask *how* we need others. Wisdom's answer to that question, the answer embodied in the spirituality of imperfection, is that human beings need each other precisely in relationships of mutuality. *Mutuality* involves not just "give or get," nor even "give and get." In relationships of mutuality we give *by* getting and get *by* giving, recognizing that we truly gain only what we seek to give and that we are able to give only that which we are seeking to gain.

That may sound complicated, but the experience of mutuality is the foundation of the very existence of Alcoholics Anonymous. This is the main discovery that Bill Wilson made in his first meeting with Doctor Bob Smith.

> Bill got sober in early December 1934. For several months he tried to help other alcoholics by sharing his newfound sobriety with them. Those he approached showed no interest.

Then, in early May of 1935, Wilson went to Akron, Ohio, on a business deal, which promptly fell through.

On the day before Mothers' Day, Bill paced the lobby of the Mayflower Hotel in Akron, getting more and more depressed. Sounds of laughter and of ice tinkling in glasses wafted from the bar, and he caught himself thinking a thought he had not had in over five months: "I need a drink!" It was hardly a new concept.

But then that impulse was pushed out of his mind by an idea that was completely new: "No, I don't need a drink—I *need* another alcoholic!" And striding purposefully away from the bar and toward the lobby telephone booths, Bill Wilson began the series of calls that led him the next day to meet Dr. Robert Holbrook Smith, who would become AA's co-founder.

Twenty years later, retelling this story at AA's "Coming of Age" convention, Wilson explained why his meeting with Dr. Bob had been different—why, after all his earlier failures, this meeting had worked.

> You see, our talk was a completely *mutual* thing. . . . I knew that I needed this alcoholic as much as he needed me. *This was it.* And this mutual give-and-take is at the very heart of all of AA's Twelfth Step work today. The final missing link was located right there in my first talk with Dr. Bob.[5]

The point is reinforced by the experience of the alcoholic who became "A.A. #3." Bill D. had already been hospitalized many times as a result of his drinking. Because of his prominence in the community, many had tried to help him. None had succeeded. Why then did he listen to Bill Wilson and Dr. Bob Smith when these two strangers confronted him? What was different about their approach?

> "All the other people that had talked to me wanted to help *me*, and my pride prevented me from listening to them, and caused only resentment on my part, but I felt as if I would be a real stinker if I did not listen to a couple of fellows for a short time, if that would cure *them*."[6]

Mutuality: the awareness that life's most precious realities—love, wisdom, sobriety—are attained only in the giving of them and are given only in the openness to receive them. A half-century after A.A.'s founding, Jean Vanier—former naval officer, former philosophy professor, former student for the Catholic priesthood—offered an understanding of *mutuality* derived from his meditation on the story of the confrontation between Jesus of Nazareth and "the sinful woman."

> He does not tell the woman who approaches him, Mary Magdalene, to get her act together; He does not *just* "forgive" her or "heal" her—which will prove, after all, to be the same. Rather he begins by exposing to her his need—he says "I need you."[7]

Vanier discovered mutuality—*giving by getting, getting by giving*—in his work with the disabled. In 1964 at the small French village of Trosly-Breuil, *"le grand girafe,"* as the tall, rumpled Canadian is affectionately referred to by his friends, founded L'Arche as a homelike setting in which non-disabled people would live with the disabled in the practical, daily understanding that each member of both groups had something to offer all the others. Vanier and his compatriots at L'Arche soon discovered two intertwined realities. First, the handicapped person needs not only to receive love but also to give love in return. And second, the weak and the broken do have much to give—they can heal us because they tap the well of our own brokenness.

> In telling the story of one of his friends, the gravely crippled Armando, Vanier suggests how mutuality heals.
>   "Because he is so broken, in some way we can allow him to reveal to us our brokenness without getting angry. . . . He is so broken that I am allowed to look at my own brokenness without being ashamed."[8]

As he spent more and more time with the handicapped, with the varieties of broken individuals so easily discarded like a kind of jetsam in the modern age of technological perfection, Vanier became convinced that "healing happens only in a *community* of love." But, he quickly goes on to insist, the "community of love" in which that healing occurs is both earthly and earthy. This is not a place of angels and refined spirits, filled with sweetness and light and heavenly bliss, but a very painful place, a place of grieving, a place of loss, a place of death. "Community is the realization that evil is *inside*," Vanier says. "Not only inside my community, but inside *me*."[9]

✧

Our need for *mutuality* arises from our very flawedness and imperfection; it originates in the fact that by ourselves we are never enough. We need others to help us; we need others in order to help them. Thus, the question "Who am I?" carries within itself another, even more important question: "Where do I belong?" We find *self*—ourselves—only through the actual practice of locating ourselves within the community of our fellow human beings. Discovering community and becoming aware of our "location" within that community involves the experience of "fitting." Real *"feeling* good," the "feeling good" that comes only from *"being* good," involves "fitting in" with others who are engaged in the quest for answers to their most anguished questions.

> The devotee knelt to be initiated into discipleship. The guru whispered the sacred mantra into his ear, warning him not to reveal it to anyone.
>
> "What will happen if I do?" asked the devotee.
>
> Said the guru, "Anyone to whom you reveal the mantra will be liberated from the bondage of ignorance and suffering, but you yourself will be excluded from discipleship and suffer damnation."
>
> No sooner had he heard those words than the devotee rushed to the marketplace, collected a large crowd around him, and repeated the sacred mantra for all to hear.
>
> The disciples later reported this to the guru and demanded that the man be expelled from the monastery for his disobedience.

The guru smiled and said, "He has no need of anything I can teach. His action has shown him to be a guru in his own right."[10]

Community is created when people seek the same spiritual reality. The key to community is the discovery that *we are all looking for, but we find what we are looking for only by being looked for.* Our fellow seekers comprise what Ignatius of Antioch first termed "the company of the saints." In such company, one is likely to find friends who are also guides: wise women and men who listen well, who offer advice and support, who help us to clarify our questions, to recognize our options and to make our choices, *and who seek and find in us the same realities.*[11]

We need "significant others"—not in the soft sense of needing others whom we cherish and are cherished by, important as this may be—but in the meaning intended by the originator of the term, the early twentieth-century philosopher and social psychologist, George Herbert Mead. Mead coined the term *significant other* to indicate the one who signifies or reflects back to us the meanings of our gestures and, in doing so, develops with us our ability to act meaningfully with others.[12]

The point is that it takes two. Being human requires more than one, for human be-ing—the behavior that flows from our humanness—never takes place in a vacuum. It is "more like a wink than a blink," to use a helpful distinction suggested by Clifford Geertz, an anthropologist sensitive to manifestations of spirituality. The blink and the wink have in common certain physiological characteristics—they look alike. But a blink is unintended, automatic, its purpose self-contained—to lubricate the eye. A wink, on the contrary, has a different kind of purpose: It conveys an intention and, as such, is *necessarily* directed toward another. Why? because the wink can succeed as a wink only if it is perceived by the other *as* a wink and not as a blink. Our most human behavior is fundamentally intentional, and intentionality becomes actualized only as effective *co*-intentionality: which means simply that it takes two to make a wink; we cannot *be* humanly in isolation from others.[13]

Unity, our own wholeness, is discovered only within community;

THE SPIRITUALITY OF IMPERFECTION

and "community" comes into being only co-intentionally, in the recognition and acceptance of mutuality. A modern teacher of spiritual mentoring makes the point with a story.

> One of the early spiritual mentors, John of Lycopolis, tells of an ascetic who lived alone in the desert where he encountered many temptations. Eventually he returns to the life of community after a dream in which an angel advises him: "God has accepted your repentance and has had mercy on you. In future take care that you are not deceived. The brethren to whom you gave spiritual counsel will come to console you, and they will bring you gifts. Welcome them, eat with them and always give thanks to God."
>
> For those of us who are spiritual mentors, the awareness that others bring us gifts and that we need to welcome them, eat with them, and always give thanks to God is one of the most important aspects of our ministry.[14]

Another story, by another modern student of spiritual direction, clarifies the other side of that mutual relationship:

> A monk once confessed to an elder: "In my cell I do all that one is counselled to do there, and I find no consolation from God."
>
> The elder said: "This happens to you because you want your own will to be fulfilled."
>
> The brother said, "What then do you order me to do, father?"
>
> The elder said, "Go, attach yourself to a man who fears God, humble yourself before him, give up your will to him, and then you will receive consolation from God."[15]

The practice of seeking out guides, mentors, or soul-friends who might give some direction in the journey toward spirituality is an ancient one. Spiritual "directors"—those who offer a sense of direction—rarely "teach" in the ordinary sense of telling truths. Instead, they serve first and foremost as *listeners,* hearers who attend in a way that elicits honesty, sincerity, truthfulness, and conscientiousness from the speaker. "Hidden things hinder wholeheartedness," observed Cassian, known as the Father of Western Monasticism, whose two great works, *The Institutes* and *The Conferences*, codified the thoughts and the practices of the Desert Fathers. By listening well, by asking the right questions, by requiring "wholeheartedness," a spiritual director helps uncover the reality of one's spiritual condition.

For the first "mutuality"—the first reality gained by giving and given by getting—is *honesty*. Only in telling another the truth about ourselves do we discover the truth about ourselves. Honesty with others is as essential to honesty with self as honesty with self is essential to honesty with others. We can "tell" only what we know, but we come to "know" only in the telling.

Such honesty, the honesty that undergirds *wisdom*, comes not from books or beliefs, dogmas or doctrines, but from people.

> Once, when Rabbi Mordecai was in the great town of Minsk expounding the Torah to a number of men hostile to his way, they laughed at him. "What you say does not explain the verse in the least," they cried.
>
> "Do you really think," he replied, "that I was trying to explain the verse in the book? That doesn't need an explanation! I want to explain the verse that is within me."[16]

❖

The spirituality of imperfection begins, as the Desert Fathers and Mothers suggested, with "disciple approaching master, asking for words of advice." This process of *identification and seeking* is common to all traditions at all times. The sixteenth-century mystic John of the Cross summed up the insight: "The virtuous soul that is alone and without a master is like a lone burning coal. It will grow colder rather than hotter."[17]

Irish spirituality produced a saying with similar meaning: *Colainn gan cheann duine gan anamchara* ("a person without a soul-friend is a body without a head"). Eastern Christianity, in the person of Symeon the New Theologian, stressed "the vital need for living, personal direction in the spiritual life." The Hasidic master Rabbi Jacob Yitzhak was known for his insistence that "the way" can only be communicated from person to person.[18] And, of course, there is a story.

In the days when Rabbi Bunam still traded in lumber, a number of merchants in Danzig asked him why he, who was so well-versed in the sacred writings, went to visit *zaddikim*. What could they tell him that he could not learn from his books? He answered them, but they did not understand him.

That evening, they invited him to go to the play with them, but he refused. When they returned from the theater, they told him they had seen wonderful things. "I know all about those wonderful things," said he. "I have read the program."

"But from that," they said, "you cannot possibly know what we have seen with our own eyes."

"That's just how it is," he said, "with the books and the *zaddikim*."[19]

The meeting between the novice and the experienced practitioner is essential not because the elders are necessarily wiser or holier, but because the seeking itself signifies the humility and willingness to learn that makes spiritual wisdom possible. All true wisdom must be grounded in accurate self-knowledge, and the self-knowledge that is wisdom comes not from "answers" but from identification.

Rabbi Leib, the hidden *zaddik* who wandered over the earth, said this: "I did not go to the maggid in order to hear Torah from him, but to see how he unlaces his shoes and laces them up again."[20]

Through the process of *identification*, the spirituality of imperfection is transmitted from person to person. Indeed, one large chapter in the history of spirituality may be summarized in an ever-recurring story found in one form or another in every tradition.

The disciple, the would-be initiate, approaches the master and says: "Teach me."

And the teacher replies: "Come, *follow* me."

Sometimes, the newcomer tries to insist: "No, I mean *tell* me."

And the adept can only smile a welcoming love that cannot be "told."

More often, like the good and intelligent aspirant in Luke's gospel, the now-no-longer-neophyte turns sadly away.

Spirituality is a reality that one approaches not by "learning," but by *following.*[21]

This "following" is *identification,* and like love, it involves a kind of fusion of the knower with the known. The medieval monks termed this identification *imitatio,* presenting it as a two-part process. The first part—*imitatio effectus operis*—involved an external imitation of the deeds and gestures described in the stories that narrated the life of Christ and the lives of the saints. There would follow, it was hoped, the second (more difficult) part, *imitatio affectus mentis*—the *internalization* of the attitudes, emotions, and self-awareness appropriate to the story.[22]

The two parts were, of course, understood to be mutually reinforcing: External actions both signal and shape internal attitudes. Later thinkers in the tradition conveyed this insight more colloquially, from William James's "Act yourself into a new way of thinking" to A.A.'s axiom, "Bring the body, the mind will follow." But the ancient monastic appreciation of identification as a two-part process remains useful because it helps to clarify the important distinction between true identification and mere imitation.

When Rabbi Noah, Rabbi Mordecai's son, assumed the succession after his father's death, his disciples noticed that there were a number of ways in which he conducted himself differently than his father, and asked him about this.

"I do just as my father did," Rabbi Noah replied. "He did not imitate, and I do not imitate."[23]

Psychoanalyst Annie Reich suggests a useful way of distinguishing identification from "imitation."

It is imitation (magical identification) when the child holds the newspaper *like* his father. It is identification when the child learns to read. Imitation means trying to *be* the envied parent but not necessarily to *become* it. This is the domain of magical achievements.[24]

The desire to *become* and the commitment to do whatever is necessary to *become* distinguish identification from imitation. Imitation indicates wishing: "it would be nice" to be like so-and-so. Identification involves *willing* and especially *willingness*—the *openness* to do whatever is necessary to become like the model, the willingness that accepts that one can never "be" another.

> The Rabbi of Kotzk said: "Everything in the world can be imitated, except truth. For truth that is imitated is no longer truth."[25]

Many stories in many traditions illustrate the difference between wishing and willing, between imitation and identification, between demanding to be, which is easy, and the willingness to become, which is rare:

> When the King visited the monasteries of the great Zen master Lin Chi, he was astonished to learn that there were more than ten thousand monks living there with him.
> Wanting to know the exact number of monks, the King asked, "How many disciples do you have?"
> Lin Chi replied, "Four or five at the very most."[26]

Identification has been called "the half-way house between self-love and other-love." It is a reaching out from the self toward another whom one admires and respects, but it stops short of trying to *be* other than who one is. Each of us is and can be only our own self. Yet learning how to be a person—or, more accurately, learning to *be* the particular *kind of* person we are—originates through identification, and identification takes place in community. The question "Who am I?" really asks, "Where do I *belong* or *fit*?" We get the sense of that "direction"—the sense of moving toward the place where we fit, or of shaping the place toward which we are moving so that it will fit us—from hearing how others have handled or are attempting to handle similar (but never exactly the same) situations. We learn by listening to their stories, by hearing how they came (or failed) to belong or fit.

> Knowing how another human being lives and functions on the inside —how he or she handles the vicissitudes of life, copes with its joys and frustrations, faces critical choices, meets failure and defeat as well as challenge and success—is what enables us to feel prepared for life.
>
> It is the availability of appropriate individuals with whom we can identify, individuals who also permit us to do so, which quiets the inner yearning [of the need] for preparedness, for an external model that may serve as an internal guide for the self.[27]

". . . *the availability of appropriate individuals with whom we can identify.*" One all-important question remains. With whom do we *choose* to identify? A Sufi story addresses this ancient concern.

> A man walking through the forest saw a fox that had lost its legs, and he wondered how it lived. Then he saw a tiger come up with game in its mouth. The tiger ate its fill and left the rest of the meat for the fox.
>
> The next day God fed the fox by means of the same tiger. The man began to wonder at God's greatness and said to himself, "I too shall just rest in a corner with full trust in the Lord and he will provide me with all that I need."
>
> He did this for many days but nothing happened, and he was almost at death's door when he heard a voice say, "O you who are in the path of error, open your eyes to the truth! Stop imitating the disabled fox and follow the example of the tiger."[28]

"If you have decided you want what we have . . ." begins what some members term "the most important words in the book *Alcoholics Anonymous.*" That those words invite identification rather than mere external imitation is clear from their placement; they introduce A.A.'s Twelve Steps. Real human-hood involves not sheer physical exertion but moral and spiritual vigor. In a gentle mockery of his contemporary Theodore Roosevelt's brawny image of muscular potency, the philosopher William James chose to name the energy that goes into this process of identification "the strenuous mood." The following passage by Don S. Browning, who brings a profound spiritual sensitivity to his study of James, eloquently captures the philosopher/psychologist's meaning:

> [James's] strenuous mood is the opposite of the "easygoing mood" and the attitude of "I don't care." It is a positive attitude of care— care for oneself, one's family, the wider community, and possible future communities which may extend beyond the limits of one's individual life. The strenuous mood entails a personal identification of one's self with a wider range of people and communities, both present and future. It involves heightening one's sympathies and overcoming what James called that "certain blindness" in human beings which makes it difficult for us to appreciate and respect the inner meaning of another's experience.[29]

To appreciate "the inner meaning of another's experience" requires something not often considered part of "the strenuous mood" —the ability to *listen* truly and well. All "community" begins in *listening.* "Spirituality," "wisdom," "that-which-all-seek" is initially transmitted from one person to another by *attending,* one of James's favorite words, which means to be present in a *hearing* way, to *listen to* others in such a way that we are willing to surrender our own worldview. Only by such "attending" can we discover the way of life that we really seek—a way of life that is more than mere "worldview" in the same way that wisdom is more than knowledge and love is more than acquaintance. What happens first, in any "community," is that those who would participate in it *listen.*[30]

But if we would listen, we must also tell; and if we would tell our stories, we need places where we can tell and listen. In this mutuality between telling and listening, between speaking and hearing, lies the deepest spiritual significance of mutual-aid groups (sometimes erroneously termed "self-help groups"), like Alcoholics Anonymous. Those wrestling with spiritual dilemmas do not need answers but presence—permission to confront the dilemma and struggle with it aloud.[31]

Thus, if an essential component of spirituality is attending—listening—it is also a human truth that we are able to listen only when we know that in time, we will be able to tell our own story. Perhaps the main benefit of the storytelling format, whether in the Egyptian desert, the Eastern European *shtetl*, or a meeting of Alcoholics Anonymous, is that it invites, enables, and teaches *listening*. When we are able to tell our own stories, when we are urged to stand up and tell them, we learn respect for other peoples' stories and for their need to tell them. The practice of telling stories gives birth to good listeners.

And practice in listening produces good storytelling. *Ausculta*— "Listen" insists the first word of the sixth-century Rule of Saint Benedict, the longest-flourishing monastic canon. As Bernard of Clairvaux urged: "You wish to see; Listen." The world has always needed good listeners, for only good listeners are truthful tellers. "Good listening" involves the surrender of a self-centered view of the world; it entails the equation of trust and love that flows from that surrender. To listen, to surrender, to trust, to love: These are to be open to discovery. Spirituality flourishes in discovery, and especially in the discovery of shared story—the discovery that creates community. For *community* is where we can learn and practice storytelling and its virtues, "humility" and "obedience"—two painfully misunderstood qualities that are really *the arts of listening*. Humility involves the refusal to coerce, the rejection of all attempts to control others; real listening may be the most humanizing act of humility. Obedience—to *obey*—means simply to "listen thoroughly."

> It is reported that in the early days of his move to the desert, Evagrius visited an old Desert Father, perhaps Macarius of Egypt, and asked him, "Tell me some piece of advice by which I might be able to save my soul." The reply was, "If you wish to save your soul, do not speak before you are asked a question."[32]

A modern-day lament by a nursing-home resident captures both the importance of listening thoroughly and the utter despair that occurs when there is no one available or willing to listen:

> "Heard . . . If they only understood how important it is that we be heard! I can take being in a nursing home. It's

really all right, with a positive attitude. My daughter has her hands full, three kids and a job. She visits regularly. I understand.

"But most people here . . . they just want to tell their story. That's what they have to give, don't you see? And it's a precious thing to them. It's their life they want to give. You'd think people would understand what it means to us . . . to give our lives in a story.

"So we listen to each other. Most of what goes on here is people listening to each other's stories. People who work here consider that to be . . . filling time. If they only knew. If they'd just take a minute to listen!"[33]

Long before his first meeting with Bill Wilson, the meeting that has been referred to as the founding moment of Alcoholics Anonymous, Dr. Robert Holbrook Smith joined the Oxford Group in the hope of finding a "cure" for his alcoholism. It didn't work. He went to the meetings, read the books, sought and practiced "guidance" by seeking direction from both God and other group members . . . and consistently went home and got drunk again. Then, in November 1934, Bill Wilson had his last drink, and in May 1935, he happened into Bob Smith's life.

On that Sunday evening, as the two men alternately sat and paced for more than five hours in the library of Henrietta Sieberling's residence in Akron, Ohio, something was added to the Oxford Group message. The *identification* that sprang from their listening to each other helped both Bill Wilson and Dr. Robert Smith to the understanding—the vision—that the purpose of life wasn't to get but to give . . . for only when you give, do you get! The religious rigor of the Oxford Group had afforded only a kind of monologue: Many people spoke, but few of even the silent seemed ever to listen. In their first meeting with each other, Bill W. and Dr. Bob did listen, avidly, and in that listening both came to the realization that what they needed was a dialogue, and that in their shared alcoholism, on the basis of their common imperfection, they had found it.[34]

Years later, Dr. Bob explained in liquid terms singularly appropri-

THE ROOTS OF WISDOM

ate for an alcoholic the most profound message he had learned from
Bill W.

**The spiritual approach was as useless as any other if you
soaked it up like a sponge and kept it to yourself.**

Part Two

THE DISCOVERIES OF ALCOHOLICS ANONYMOUS

❖

More than most people I think alcoholics want to know who they are, what life is all about, whether they have a divine origin and an appointed destiny, live in a system of cosmic justice and love.

Bill W.[1]

✧

Ancient thought about the paradox of being human was transported into twentieth century life by the most unlikely group imaginable: a handful of "hopeless" drunks. The founding members of Alcoholics Anonymous did not intentionally resurrect the spirituality of imperfection, nor were many of them even aware that they had tapped ancient wisdom in their search for a new way of life. And so the story of *how* they achieved this becomes all the more fascinating.

The historical context is important. In the mid-1930s, alcoholism was viewed by medical practitioners as a "hopeless" disease; the only cure medicine suggested was a "moral psychology" capable of inducing "an entire psychic change" of sufficient magnitude that it could overcome the "compulsion" to drink. The earliest members of A.A. knew about "hopeless" from their own experience of the disease and their previous efforts at recovery. Drawing on those experiences, as well as on their origins in the Oxford Group and on the philosophies of William James and Carl Jung, they set out to fashion a way of life that would allow them to live with their "hopeless disease," with their basic imperfection.[2]

In this process, they re-discovered four insights that reflected the teachings of spiritual thinkers from all ages and all traditions. What they discovered were not commandments—*Thou Shalts* or *Thou Shalt Nots*—nor even suggestions, as A.A.'s Twelve Steps are sometimes presented. They found instead what might be thought of as beacons or signal lights that guide those who seek a spirituality that fits their imperfect condition, safeguarding them from the rocks, shoals, and other avoidable traps that could abort or impede their journey.

Although we can describe these guiding insights as "discoveries

THE SPIRITUALITY OF IMPERFECTION

made for the modern age by the earliest members of Alcoholics Anonymous," these discoveries cannot be made for us, or for anyone else, by someone else. Nor are they ever found once and for all. For these are truths that must be rediscovered, sometimes on a daily basis, by each person interested in spirituality. Because others have gone before, the way is in some sense easier; yet it remains true that spirituality, like *daily bread,* comes "one day at a time." Each day requires constant rediscovery and continually new insight into what it means to be human, what it means to exist as a fully human being.

What were these "discoveries of Alcoholics Anonymous"? Four such insights can be discerned—insights that, although they did not and do not flow in any straight-line fashion, nevertheless do reveal a pattern, a kind of order, in how they tend to be discovered . . . or at least such a pattern emerges from the experience of Alcoholics Anonymous.

The first discovery made by those earliest members of Alcoholics Anonymous was that spirituality is *essential* but *different: essential* to their recovery of human be-ing, but *different* from what anyone imagines it to be on first hearing that statement.

Second came the discovery that there exists a vast difference between magic and miracle, between magic and mystery—and that spirituality involves not magic's manipulation, but the wonder inherent in *mystery* and *miracle.*

The third discovery of those earliest members was that spirituality is essentially *open-ended;* unable to be "grasped" or "possessed," it is more at home with questions than with answers.

Fourthly and finally, they discovered that any true spirituality must *pervade* every aspect of one's existence—that spirituality is a reality that touches everything in one's life, or it touches nothing of one's life.

❖

Each of these discoveries comes only by *experience.* One "discovers" not by being told, but by *doing;* the spirituality of imperfection is necessarily pragmatic. And so those earliest members of Alcoholics Anonymous made their discoveries by putting them into practice—trying them on and trying them out, in the awareness that we learn first, and most, from our own successes and failures, our own triumphs and tragedies, our own story. The first A.A.s borrowed amply and widely for their Twelve Steps, but they tested everything against their own experience. "The spiritual life is not a theory," their Big Book states. *"We have to live it."*[3]

How Bill Wilson, Dr. Bob Smith, and those who followed them made that discovery and how they put into practice what they discovered is the story we will tell in Part Two.

Chapter 7

SPIRITUALITY IS ESSENTIAL . . . BUT DIFFERENT

❖

. . . an illness which only a spiritual experience will conquer.

Alcoholics Anonymous, p. 44.

Dr. Bob Smith and Bill Wilson looked down at the falsely hearty, still shaking figure on the hospital bed. Both men knew the torn feelings and the desperate hope that hid under that facade. Wilson had been sober six months; Dr. Smith for barely a week. The spectre of what they had once been stared back at them both, and they endured a moment of doubt. Had they bitten off more than they could chew?

The nurse had filled them in on some of the details of this case. Bill D., a prominent attorney, was a former city councilman and church vestryman. He was also, the weary nurse confided, a "real corker." This was his eighth detoxification in six months, and within minutes of entering the hospital he had physically assaulted two nurses, leaving both with black eyes.

The three men chatted for a while, and it quickly became apparent to Bill D. that his visitors knew what they were talking about, that they were real drunks who were now happily sober—an earth-shattering concept if there ever was one —and maybe he'd better listen up, see if he could learn something. But like most alcoholics, Bill D. was better at talking than listening, and he droned on and on about his drinking, his despair, and the utter ruin of his life.

Wilson finally interrupted, explaining that he and Dr. Smith had to give their "program" to someone else if they were to stay sober themselves. And so they had to know: was Bill D. really certain that he wanted it? Because if he wasn't certain, he was doing something much worse than wasting their time—he was actually endangering their sobriety. They wouldn't stay around and nag at him if he wasn't ready; they would have to "be going and looking for someone else."

Entranced by the clear-eyed enthusiasm of these two men even as they spoke of their own hopelessness, Bill D. declared that Yes, he wanted the program. But when his visitors began talking about "a spiritual program" and a "Higher Power," he shook his head. "No, no," he said emphatically. "It's too late for me. I still believe in God all right, but I know mighty well that He doesn't believe in me any more."

Smith and Wilson were not about to give up on their first recruit. They told Bill D. they understood how he felt, and then they left, promising to visit again the next day. They did return, and over the next several days, they visited again and again. One morning they arrived to find Bill D. sitting up in bed, talking excitedly with his wife. During the previous night, he explained, "hope had dawned," and he understood that "if Bob and Bill can do it, I can do it. Maybe we can all do together what we could not do separately."

A few days later Dr. Smith, the more conventionally religious of A.A.'s two co-founders, stopped by on his daily visit with Bill D., who would some years later be known as "Alcoholics Anonymous Number Three." As they chatted, something in one of this first recruit's remarks—a bit of cynicism about help from "a power greater" than himself—caught the surgeon's attention, and he decided to confront him. "Young man," Dr. Smith challenged in his resonant baritone. "Have you abandoned your God?"

Bill D. was not even momentarily taken aback. Calmly, but with a great deal of quiet pain, he answered: "Gee, no,

Doc, I don't think so . . . but I sure feel that my God has abandoned me."[1]

❖

That cry of abandonment captures the experience of so many human beings who live in despair, who search endlessly for meaning in a cruel, chaotic, unjust world. The "hidden God" is a challenge, for if there is a God—and just about everybody at one time or another doubts even this part—He, She, or It seems to be *hiding*. This may sound like a very modern malaise, but the complaint is not new.

> The favorite disciple of Rabbi Pinchas complained to him that it was very difficult in adversity to retain perfect faith in the belief that God provides for every human being. "It actually seems as if God were hiding his face from such an unhappy being," he exclaimed.
>
> "It ceases to be a hiding," replied Rabbi Pinchas, "if you know it is hiding."[2]

The same Hasidic tradition reminds that there is another way of understanding this experience.

> The Medzibozer's grandson, Yechiel Michel, was playing hide and seek with another child. He hid himself for some time, but his playmate did not look for him. Little Yechiel ran to Rabbi Baruch and said amid tears: "He did not look for me!"
>
> The Rabbi said: "This is also God's complaint, that we seek Him not."[3]

Yet the problem is not "finding" God; as C. S. Lewis observed: "To speak of man's search for God is like speaking of the mouse's search for the cat." In *The Hound of Heaven,* poet Francis Thompson offered in his title-image an understanding that comes even closer to the insight that infuses the spirituality of imperfection. For the problem is not "finding" God, but how do we let ourselves be found by a Hidden God.

Once upon a time, a carefree young girl who lived at the edge of a forest and who loved to wander in the forest became lost. As it grew dark and the little girl did not return home, her parents became very worried. They began calling for the little girl and searching in the forest, and it grew darker. The parents returned home and called neighbors and people from the town to help them search for their little girl.

Meanwhile, the little girl wandered about in the forest and became very worried and anxious as it grew dark, because she could not find her way home. She tried one path and another and became more and more tired. Coming to a clearing in the forest, she lay down by a big rock and fell asleep.

Her frantic parents and neighbors scoured the forest. They called and called the little girl's name but to no avail. Many of the searchers became exhausted and left, but the little girl's father continued searching throughout the night.

Early in the morning, the father came to the clearing where the girl had lain to sleep. He suddenly saw his little girl and ran toward her, yelling and making a great noise on the dry branches which awoke the girl.

The little girl saw her father, and with a great shout of joy she exclaimed, "Daddy, I found you!"[4]

We are all looking for, but we find what we are looking for only by being looked for. Members of Alcoholics Anonymous discover that the most important discovery is that one *has been* discovered; however it happens, some version of this kind of discovery is essential to sobriety and to living a fully human life. The conviction that there is some reality *beyond* self, some "power greater than ourselves," has brought hope into thousands of alcoholics' lives—people just as "hopeless" as Bill D., just as leery of other alcoholics ("I'm not like them!") and just as wary of anything even remotely connected to "God," "religion," or the "spiritual."

Most actively drinking alcoholics have Bill D.'s image of "God" fixed firmly in their minds: something that has gone away and abandoned them, probably because it never existed in the first place. Within Alcoholics Anonymous, they learn that they can reclaim "God," calling that "higher power" anything they want, as long as they are ready to admit that they cannot control everything in life. In order to stay sober, they must admit their own helplessness to stay sober by themselves, by their own power.

"First of all, we had to quit playing God," declares the book *Alcoholics Anonymous*. Spiritual thinkers throughout the centuries have said the same thing in virtually the same words. A.A.'s genius can be found in the next sentence: "It didn't work." But recognizing the effort to "play God" taught something: One cannot escape "the spiritual" even in the midst of efforts to deny it. And so early on, the fellowship of Alcoholics Anonymous rediscovered a truth familiar to the ancients, but lost for the most part to the modern world: "The spiritual" is essential to being human, but "the spiritual" is *different* from what one imagines it to be on first hearing that claim.

The earliest members of Alcoholics Anonymous learned the hard way about the spiritual being "essential." A January 1940 letter from Bill W. to the wife of early member Clarence S., who founded the fellowship in Cleveland and was the first to call its gatherings "meetings of Alcoholics Anonymous," tells that story well.

> During the past 12 months we have had quite a number who felt that the fellowship, the helpful attitude toward others, the warming of the heart at social gatherings, was going to be sufficient to overcome the alcoholic's obsession. Taking stock at the year's end, we find that this school of thought has few survivors, for the bottled heat treatment has persuaded them that we must find some sort of spiritual basis for living, else we die. A few, who have worked ardently with other alcoholics on the philosophical, rather than the spiritual plane, now say of themselves "We believed that Faith without works was dead, but we have now conclusively proved that works without Faith is dead also."[5]

In another letter written a few months later, Wilson makes the point even more forcefully. Writing to a member who was trying to get A.A. started in a new city, Bill began by explaining why he chose to emphasize "what in the last analysis, really makes A.A. tick—i.e., the spiritual angle":

> I explain this at some length because I want you to be successful with yourself and the people with whom you work. We used to pussyfoot

on this spiritual business a great deal more out here [New York City] and the result was bad, for our record falls quite a lot short of the performance of Akron and Cleveland, where there are now about 350 alcoholics, many of them sober 2 or 3 years, with less than 20% ever having had any relapse. Out there they have always emphasized the spiritual way of life as the core of our procedure and we have begun to follow suit in New York for the simple reason that our record was only half as good, most of the difficulties being directly attributable to temporizing over what it really takes to fix the drunks, *i.e., the spiritual*.[6]

Bill Wilson and the other early A.A. members discovered that "the spiritual" was *essential*—it was, in other words, *what it really takes to fix the drunks*. But they also discovered that whatever this spirituality was, it was *different*—it was not what anyone ever imagined it to be, and especially it was not what any one envisioned on first hearing the claim that the spiritual was "essential."

Every newcomer to Alcoholics Anonymous brings along two false stereotypes. The first is the image of the alcoholic as hopeless degenerate, dissolute and unkempt or, at best, spineless and weak-willed. This notion begins to break up the minute some clear-eyed member introduces himself as "an alcoholic," and it is shattered into ever smaller pieces each time a sober alcoholic embraces that identity. Ears perk up, twitching fingers scratch flushed foreheads, and old ideas are shredded as the at-first-disbelieving new member listens to maturely sober individuals describe what only an alcoholic can experience, thus testifying by their very presence that the term *alcoholic* can signify something other than "drunk."

The second erroneous stereotype, which generally takes a bit longer to subvert, involves spirituality. The typical newcomer to Alcoholics Anonymous hears in "the spiritual" another name for religion—a program for perfection, a fellowship of those who claim to be, or at least hope to become, "holy." Such a way of life holds little appeal for a down-and-out drunk, even if he is at the moment a nondrinking drunk. Who wants to sit in a church, even if only in the church basement, and pretend to be saintly? And what high-toned spiritual program would let in a bunch of drunks, anyway?

But in meeting after meeting, as sober alcoholic after sober alcoholic stands up to tell his or her story, occasionally peppering the narratives with words that "would make a sailor's parrot blush" (as Wilson's biographer Robert Thomsen put it in describing A.A.'s early meetings), a new image of spirituality takes root. This isn't a program of perfection but a way of life that accepts imperfection *as* imperfection! This isn't a room full of saints, but a fellowship of sinners! For if words like *love, honesty,* and *trust* can be mixed in with the sadness, fear, despair, and degradation of any alcoholic's life, then maybe spirituality is something that alcoholics *can* claim, maybe there is something to this "higher power" stuff, something that can bring release, gratitude, humility, tolerance, and forgiveness back into lives that had lost all hope of ever experiencing them again.[7]

"God comes through the wound": The descent to the depths brings the realization that without help one is lost. The spirituality of imperfection is the spirituality of the weak and the broken, the poor and the humble. It is and always has been a spirituality for people with large and strong passions, with troubled pasts and uncertain futures, a spirituality both ordinary and unconventional.

For those who live a spirituality of imperfection seem always, somehow, to combine those two paradoxical qualities, to be both "ordinary" and "unconventional." Socrates quietly declined to wear shoes, Jesus Christ turned the other cheek, Francis of Assisi watched placidly as "Brother Fire" consumed his home. Julian of Norwich encouraged the contrite that God wants saints who have been sinners, Caussade insisted that the fruit of grace is discovered in the "abyss" of our "wretchedness," Gandhi and Martin Luther King practiced passive resistance in extraordinarily violent times, Mother Teresa discovered her God among the destitute outcasts of Calcutta. . . .

The spirituality of imperfection, of which Alcoholics Anonymous forms a modern tributary, has always flowed in unpredictable directions. In fact, the whole story of Alcoholics Anonymous might be summed up as an ongoing quest for a nonconventional spirituality. For that is how A.A. began, according to Bill Wilson, who always insisted that the roots of Alcoholics Anonymous were planted several years before his first meeting in 1935 with Dr. Bob Smith.

Sometime in 1931, Rowland H., talented scion of a prominent Connecticut family, found himself on the verge of despair

over his inability to control his drinking. Having attempted virtually every other cure, he traveled to Zurich, Switzerland to place himself under the care of one of the greatest psychiatric talents of the time, Dr. Carl Gustav Jung. For almost a year, Rowland worked with Jung, finally leaving treatment with boundless respect for the physician and almost as much confidence in his new, sober self.

To his profound dismay, Rowland soon began drinking again. Believing that Jung was his last resort, he returned to Zurich and the psychiatrist's care. There followed, in Bill Wilson's words written to Dr. Jung in 1961, "the conversation between you [and Rowland] that was to become the first link in the chain of events that led to the founding of Alcoholics Anonymous." That conversation, Bill continued in his letter, made two crucial points. "First of all, you frankly told him of his hopelessness, so far as any further medical or psychiatric treatment might be concerned." Second, in response to Rowland's frantic query whether there might be any other hope, Jung had spoken of "a spiritual or religious experience—in short, a genuine conversion," cautioning, however, "that while such experiences had sometimes brought recovery to alcoholics, they were . . . comparatively rare."

This slender thread of hope led Rowland H. to join the Oxford Group, a nondenominational evangelical movement that emphasized the principles of self-survey, confession of sins, restitution to those one had harmed, and the giving of self to others. Within the Oxford Group Rowland found, as Bill wrote later, "the conversion experience that released him for the time being from his compulsion to drink."

In August 1934 Rowland led his old friend Ebby T. to the Oxford Group and three months later Ebby, sober and flushed with confidence and enthusiasm, sought out the most hopeless and self-destructive drinker he knew—his old friend, William Griffith Wilson.[8]

Alcoholics Anonymous thus came honestly to its openness to unconventional spirituality. This was perhaps the greatest contribution to its program of not only the Swiss psychiatrist, Dr. Carl Jung, but of the American philosopher-psychologist William James. Both were figures of intellectual world-renown who took religious insight seriously; neither was "religious" in any conventional sense of that term. That "the spiritual" could mean something different from what most thought when hearing that word was the most important lesson of the lives of both of these thinkers honored by Bill Wilson as among A.A.'s remote "founders."

But there was a further dimension to Jung's contribution. In 1961, Wilson wrote to the psychiatrist, telling him of his role in A.A.'s origins and thanking him for that inspiration. Just months before his death, Jung responded in a letter that illuminated not only his understanding of spirituality but also the profundity of the instinct that connected his understanding with Alcoholics Anonymous.[9]

In his letter Jung explained that he had not been able to reveal to Rowland H. the full extent of his belief that spirituality is essential to recovery, for he feared that any talk of spirituality would be misinterpreted. "How could one formulate such an insight in a language that is not misunderstood in our days?" he asked. But he took the risk in his letter to Wilson, explaining his intuition of the connection between spirituality and recovery.

> [Rowland's] craving for alcohol was the equivalent, on a low level, of the spiritual thirst of our being for wholeness, expressed in medieval language: the union with God. . . .
>
> You see, "alcohol" in Latin is "spiritus" and you use the same word for the highest religious experience as well as for the most depraving poison. The helpful formula therefore is: *spiritus contra spiritum*.[10]

The phrase *spiritus contra spiritum* captures a paradox that serves as a beacon lighting the unconventional pathway—the road less traveled—of a spirituality of imperfection. Long before Jung offered that helpful dictum, the earliest members of Alcoholics Anonymous groped their way along, seeking sobriety, looking for some kind of map that might guide them toward that goal—a map that would give a sense of direction and help them gauge progress, with suggestions of what to look for and warnings of possible pitfalls along the way. Past experience taught them that the available maps purporting to guide the way out of alcoholism, whether offered by churches, physicians, or psychiatrists, did not work. The shards of insight they garnered from reading William James and from repeating the story of Rowland's encounters with Carl Jung at least set them on the right trail. But after their departure from the increasingly perfectionistic demands of the Oxford Group, how did they discover how to continue?

Clumsily, even unwittingly, A.A.'s first members stumbled down the path to find their own answer, occasionally falling, picking themselves up, only to fall again, but gradually developing not only a message of hope, but a way of passing on that hope. Exploring "what it takes to fix the drunks," they discovered that sobriety involved not only *not* drinking, it also required throwing out the old way of life—the old map that was their former way of interpreting reality—and learning to follow a new map, a new way of life that would allow them to be both sober and alcoholic. And that *way of life,* they discovered, could be learned and taught only through the process of telling stories —stories that "disclose in a general way what we used to be like, what happened, and what we are like now."

Psychologists speak of this process as "re-framing," but within the context of a spirituality of imperfection, the term *re-mapping* far more accurately conveys the idea of journey as well as the sense of discovering a new "map" through storytelling. When newcomers to Alcoholics Anonymous become immersed in storytelling and storylistening, they begin to see the form and outline of a new map, which details where they are, and how they got there, and—most importantly—the way to get where they want to go.

The active alcoholic does have a "way of life," a map—but it is the *wrong* map. A traveler's story suggests the point.

Several years ago, I flew from Atlanta, Georgia, to Detroit, en route to a meeting in northern Michigan. Renting a car, I laid out a book of maps on the passenger seat and proceeded to set out for the northern Michigan peninsula. The map of the metropolitan area was beautifully detailed, showing the airport on the west of the city, the large body of water to the city's east, and route 94, the interstate highway. But after almost an hour of wandering around looking at road signs that failed to match the map and obviously getting nowhere, the realization slowly dawned: the Ford Freeway on which I was driving would *never* turn into the Edens Expressway shown on the map. The map of Detroit didn't work because it was the wrong map: It was a map of Chicago.[11]

This traveler's situation is not unlike the bewildered wandering about of the active alcoholic in search of a solution to his "drinking problem"; nor, in fact, does it differ much from the restless stragglings of so many of us who fall into the easy trap of seeking spirituality where it cannot be found. The "wrong map"—drinking alcohol as a means of easing pain or finding wholeness, for example—helps neither in getting out of the "wrong" place nor in finding the "right" place. As an A.A. member once observed: "The drinking alcoholic is trying to find his way around on Earth with this beautifully detailed map of Venus."

Through the practice of hearing and telling stories, we discover and slowly learn to use a new "map," a map that is more "right" because it is more useful for our purposes. Using this map gives some sense of *place,* of how things are located and how they fit; and this flows into a developing sense of how *we* fit, of *self* as "fitting" . . . fitting into some meaningful whole. That "meaningful whole" is two-fold: It involves first our *relationships,* for that is one name for our "fittings," but it also involves and, indeed, is our very *identity*—who we are. In a very real sense, we are defined by our relationships, our connections with *all* reality; what happens in the re-mapping of storylistening and storytelling is that in telling our *own* story, we come to *own* the story that we tell.

From the very beginning of our lives, most of us have been subjected to other peoples' attempts to map out our lives. Parents, teachers, and others assign us roles and present us with a "map" that we supposedly fit into . . . or are "supposed to" fit into. In the process of growing to adulthood, we begin to accept the responsibility of defining ourselves, of finding and designing our own map, of *owning* ourselves. At times, however, adulthood seems to consist of fending off others who try to impose on us their ideas of what our roles should be, *their* versions of *our* stories. Our spiritual problems stem, at least in part, from the fact that we continue to allow someone else to tell us *our* story. As R. D. Laing observed:

> Others tell one who one is. Later one endorses, or tries to discard, the ways others have defined one. It is difficult not to accept their story. One may try not to be what one "knows" one is, in one's heart of hearts. . . . [But all too often,] we learn to be whom we are told we are.[12]

Or, as Dr. Tom Szasz has put it: "In the animal kingdom, the rule is, eat or be eaten; in the human kingdom, define or be defined."

A fool went to the rabbi and said: "I know I'm a fool, Rabbi, but I don't know what to do about it. Please advise me what to do."

"Ah, my son!" exclaimed the rabbi, in a complimentary way. "If you know you're a fool, then you surely are no fool!"

"Then why does everybody say I'm a fool?" complained the man.

The rabbi regarded him thoughtfully for a moment.

"If you yourself don't understand that you're a fool," he chided him, "but only listen to what people say, then you surely are a fool!"[13]

In the area of "the spiritual," others—parents, teachers, friends, employers, advertisers, whoever—cannot tell us who we are. The spiritual teachers universally recognized as "great" did not give commandments nor did they impose their way of life on others. They knew that when *any* "map" was mistaken for the territory, it became more hindrance than help. And so they invited their followers to question the handed-down maps by making available their own maps —their *own* stories. Rather than trying to tell their listeners' stories, rather than imposing interpretation, the sages and saints told the kind of stories that invited *identification*. For they understood what the ancients had discovered: *The best way to help me find my story is to tell me your story.*

But if we are to hear a story—any story—in a way that will help us discover our story, our spirituality, we must be open to the reality of "essential but different," open to the experience of *wonder*. Some people find that difficult.

> A man took his new hunting dog out on a trial hunt. Presently he shot a duck that fell into the lake. The dog walked over the water, picked up the duck, and walked back to his master, laying the duck at his feet. The man was flabbergasted! He shot another duck. Once again, the dog walked over the water and retrieved the duck.
>
> Hardly able to believe what he had seen, the man returned home and called a friend, inviting him to go out for a shoot on the following day. Once again, each time he or his companion hit a bird, the dog would walk over the water and bring the bird in. The man said nothing. Neither did his friend. Finally, unable to contain himself any longer, the hunter blurted out, "Do you notice anything strange about that dog?"
>
> The neighbor rubbed his chin thoughtfully. "Yes," he finally said. "Come to think of it, I do! The son of a gun can't swim!"[14]

Honest openness to "the different" requires willingness to be surprised. The A.A. Big Book's appendix, "Spiritual Experience," comments on the essential but different nature of spirituality by concluding:

> *Willingness, honesty and open mindedness are the essentials of recovery. But these are indispensable.*[15]

"Willingness, honesty and open mindedness" are also essential and "indispensable" to recovering our own story—our own spirituality.

Chapter 8

NOT MAGIC, BUT MIRACLE

❖

The problem of evil has baffled mankind since Eden; perhaps because it can only be approached through facing the mystery of good, and we do not like to acknowledge that good is a mystery.

D. M. Dooling

"Miracle" is simply the wonder of the unique that points us back to the wonder of the everyday.

Maurice Friedman[1]

One of the early issues of *The Grapevine,* A.A.'s unofficial monthly publication, reported on a bantering conversation about "Why A.A. Works." Opinions varied from "moral philosophy" to "behavior conditioning," from extolling the joys of sober fellowship to emphasizing the usefulness of reminders to "Remember When." Finally Bill Wilson spoke up.

> Why A.A. works is fundamentally a mystery. When we consider that for thousands of years, few alcoholics escaped from their misery and that we are now witnessing a wholesale escape, that adds up to a miracle. And a miracle is a mystery.[2]

And *miracle,* Bill and the other early A.A.s knew from their own experience of alcoholism and recovery, is exactly the opposite of magic. *Miracle* involves openness to mystery, the welcoming of surprise, the acceptance of those realities over which we have no control. *Magic* is the attempt to be in control, to manage everything—it is the claim to be, or to have a special relationship with, some kind of "god."

118

Spirituality is aligned not with magic and the effort to control, but with miracle, "the wonder of the unique that points us back to the wonder of the everyday."

Novelist Nikos Kazantzakis re-tells this story:

In the remote mountains of northern Greece, there once lived a monk who had desired all of his life to make a pilgrimage to the Holy Sepulchre—to walk three times around it, to kneel, and to return home a new person. Gradually through the years he had saved what money he could, begging in the villages nearby, and finally, near the end of his life, had enough set aside to begin his trip. He opened the gates of the monastery and, staff in hand, set out with great anticipation on his way to Jerusalem.

But no sooner had he left the cloister than he encountered a man in rags, sad and bent to the ground, picking herbs. "Where are you going, Father?" the man asked. "To the Holy Sepulchre, brother. By God's grace, I shall walk three times around it, kneel, and return home a different man from what I am."

"How much money to do that do you have, Father?" inquired the man. "Thirty pounds," the monk answered. "Give me the thirty pounds," said the beggar. "I have a wife and hungry children. Give me the money, walk three times around me, then kneel and go back into your monastery."

The monk thought for a moment, scratching the ground with his staff, then took the thirty pounds from his sack, gave the whole of it to the poor man, walked three times around him, knelt, and went back through the gates of his monastery.

He returned home a new person, of course, having recognized that the beggar was Christ himself—not in some magical place far away, but right outside his monastery door, mysteriously close. In abandoning his quest for the remote, the special, the somehow "magical," the monk discovered a meaning far more profound in the ordinary experience close to home. All that he had given up came suddenly rushing back to him with a joy unforeseen.

To be surprised by grace is a gift still to be prized.[3]

We do not create miracles, we witness them. In witnessing them, we must acknowledge that they exist. In acknowledging that they exist, we must admit that we do not know "why" or "how." Somehow above and beyond human reason, miracle, like mystery, is inexplicable, unsolvable, incomprehensible.

Underlying the very concept of *miracle* is the simple acceptance that we are not in ultimate, total control. This is also, of course, the inherent, eternal, fundamental message of spirituality: *You cannot control everything. You are a human being, and human beings make mistakes, and that's okay—because you are a human being, not a God.*

At the heart of all spirituality is a sense of wonder and surprise, the awe that accepts that it can only marvel and delight—whether at the magnificence of a landscape, the sublimity of a symphony, or the incomprehensible beauty of self-sacrificing love. "Awe," one writer suggests, "is a reflex of the spirit." One penalty inflicted by the need-to-control is the failure of awe and wonder, and the consequent inability to "see" miracle. Anxious determination to take control, to be in charge, reveals the failure of spirituality.[4]

Addiction represents the ultimate effort to control, the definitive demand for magic . . . and the final failure of spirituality. Turning to the "magic" of chemicals signifies the desperate (and doomed) attempt to fill a spiritual void with a material reality—to make "magic" a substitute for miracle. Addiction has been described as the belief that whenever there is "something wrong with me," it can be "fixed" by something outside of me. That false start generates ever more drastic illusions. The search for "the quick fix," inevitably unfulfilled by drugs and unsated by material things, leaps next to spiritual realities and the search for "instant spirituality"—some sort of quick "spiritual fix." It is no wonder, then, that "locating divinity in drugs" becomes a kind of spiritual death.[5]

For a profound relationship exists between spirituality and addiction, as suggested by the ancient metaphor of *thirst* and the Jungian formulation *spiritus contra spiritum.* "Drunkenness can be a kind of shortcut to the higher life, the [attempt to] achieve a higher state without an emotional and intellectual effort," observed Dr. E. M. Jellinek, a pioneer in alcoholism theory and treatment and formulator of the modern disease-concept of alcoholism.[6] Alcohol is the perfect "magic" for the alcoholic, at least for a time. Many alcoholics describe how, right from the start, the feeling they got from alcohol was "magic"—instant, fabulous, incredible. With no work and little time invested, a drink brought them face to face and heart to heart with divinity.

But shortcuts, alcoholics learn the hard way, are dead ends, and recovery from addiction requires giving up the claim to be God, the demand to control experience, the search to achieve "magical" solutions. The discovery that spirituality involves mystery and miracle rather than magic was critically important to the early members of Alcoholics Anonymous because the search for magic had proved fatal time and time again; those recovering alcoholics who sought magical solutions as a way of dealing with life's ongoing problems inevitably returned to drinking. The early A.A.s knew from their own experience that, for the alcoholic, nothing in this world is as reliable or as immediate as the magic of alcohol, and they also knew that alcohol's "magic" inevitably destroyed spirituality. And so they discovered that whatever spirituality they would find in sobriety would have to be "earned"—*earned* in the original sense of "made one's *own*," by the work, the building, the journey, the "toil, sweat, and tears" that the ancients insisted was necessary if the soul was to "ripen."

Alcoholics, of course, are not the only people who have to "earn" spirituality. An ancient Sufi story uses the metaphor of thirst to teach about the foolishness of the search for the "quick spiritual fix."

A certain person wished to see the blessed Messenger [Mohammed] in a dream, but he seemed to be incapable of achieving this vision. He therefore approached a noble saint, imploring his advice. That noble being was an intimate friend of Allah. He said: "My son, on Friday evening you must eat a lot of salted fish, then perform your prayer and go to bed without drinking any water. Then you will see."

The man followed this advice. He spent the whole night dreaming that he was drinking from streams, fountains and springs. When morning came, he ran crying to the saint: "O Master, I did not see the Messenger. I was so thirsty that all I dreamed about was drinking from fountains and springs. I am still on fire with thirst."

The saint then told him: "So, eating salted fish gave you

such a thirst that you dreamed all night of nothing but water. Now you must feel such a thirst for Allah's Messenger and you will then behold his blessed beauty!"[7]

❖

The core discovery in this area of "not magic but mystery and miracle" concerns *limits* and *responsibility*—what we human beings can and cannot do, can and cannot will. The difference between magic and miracle reflects the difference between willfulness and willingness. *Willfulness* involves the demand for change—usually some change in realities outside the self, but also, at times, the demand for change in oneself. *Willingness* involves the acceptance that one is not in absolute control, thus opening up the possibility of *being* changed—being open to what change is possible even if one is not in control.

Spiritual thinkers have always distinguished between claims to change ("I've changed!") and openness to being changed ("Humbly asked Him to remove our shortcomings"), a distinction that underlies all discussions of "conversion." Members of Alcoholics Anonymous have traditionally been wary of the word *conversion* because of its "religious" connotations. But as early as 1944, Bill Wilson, urged on by friend and mentor psychiatrist Harry Tiebout, who was fascinated by the "surrender" and "conversion" that A.A. made possible, did address those subjects in several of his talks to physicians. Referring to the "spiritual awakening" mentioned in the program's Twelfth Step, A.A.'s co-founder described it in terms of "a personality change," "transformation," "a new state of consciousness and being," "a profound alteration in one's reaction to life": "a mysterious process of conversion . . . the very thing most alcoholics have sworn they would never have."[8]

Such changes need not occur with the trappings of drama. A few years before his first Medical Society presentation, in the A.A. Big Book's discussion of "Spiritual Experiences," Wilson assured readers that overwhelming transformations, "though frequent, are by no means the rule. Most of our experiences are what the psychologist William James calls the 'educational variety.'"[9] The drama, in other words, can be quiet. A modern spiritual writer captures this reality in his description of his own "transforming experience," for such experiences do not happen only within Alcoholics Anonymous.

I was neurotic for years. I was anxious and depressed and selfish. Everyone kept telling me to change. I resented them, and I agreed with them, and I wanted to change, but simply couldn't, no matter how hard I tried.

What hurt the most was that, like the others, my best friend kept insisting that I change. So I felt powerless and trapped. Then, one day, another friend said to me, *"Don't change. I love you just as you are."*

Those words were music to my ears: *"Don't change. Don't change. Don't change . . . I love you as you are."* I relaxed. I came alive. And suddenly I changed!

Now I know that I couldn't really change until I found someone who would love me whether I changed or not.[10]

Sensitivity to the distinction between mystery and magic—to the difference between the *willfulness* that demands a kind of magical control over change and the *willingness* that creates an openness to being changed—lies at the heart of spirituality's horror of "idolatry." Idolatry represents the attempt to wrest control, even of mystery, trying to twist it into some kind of magical talisman. The sages and saints have always sought help to remind themselves of this danger, often turning to stories. The Trappist monk Thomas Merton was no exception.

One of Merton's favorite figures was Tan-hsia, a ninth-century master who often is pictured warming his bare backsides at a fire which he had made with a wooden image of the Buddha. In the Zen tradition, it is understood that idols of every sort are to be relentlessly smashed—whether they be one's dependence upon the ego, doctrine, scriptures, or even the Buddha.[11]

Most of us living in the modern world have difficulty understanding the concept of "idolatry." But we have our own *idols,* less subtle but no less dangerous manifestations of that same quest for magic. Perhaps the most pervasive modern-day idolatry is the worship of "technique." Used fittingly, technique—attention to method, the use of routines—enhances many areas of our lives. But there are limits to all human reality, and technique *is* a human reality. Unlimited faith in technique—the demand for procedures for everything in our lives, the refusal to acknowledge and attend to what cannot be measured or manipulated—indicates a rejection of our own limitation, a disowning of our very humanity. Such a denial of limitation is a form of the idolatry that demands magic and thus refuses spirituality.

For spirituality can never be "technique," although that can be a difficult lesson both to learn and to teach.

In 1988, a group of Soviet narcologists—as addiction experts are titled in the USSR—visited the United States. As a part of their research, they attended several A.A. meetings, hoping to find in those smoky rooms something that could be used to fight the serious alcohol problem in their homeland. They listened to the stories, they talked to the A.A. members, and they decided that, yes, there was something here that could help. But what was it, exactly? They couldn't quite figure it out.

At the end of one meeting they approached their hosts, several of whom were recovering alcoholics. "We want to make alcoholics like that," they said. "Teach us how."

The hosts smiled in gentle understanding. "Well, that's what we've been doing this evening," came the answer. "You see, you learn how to be like that only by being like that."

"But," the Soviets sputtered, "surely there must be something you could share with us, a technique, a certain kind of approach, some kind of trick that would make this all a little easier?"

"No," came the reply. "What you see in this room, what you want to take home with you, is *spirituality;* and if there is one thing that all alcoholics discover, it is that there are no shortcuts to spirituality, no techniques that can command it, and especially no 'tricks.' That's what we tried to find in the bottle, in booze, in alcohol. It didn't work. What we have learned is that the only 'technique' is what we call 'a four-letter word': it is spelled 'T-I-M-E.' "[12]

The Soviet scientists hoped for some *technique,* an instant answer, a magic potion, a quick way to "instant spirituality," something they could write down like a formula and carry home with them. But spirituality doesn't work that way, and that is perhaps the most difficult lesson that we all need to learn and to re-learn, day after day after day, so long as we live.

❖

Spirituality involves not magic but miracle and mystery; not willfulness but willingness. Psychoanalyst Dr. Leslie Farber, described by *New York Times* reviewer Anatole Broyard as "a poet in the field of psychotherapy," devoted much of his life to examining the psychiatrically unfashionable topic of *will*. In a delightful collection of essays entitled *Lying, Despair, Jealousy, Envy, Sex, Suicide, Drugs and the Good Life*, Farber describes and analyzes "the modern problem of willing." For we live, he suggests, in an "Age of Disordered Will."

According to Farber, our will—our ability to choose—operates in two distinct "realms." The first is the domain of *objects*, which has to do with specific entities that we can directly choose. The second realm involves *directions* or *goals*, those realities that cannot be directly grasped or chosen; in fact, Farber warns, goals and directions are distorted, even destroyed, by attempts to control them.

Some examples may help. We can, for instance:

directly will	*but not*
knowledge	wisdom
pleasure	happiness
congratulations	admiration
reading/listening	understanding
going to bed	sleeping
meekness	humility
executing a play	winning a game
dryness	sobriety

Confusing the two realms—attempting to treat *directions* as if they were *objects*—leads first to anxiety and then, inevitably, to addiction. *Anxiety* occurs because the confusion of objects with directions is doomed to failure; the split between the will and its impossible goal deepens with each futile attempt to will what *cannot* be willed. ("The harder I try to fall asleep, the wider awake I get." "The harder I try to make myself happy, the more miserable I become.")

Addiction enters because drugs can offer the illusion of healing that split, appearing to bring even "directions" and "goals" under technological control. Sleep medications can help one doze off, tranquilizers can dull nerves, and a few cocktails can create sensations of warmth and belonging. But as many alcoholics and pill-addicts will attest, there is a vast difference between falling asleep and lapsing into coma, between relaxation and numbness, between boozed-up euphoria and the warmth and comfort of real relationships. As Farber pointedly observes, addiction results not in "better living through chemistry," but in the self-destructive "location of divinity in drugs."[13]

The problem with "willing what cannot be willed" is that we step into a territory that is not ours—we stake the claim to *be* God. This attempt to wrest control from the uncontrollable has become the keynote characteristic of our "Age of Addiction." We try to command those aspects of our lives that cannot be commanded, we try to coerce what cannot be coerced, and in doing so, we ironically destroy the very thing we crave. We enter a *vicious circle:* As the ancient yet ever-new story of the magical search for the perfect aphrodisiac illustrates, seeking to control what cannot be controlled destroys precisely what we are trying to control.

The classic mythic story conveying this insight unites the quest for magic with the *logismos* of greed. It is the story of Midas, King of Phrygia and not incidentally friend of Dionysus, who granted the king his magical wish that everything he touch turn to gold. The result, of course, was that Midas then found it impossible both to eat and to embrace his beloved child.[14] A more modern version of the story diffuses the classic focus on greed to concentrate on a paradox of love.

Once upon a time, but not very long ago, in a kingdom both near and far away, there lived a canny scientist who longed for the love of a beautiful woman. Because his first love was not even science but his own knowledge, wise women were wary of the man, and so he lived a very lonely life.

One day, the man decided to use his science to win love,

and he set about to concoct a chemical that would cause the object of his affections to fall madly in love with him. Soon his research succeeded, he produced the chemical, and as luck would have it, at just that time he met a beautiful, talented and good woman—the ultimate woman of his dreams.

The scientist arranged for friends to introduce them, and at their first meeting, he poured his potion into her beverage. Lo and behold, his fantasy came true! The exquisite creature fell instantly and completely in love with him, and they soon married.

But was our hero happy? Alas, no. In a short time, he became gaunt from not eating, his work fell by the wayside, and eventually he could not even bring himself to touch his beloved, as he spent every waking moment torturing himself, trying to devise some kind of test to answer his agonized question: "Would she love me if it were not for the chemical?"

For our scientist did crave *love*, and love cannot be commanded.

To will what cannot be willed is to become, in Farber's memorable phrase, "Addicted to Addiction"—perhaps the best description as well as the most profound diagnosis of the failure of spirituality in the modern age.[15]

❖

How do we learn the difference between *willfulness* and *willingness*, the distinction between magic and miracle? The answer will come as no surprise: in the practice and process of storylistening and storytelling. "Story," the novelist John Gardner observed, "details the gap between intentions and results." Story conveys the reality of human freedom, for although "real," our freedom is limited, and although "limited," our freedom is real. To live with an awareness of story is to recognize, with philosopher Alasdair MacIntyre, that "We are never more than the co-authors of our own stories."[16]

Every story details a mixture of what Niccolò Machiavelli named *necessità, virtù,* and *fortuna*: cause, choice, and chance. The very combination of the three reveals that we are neither completely controlled nor completely in control. We can *will,* in other words, but we must also *be willing*. This can be a difficult, even painful lesson to accept, for we tend to want "either-or," especially in matters of being "controlled" or "in control." Accepting the impossibility of this willful demand—becoming willing to accept the limited freedom that is ours—is one gift of story. Stories reveal a spirituality that views life not as a problem to be solved, but as a mystery to be lived.

> **When a learned but ungenerous man asked Rabbi Abraham of Stretyn for a drug to attain to the fear of God, Rabbi Abraham offered him instead one for the love of God. "That's even better," cried the man. "Just give it to me." "It is the love of one's fellowmen," replied the rabbi.**[17]

Cause, choice, and chance. Choice *is* possible. We can choose, for example, to be willing. Because that particular choice involves a rejection of the demand for "magic," we also "choose" (insofar as that is possible) *mystery* and *miracle*. We choose, that is to say, the possibility of *being chosen*—and that is the most important choice of all.

Whenever we choose what we will be, we also close the door on other potential choices. When we close the door on magic, we open it to something else. As so often in the realm of spirituality, an apparent problem—"How choose?"—contains a valuable but hidden opportunity, if we can find it. How can we make the choices that will lead to fulfilling our humanity?

The insight of social critic Philip Rieff suggests one approach to our "problem." In his study of *The Triumph of the Therapeutic*, Rieff despaired over the profound pessimism of psychoanalytic thought. He referred to a letter written by Freud to Marie Bonaparte, in which Freud termed "insane" the hope of finding "meaning and value in life," thus abandoning humankind to a meaningless world. Rieff describes the thinking and feeling of living in that world, a world without choice.

> There is no feeling more desperate than that of being free to choose, and yet without the specific compulsion of being chosen. After all, one does not really choose; one is chosen. This is one way of stating the difference between gods and men. Gods choose; men are chosen. What men lose when they become as gods is precisely that sense of

being chosen, which encourages them, in their gratitude, to take their subsequent choices seriously. . . .

The hardest lesson to learn is not how to choose but rather how to acquire that passionate knowledge which will permit us again to be chosen.[18]

How do we acquire that "passionate knowledge which will permit us again to be chosen"? There can, of course, be no easy answer to that question. But perhaps we might suggest a place to begin. If you have never been to a meeting of Alcoholics Anonymous, go and watch what happens when a relative newcomer, sober only a few months, hesitantly and haltingly speaks publicly for the first time. Concluding her—or his—story, the speaker sighs with relief. The group stands up, cigarettes are lighted, coffee is poured, voices commingle. Then, sometimes perhaps, something very special happens. One of the listeners comes over and shyly reaches out to shake hands with the speaker. "Thanks, thanks a lot," he says. "What you said really helped me."[19]

We are all looking for, but we find what we are looking for only by being looked for. We find miracle only when we stop looking for magic.

Chapter 9

AN OPEN-ENDED SPIRITUALITY

❖

> *But as for the A.A. therapy itself, that could be practiced in any fashion that the group wished to practice it, and the same went for every individual. We took the position that A.A. was not the final word on treatment; that it might be only the first word. For us, it became perfectly safe to tell people they could experiment with our therapy in any way they liked.*
>
> Bill W.

> *Woe to the man so possessed that he thinks he possesses God!*
>
> Martin Buber[1]

A.A. co-founder Bill Wilson—chief writer of the Big Book, *Alcoholics Anonymous*, author of the handbook *Twelve Steps and Twelve Traditions* and the historical narrative *Alcoholics Anonymous Comes of Age*—intended to write one last book. To be titled *Practicing These Principles in All Our Affairs*, it would delineate "A.A. spirituality."

Bill began the project in April 1961 with an article in *The A.A. Grapevine* titled "God As We Understand Him: The Dilemma of No Faith." Subsequent articles, on "Humility for Today," "This Matter of Honesty," "This Matter of Fear," and "What is Acceptance?" followed irregularly over the next year, each labelled "one of a series." Then, in the July 1962 *Grapevine,* the series came to an unannounced end with an article titled, "Spiritual Experiences." The proposed book was never published, although Bill wrote more than twenty more articles for the *Grapevine* and lived until 1971.

"What happened to the spirituality book?" is a question never directly addressed, but one answer can be found in this story.

One evening at a meeting, during the time he was working on the book, Bill noticed an A.A. member of obvious spiritual depth. Hoping to plumb his experience, Bill approached the man after the meeting. "You seem to have a real spirituality . . ." Wilson began.

"Oh, no," the man replied, quickly cutting Bill off. "I mean, thanks, I am working on the spiritual angle; but if you want to know about spirituality, you'd better talk to Donald over there, or maybe you could look up Phil—he moved about a month ago, but look, I'll get his new telephone number for you."

"That's how I learned the most important thing about spirituality," Bill always mused in retelling the story. "Those who have it don't know that they have it!"[2]

And that is why Bill never finished that book on spirituality, for he understood the paradox all too well: Anyone who claimed to be an "expert" on the subject of spirituality would not be able to produce a book worth reading!

Spirituality is one of those realities that you have only so long as you seek it; as soon as you think you have it, you've lost it. In rediscovering this basic spiritual insight, the earliest members of Alcoholics Anonymous tapped the essence of *open-endedness* that characterizes a spirituality of imperfection. Spirituality is boundless, unable to be fenced in: We do not capture it; it captures us. As much as we might like to "wrap things up," to lock spirituality in and hold it fast, it will forever escape our grasp.

In the long story of spirituality, many images have been used in the effort to convey its open-endedness. In the modern age, we tend to favor the metaphor of *growth*. The literature of therapy and popular writings on self-help have thrived on this image, describing *growth* in biological terms, as a spontaneous and largely automatic process profoundly shaped by outside factors such as parents, teachers, and peers. Lives can thus be read like the rings of a tree, with events and experiences leaving their marks deeply and permanently embedded in our psyche; "as the twig is bent," these early aberrations can never be entirely undone.

The classic literature on spirituality suggests a more ancient image for the spiritual life—that of *building,* in which our life's time is occupied in the construction of a spiritual edifice, a kind of "home." The rich metaphor of *architecture* offers several advantages. It invites thinking in terms of tools, materials, and choices: Which tools, which materials do we choose to use in shaping our spiritual abode? Building also requires a plan, or at least planning, and so *thinking*—how and what one *chooses to see*—makes a difference to the outcome. And finally, although the task of construction is laborious, mistakes can be undone, and what is learned from them can be used to improve the structure as a whole.[3]

While both *growth* and *building* add useful shades of meaning to the experience of spirituality, the spirituality of imperfection offers an alternative image for the spiritual life: that of *journey.* And the practice of storytelling brings the metaphor of journey to life, for the narrative format of "what we used to be like, what happened, and what we are like now" suggests the particular kind of journey that is *pilgrimage.* That "plot" bestows on the storyteller the "identity" revealed by the story, the identity of the kind of "journeyer" who is a *pilgrim.*

The pilgrimage metaphor conveys spirituality's open-endedness by reinforcing the essential distinction between confident certainty and the mysteries of uncertainty. A pilgrimage involves not a settled and determined lockstep march to a fixed point, but a winding, turning, looping, crisscrossing, occasionally backtracking *peregrination*—the ancient name for "pilgrimage" that conveys its wandering essence. It is no accident that Bill Wilson's favorite image, repeated literally thousands of times in letters to people who sought his advice, depicted sobriety as "a kind of Pilgrim's Progress." "We claim spiritual progress rather than spiritual perfection," reminds the A.A. Big Book.

An unlikely modern source provides a helpful picture of the open-ended journey that is traditional spirituality.

Several years ago, the cartoon strip *Family Circus* showed little Billy, in all his open-faced innocence, arriving at his front

door, schoolbooks in hand. His mother gazed down on him with a relieved but sternly questioning look on her face.

"Honest, Mom," he was saying, his round face gleaming with puzzled truthfulness, "I came *straight* home from school!"

Sketched out in a dotted line behind Billy, cartoonist Bil Keane indicated the "straight" route he had taken—a rambling circuit of loops and twists, zigzags and meanderings, as he tested every swing, picked up every errant ball, petted every dog, waded through every mud puddle.[4]

And yet Billy was telling the truth—he had come "straight home" in the sense that his goal was his home, and he had been moving toward it, never abandoning that goal despite all the distractions that might have seemed to his mother intermediate destinations. Billy's mother, of course, is not alone in her inability to square "rambling" with "straight." In this age of modern airplane or superhighway travel, most of us have lost all sense of journey as open-ended pilgrimage. "Where are you going?" we ask a friend who is planning a trip abroad. "To Europe," comes back the answer, "four days in London, then three in Paris, four in Rome, two in Vienna." Our trips tend to be planned out to the last excruciating detail, fixed in time, carefully bundled into the most efficient package available. Or, at the other extreme of modern travel, we meander in totally unplanned fashion, content to drop in here for a week, sleep there for another few nights —an aimless, totally random excursion.[5]

Both extremes of modern travel—the "Are we there yet?" and the "Who cares where we are?" syndromes—fail to grasp the nature of the *pilgrimage* journey, which is neither a straight-line "trip" nor mere "meandering around." The word *journey* originally meant "the distance traveled in one day"; a journey becomes a pilgrimage as we discover, day by day, that the distance traveled is less important than the experience gained. "When you're on a journey, and the end keeps getting further and further away, then you realize that the real end is the journey," quoted Joseph Campbell.[6]

Neither randomly spontaneous nor totally premeditated in every detail, *pilgrimage* is the kind of journey that is characterized by *vicissitudes*. A favorite term of both the French Jesuit Jean-Pierre Caussade and the American pragmatist William James, *vicissitude* conveys a different emphasis and therefore a different attitude toward the spiritual life than do the more common metaphors of *progress* and *growth*. *Vicissitude* accentuates not the actual movement in the journey, real though it might be, but the agonizing process of falling down and getting up again and the painful reality that even for the pilgrim, identity is found rather than seized.

For just as we cannot capture spirituality, so we cannot "seize" an identity. Identity captures us, overtaking us especially in moments of pain and anguish—when we are lost and searching, stumbling and falling. Thus, while the pain cannot be denied, the falls are never merely failures, because it is precisely the alternation between successes and failures that builds spiritual identity. As the fourth-century monk Macarius emphasized, all improvement in spirituality is "a matter of falling and getting up again, building something up and then being knocked down again."[7]

This kind of journey necessarily involves uncertainty and incongruity, often taking us to places we never expected to go. Embarking on such an unpredictable expedition thus implies a commitment to *flexibility*, for the pilgrim recognizes that danger lurks in the rigidity that is the antithesis of open-endedness. Our old friend Barsanuphius had this advice for the spiritual pilgrim:

> Do not give yourself any absolute regulations, because it will only lead you into conflicts and anxieties; instead, probe what is at hand at each moment. . . . Give yourself no regulations. Be obedient and humble, and demand an account of yourself each day. The prophet indicated this day by day principle with the words, "I said, now I have begun," and so did Moses when he said, "Now, O Israel." So you too should hold fast to the "now."[8]

Later spiritual writers reinforced the theme that rigid regulation is dangerous because it stifles the flexibility in which spirituality flourishes. The unknown author of the medieval "Cloud of Unknowing" pointed out that since we cannot ever work out any way of "getting God," it is wise to avoid tying ourselves down to any particular regimen. "Set practices" leave us unable to respond to the real demands of actual situations, with the result that, "under colour of holiness," we enslave ourselves.[9] Jean-Pierre Caussade cautioned against being "enslaved by devotional practices, whether bodily or interior." In Caussade's vision, as author Simon Tugwell points out:

> Too many people identify spiritual prowess with "being perpetually busy. . . ." We can come to be as dangerously attached to our own will in matters of piety and holiness as we can in worldly things, and such "pious pigheadedness" is still self-love, however spiritualized.[10]

These spiritual masters understood that a spirituality that begins in the acceptance that one is not "in control" necessarily involves a *flexible* attitude, which requires a mistrust of the rigidities of certainty. If life is "unmanageable"—and, of course, at times it is—there will necessarily be sudden surprises, unexpected twists and turns, unforeseen detours. In recognizing spirituality's—life's—open-endedness, we learn to be flexible and adaptable, thus protecting ourselves from the tendency to want to fix things "once and for all." *Hold fast to the "now"* means "hang on and enjoy the ride," for we never know (and we can't control) where the vicissitudes of the pilgrimage that is spirituality will take us.

The modern mind—so enthralled by technique, so oriented to efficient production and "bottom-line" results, so obsessed with comfort and predictability—approaches the concept of *pilgrimage* with wariness and puzzlement. Why backtrack and sidestep when you can march straight ahead? The word *vicissitudes,* with its promise of ups and downs, its suggestion of successes and failures, its reminder that we *cannot* "march straight ahead," is unsettling and disorienting for those who equate progress with perfection. Perhaps an exercise of imagination will help us to regain an appreciation of this "progress not perfection" aspect of the spirituality of imperfection. Let's go back in time to the fourteenth century.

You are an adolescent shepherd in a tiny English village, in Sussex. Each day you take your flock to the hills, where you lie on your back, searching out images in the cloud

formations, one ear always cocked for sounds of possible danger.

One afternoon, you return to find your village astir with anticipation. A stranger has arrived, a pilgrim returning from the great shrine at Canterbury. In exchange for a meal and a night's lodging, the stranger will sit at the village fire that evening and tell the tale of his travels. Eagerly, you join in the preparations. At the supper, you are so anxious to hear the pilgrim's story that you gulp rather than savor the rare rich meal. Ages seem to pass before everyone is finished eating, and the site is tidied. As the villagers settle in to hear the traveler's tale, you scramble to gain a place near the front so that you can see and follow the expressions on his face.

The stranger begins, recounting both the perils and the happy coincidences of his journey, describing his fellow-pilgrims, and finally detailing the magnificence of the great shrine of Canterbury and the wonders to be beheld there. You hang on every word, picturing every nuance of his story in your imagination. Long after the story is over and you lie abed in your hut, your mind leaps into those pictures, trying to make the stranger's adventures a part of your own life. The next day, as you return to the hillside with your flock, you see in the clouds the shapes described by the storyteller, and you long to make a similar pilgrimage. But that is impossible. Young shepherds whose work is needed to help sustain their families do not make pilgrimages.

Several months later, a sheep-plague strikes the area, and most of the villagers' sheep die. You soon realize that you have become more a liability than an asset to your family and that for their sake as well as your own, you must make your way to the great city of London, perhaps to learn some new skill, at least to find a way of living.

But you need not go to the city directly or at once. Indeed, for your spiritual welfare as well as to ask God's blessings on your ambitions, you decide to journey by way of Canterbury, finally making the long-dreamed of pilgrimage. But how to get there? There are no maps; only barons and their knights have those. Still, you do not worry, for starting out is simple: There is but one road through your village, and you know the direction from which the stranger came.

You also know the habits of pilgrims—how your stranger had stopped in a similar way the evening before arriving in your village. After a day's journey, you might be fortunate enough to stop where he had stopped, and there you might find someone who can point you in the right direction for the next leg of your own pilgrimage. And so you set off, not knowing exactly where you are going nor exactly how to get there, but hoping to find on the way others who are interested in the same quest and who can help to guide your own.

And, of course, you do. Travelers are rare in that age, and strangers rarely meet except when traveling. The people you meet thus answer the question, "Who are you?" by detailing "how I come to be *here.*" Each person who joins the quest tells *how* she heard of the goal and *what* he knows of it. In the process of telling the stories of their lives, the pilgrims band together, pooling their knowledge about the journey, merging bits of wisdom remembered from the stories told by others who had made the same journey. "The route through that wood is attacked by robbers." "The rockier trail is the best way around the hill." "After a rain, that stream can be forded only above its rapids." In less stressful moments, the journeyers share expectations and hopes: "I heard that a man with a leg more crippled than mine was cured." "When the procession of the Sacrament begins, it is as if the angels were singing." "Even lawyers have become humble when standing at that altar."

Thus it is that, on the way, you learn more not only about the goal you are seeking—the Canterbury of Becket, who preferred the risk of a king's wrath to the risk of God's judgment —but also about yourself as the seeker of that goal. What risks are you willing to take? Which do you refuse? What kind of people have hopes such as your own? Whom would you like to be like? Whose help do you accept? Whose do you suspect?

And, of course, the paramount discovery gradually dawns as the pilgrimage continues—the realization that the ultimate goal you seek is not some reality "out there," but the awakening of an identity that lies *within.*[11]

"Our destination is never a place, but rather a new way of looking at things," writer Henry Miller noted. Such a destination fits T. S. Eliot's description in concluding "Little Gidding."

> We shall not cease from exploration
> And the end of all our exploring
> Will be to arrive where we started
> And know the place for the first time.

The goal of the pilgrimage that is spirituality is, simply, to keep moving—*spiritually*—one step at a time. While we are not always well-situated to judge "progress," at least we know with Rilke that "Staying is nowhere." Or as Confucius said, "It does not matter how slowly you go, so long as you do not stop."

When a monk asked, "What is the Tao?" Master Ummon replied, "Walk on."[12]

In seeing life as pilgrimage, the vision that is spirituality's open-endedness recognizes that it is not how far one has come that is significant, but how far one has yet to go. Remember the man whom Bill Wilson approached about "spirituality" in the story at the beginning of this chapter? He responded as he did to Bill's query because those who are "on the way" are less aware of the distance they have come than of how far they have yet to go. The pilgrimage image suggests that the goal of this particular journey known as life is not to prove that we are perfect but to find some happiness, some joyful peace of mind in the reality of our own imperfection. Rather than thinking, "If I'm not farther along than I was yesterday, something's wrong with me," the pilgrim thinks, "I'm in a different place from where I was yesterday, and isn't this interesting?" In this realization, in this kind of looking forward from where you are (no matter where that happens to be), resides the classic virtue of *hope.* "Hope is born while facing the unknown and discovering that one is not alone."[13]

❖

Rarely will we find a clearer example of being open to change and learning from *continuing* experience, than in the beginnings of Alcoholics Anonymous. Born within the Oxford Group, A.A. left those auspices precisely because of the Groupers' harping on their "Four Absolutes": absolute honesty, absolute purity, absolute unselfishness, and absolute love. The welcoming of degrees and differences was not an Oxford Group trait, as their insistence on being "really maximum" relentlessly reminded. "The alcoholics couldn't stand the pace," Bill W. wrote to one correspondent, explaining the early members' departure. "They simply did not want to get 'too good too soon.' "

The fellowship built upon that insight as its own pilgrimage proceeded. The original foreword to *Alcoholics Anonymous* described the A.A. membership criterion as follows: "The only requirement for membership is an honest desire to stop drinking." In 1949, the word *honest* was dropped; eventually, this "official" explanation was offered:

> As A.A. has matured, it has been increasingly recognized that it is nearly impossible to determine what constitutes an "honest" desire to stop drinking, as opposed to other forms in which the desire might be expressed. It was also noted that some who may be interested in the program might be confused by the phrase "honest desire." Thus . . . the descriptive adjective has been dropped.[14]

Imagine a drinker at bottom, hurting, shaking, tortured by the tortuous rationalizations that characterize the alcohol-sotted brain, looking at the word *honest* and trying to make sense of it. *"Honest?* What does that mean? Could I honestly say that I honestly want to stop drinking? Sure, I want to end the pain in my life . . . that I can say honestly, but can I honestly say I have an 'honest desire to stop drinking'? How important is this 'honest'? If I'm not absolutely honest, are the doors of this program closed to me?" Those who had been there knew this "thought process" (if it can be dignified by that name). They recognized that for the drunk at bottom, even the simple word *honest* was not open-ended enough—it was too absolute! And so Alcoholics Anonymous summarily excised from its membership criterion the word that played so central a role in its description of "How It Works," in the first paragraph of which the term *honest* appears three times.[15]

The wariness of absolutes that led A.A.'s earliest members to leave the Oxford Group is perhaps the greatest contribution that Group made to A.A. spirituality. As Bill Wilson noted to one correspondent, "The earliest members say that the main thing we learned from the Oxford Group was what would *not* work for drunks!" For at the heart of Alcoholics Anonymous thrives the paradoxical philosophy that there are no absolutes but one: "I am not absolute."[16]

I am not absolute. Such an approach invites humility, flexibility, and openness—in the fellowship itself as well as in its individual members. A.A. has always understood its own limitations. "We have no monopoly on God," its Big Book reminds. As an association of alcoholics, A.A. has been and always will be human, not God; it contains no dogma, no commandments, no absolutes, no requirements beyond "the desire to stop drinking." As for "God," old-time members sometimes comment that "A.A. has only two things to say about the subject: First, there *is* one. And second, you're not it. From there, you're on your own."*

In this acceptance of its own imperfection, Alcoholics Anonymous offered its members something new, something indeed unique in the context of its birth: *a spirituality of "not having all the answers."* Such a spirituality remains open to change—ready to try new directions, to turn back, to cover the same territory again and again. *How* A.A.'s "spirituality of not having all the answers" works in practice is, however, paradoxical. Confused outsiders (especially if they are professionals examining the program from an objective distance) have been driven to shake their heads and mutter: "These members of Alcoholics Anonymous seem to think they have an answer for everything!"

On the most obvious level, that observation seems to ring true. If

---

* More accurately, since Alcoholics Anonymous strives so carefully to be "spiritual rather than religious," the substance of this comment is: "There is *something* greater than yourself."

you go to a meeting and tell someone that you are thinking of getting drunk, you will receive the advice: "Don't drink, and go to meetings!" Tell someone else at another time that you fear losing your job, and you will again be told, "Don't drink, and go to meetings!" On yet another occasion you confide to still another A.A. member that your marriage is in trouble, and by now you can anticipate the ritual response: "Don't drink, and go to meetings!" *Whatever* your problem, just about every A.A. member has the answer!

The only thing is—*it's always the same answer*. The very refrain—*Don't drink, and go to meetings!*—reminds that no one has "*all* the answers." A.A. presents itself as having "the answer" only to "What do I do about my alcoholism?" Take care of that, and perhaps you will be able to find other answers to your other concerns. Meanwhile, in the absence of answers: *Don't drink, and go to meetings!*

"Don't drink" is, of course, obvious. But why "go to meetings"? What happens there that is so special? In the absence of answers, what can one learn there? Well, perhaps one can learn how to live with the absence of answers.

In the backwoods of rural north Georgia, members of an A.A. group listened respectfully as old John told his story once again. They had heard the story many times before, but each time "Jaw-un" retold it, something special seemed to happen in the ancient shack that housed the meeting.

Wrinkled, wizened, dirt permanently embedded in the cracks in his hands, teeth stained with tobacco, John slowly shook his head as his face softened into a smile that still harbored a tinge of pain. "Back when I was drinking," he began in his accustomed fashion, "I used to think that I knew everything." Glancing at each face in the group of people sitting on the rickety chairs surrounding the old picnic table, he rested on their gentle smiles as tears welled up in his own eyes. "A.A.'s great gift to me," he continued, "what you people gave to me . . ." John searched for the words for a moment and then gently struck the table with his large, gnarled hand. "Well, dammit, you helped me be . . . you made me . . . teachable."

"*Teachable*," he repeated again and again, and with each

repetition, old John struck the table with the palm of that work-ravaged hand, softly but firmly, as if to drive home the point.

Silently, as always, the group waited. Finally, as always, it came: "Thank you," John concluded. "Thank you."

Everyone loves to teach, but rarely do any of us take unsought advice well, and even more rarely are we truly *teachable*. Being teachable means being open to learn. In order to learn, one must listen, and we learn to listen only if we know the most important thing—that we do not know everything, that we do not have "all the answers." Shunryu Suzuki captures the point well:

> The goal of practice is always to keep the beginner's mind. [The beginner's mind is] always ready for anything; it is open to everything. In the beginner's mind there are many possibilities; in the expert's mind there are few.[17]

In the long history of spirituality, those recognized as somehow spiritually "great" have consistently been called "Teacher"—they help others to learn, to become teachable. Spiritual teachers (who are never "experts") do three things: First and foremost, they listen. Second, they ask questions. Third, they tell stories. Each practice reflects the acceptance of not having all the answers, and each teaches the essential truth of spirituality's open-endedness.

> The Master gave his teaching in parables and stories, which his disciples listened to with pleasure—and occasional frustration, for they longed for something deeper.
>
> The Master was unmoved. To all their objections he would say, "You have yet to understand, my dears, that the shortest distance between a human being and Truth is a story."
>
> Another time he said, "Do not despise the story. A lost gold coin is found by means of a penny candle; the deepest truth is found by means of a simple story."[18]

And we learn that from stories, which is why stories give life itself, as an ancient Swahili tale conveys.

The poor man's wife flourishes, the Sultana gets thinner by the minute. So the Sultan sends for the poor man and demands the secret of his wife's happiness. "Very simple," he replies. "I feed her meat of the tongue."

The Sultan buys ox tongues and larks' tongues; still his wife withers away. He makes her change places with the poor man's wife and she immediately starts thriving, while her replacement soon becomes as lean and miserable as the former queen. For the tongue meats that the poor man feeds his wives aren't material, of course. They're stories, jokes, songs; in this fable from Kenya, this is what makes women thrive.[19]

For women *and* men, for alcoholics *and* non-alcoholics, spirituality is one of those realities that we have only so long as we seek it; as soon as we stop seeking, we stop finding; as soon as we think we've got it, we've most certainly lost it.

Chapter 10

A PERVASIVE SPIRITUALITY

❖

Step 6. Were entirely *ready to have God remove* all *these defects of character. . . .*

Step 8. Made a list of all *persons we had harmed, and became willing to make amends to them* all. *. . .*

Step 12. Having had a spiritual awakening as the result of these steps, we tried to carry this message to alcoholics, and to practice these principles in all *our affairs.*

From *The Twelve Steps Of Alcoholics Anonymous*
(Emphases Added)

A few years ago at an alcoholism treatment center in the suburbs of Chicago, staff members reported an intriguing discovery. Many of them lived at some distance from the facility, each day braving the hazards of tollway traffic in commuting to and from work. Then one day, the State of Illinois instituted "honor system" toll collection booths in that area: no attendant, no barrier-gate, just a basket into which motorists were expected to throw their coins.

Data are unavailable about how well the method served in meeting the highway department's fiscal and traffic-flow needs, but counselors at the treatment center collected observations that soon added up to an axiom: "Those who don't throw their money in, their patients don't get well." As one counselor put it in telling the story: "How can you pass on an 'honest program' if you aren't honest yourself? Honesty is indivisible."[1]

Spirituality is a reality that must touch *all* of one's life or it touches *none* of one's life. Spirituality is pervasive for the same reason that spirituality cannot be analyzed: the *spiritual* has no parts. And because the spiritual has no parts, it cannot touch only part of us. Spirituality's pervasiveness, then, has two dimensions: "The spiritual" not only touches all of our surface—it penetrates to all of our depths. We must live it, think it, feel it, and, most important, act it in our own lives, for only if we *do* it, only if we practice it, will we come to understand what it is.

Spirituality thus resides at our center, flowing into all that we are and do; it is at the very core of our be-ing. We cannot "borrow" it, putting it on for an hour or a day, using it like a cloak to cover the hardness in our heart or the angry or jealous thoughts in our mind. Spirituality is not a pet project that we can take up for a month or two; it is never "hobby."

"Pervasive" is an extraordinarily difficult concept to convey. Perhaps a story will help.

Some years ago a student of Twelve-Step spirituality offered a presentation at the newly established Renewal Center at Hazelden, one of the oldest and most renowned centers for the treatment of alcoholism and other chemical dependencies. As he was laboring to make his point about the pervasive nature of spirituality, one of the participants asked for an image to help her "picture" the words. "What is it like?" she asked, her expression earnest and intent. "I think I understand what you mean, but can you give me a picture?"

Momentarily stumped, the presenter sat for several frustrating minutes staring across the conference-lounge at the massive stone fireplace, so carefully fashioned out of rock deposited in the locality during Minnesota's glacial era. Late afternoon sun streamed into the room, warming the stones with light. Suddenly the stones themselves came into focus— perhaps he could use them for an image! The deep reddish rocks, flecked with golden specks; the green-hued pieces, irregularly marbled in white; the many-shaded blue slabs, their shallow niches sparkling as if with silver. Which of these stones could best represent "the spiritual"?

"Physical, mental, spiritual"—the phrase reverberated in his mind, but which of the rocks provided the best image for each of those realities? The workshop participants, ever polite and patient, shifted quietly in the rare silence. Then, suddenly, the image came! Looking at the stones, wondering at their beauty, the presenter's vision made one of those *gestalt* switches, and he saw not the individual stones but the chimney itself.

The mortar—the bland, grayish, pebbly "stuff" that held all those stones together—*that* was "the spiritual"! The spiritual is not some separate category, one specific type of stone or a particular stone of great beauty, but the substance that holds everything together.

"Spirituality is like that mortar in the fireplace," he offered pensively, finally breaking the long silence. "Just as the mortar makes the chimney a chimney, allowing it to stand up straight and tall, beautiful in its wholeness, 'the spiritual' is what makes *us* wholly human. It holds our experiences together, shapes them into a whole, gives them meaning, allows them—and us—to be whole. Without the spiritual, however physically brave or healthy or strong we may be, however mentally smart or clever or brilliant we may be, however emotionally integrated or mature we may be, we are somehow not 'all there.' "[2]

As usual in such settings, the presenter did not have the last word. Around the kitchen tables after the formal session, over steaming cups of coffee and cocoa, the workshop participants added to the image. Someone pointed out that the individual stones, before they were shaped into fireplace and chimney, had been lying around—heavy, irregular, useless pieces of rock. Beautiful stones, perhaps, but scattered meaninglessly or just piled up uselessly, they really didn't amount to much, did they? The mortar had transformed them, putting them all together in a way that gave each stone purpose and meaning and a wholly new kind of beauty.

"I get the point," another participant spoke up. "Spirituality is not something spectacular, even something spectacularly beautiful, like I sort of expected and maybe even feared. I was thinking of angels, saints, perfection, the great works of religious art. But this . . ." He walked over to the fireplace and ran his hand across the irregular surfaces, his finger along the troughs of mortar. "This is something I can handle. If my life, my experiences, are like that great big pile of rocks, if I'm going to make something of them, I need some mortar—some plain, ordinary mortar. I need something to make everything stick together. Yeah, that's the kind of spirituality I need."

❖

Spirituality is a reality that must touch *all* of one's life or it touches *none* of one's life. The earliest members of Alcoholics Anonymous rediscovered this classic truth early on, the hard way, as the main thrust of the "Into Action" chapter of their Big Book makes clear. In insisting on the *thoroughness* required in the Fifth Step, that first-generation-of-the-newly-sober explained in simple terms what their experience had taught them about why "pervasiveness" is so crucial: "Time after time newcomers have tried to keep to themselves certain facts about their lives. . . . Almost invariably they got drunk."[3]

The remedy for "keeping something to oneself" is not "letting it all hang out," which is a modern-day perversion of pervasiveness. From the very beginning, A.A. respected its members' rights to privacy, recognizing the difference between the concealment that is part of cowardice and the modesty that is an aspect of humility. A Hasidic learning tale sheds some light on the connection between appropriate reticence and inappropriate secrecy.

When young Rabbi Eleazar of Koznitz was a guest in the house of Rabbi Naftali of Roptchitz, he once cast a surprised glance at the window, where the curtains had been drawn. When his host asked him the cause of his surprise, he said: "If you want people to look in, then why the curtains? And if you do not want them to, why the window?"

"And what explanation have you found for this?" asked Rabbi Naftali.

147

"When you want someone you love to look in," said the young rabbi, "you draw aside the curtain."[4]

"Keeping something to oneself" is equivalent to a curtain always half-drawn; it indicates a holding back, a half-heartedness, a refusal to believe in love that leads to a hiding of part of the self from the Twelve Steps. Because alcoholism impacts every aspect of the alcoholic's life, recovery from alcoholism has to do the same. The principles that help keep the alcoholic sober must be applied to *all* concerns.

The early A.A.s learned this lesson despite many of their own concerted efforts to deny it. Ernie G.'s reservations over being "too young to be a *real* alcoholic," Hank P.'s resentments of Bill W.'s increasing popularity, Florence R.'s attempts to separate her social life from her sober life, even Ebby T.'s frequently renewed hopes of keeping his love life distinct from his A.A. life—each case and many more taught the truth that spirituality had to *pervade* one's whole life. Those who did not make this particular spiritual discovery got drunk again, and for a good number of those earliest members, to drink again was to die.[5]

A.A.'s Twelve Steps emphasize the importance of "pervasiveness" to the A.A. way of life in stunningly clear form. Step Four suggests "a *searching and fearless*" inventory. Step Five speaks of the need to admit "the *exact* nature of our wrongs." Step Six talks of becoming "*entirely* ready to have God remove *all* these defects of character." Step Eight suggests making "a list of *all* the people we had harmed" and of becoming "willing to make amends to them *all*." The closing words of Step Twelve speak of practicing "these principles in *all* our affairs." (Emphases added.)

All those *all*s point to the recognition, gained through painful and, for some, fatal experience, that spirituality is the kind of reality that unless it touches *all* of your life touches *none* of your life. The earliest version of Step Seven, in fact, read: "Humbly on our knees asked Him to remove *all* our shortcomings, *holding nothing back*."[6] Those who tried to hold something back almost invariably "slipped" and started drinking again.

Holding nothing back: a tall command, but one of the first—and great—gifts of a "spirituality of imperfection," for it is the acceptance of imperfection that makes "holding nothing back" possible. A.A.'s inspired choice of the terms *defects of character* and *shortcomings* in the Twelve Steps reinforces the insight. As opposed to guilt-laden words such as *sin* and *evil* or shame-inducing expressions such as *latent perversion* or *oral fixation*, the terms *defects* and *shortcomings* suggest the imagery of falling short (the original but long-lost meaning of the word *sin*). Such words and imagery first allow and then invite the owning of *all* of one's self. Alcoholics are not in A.A. to escape themselves, but to accept themselves as they are—flawed, imperfect, wounded, *alcoholic*—and through that acceptance to be healed, to be made whole, by being integrated into the reality of their *own* reality. *Healing* means not the elimination but the embracing of imperfection, for only thus is it possible to find wholeness.

The importance of spirituality's *pervasiveness* came clear to one of the authors when he began a brief stint of work at a treatment facility for alcoholic Roman Catholic clergy.

Shortly after my arrival, the House Director came down to my office one day and with a twinkle in his eye asked in his resonant Irish tenor: "Ah, Dr. Kurtz, would you like to have a reputation as being wondrously wise?"

"Of course," I answered, smiling back at the ruddy-faced Celt, "anyone would want such a reputation. Tell me, Ed, how?"

"Well," our resident genius replied, "as you may suspect, not all of our men make it on the first try. Some of them try a wee sip of 'the creature' again, and so eventually they end up back here. And because I am the Director they come to me to be interviewed as they are re-admitted, and when they do, I start off by asking them two questions, and oh, they think I am so wise . . . that I can see into their very souls."

After a maddeningly long pause, Ed continued: "The first question I ask, of course, is, 'When did you stop going to meetings?' And the second question I ask them is, 'And what are you hiding?' "

"*What are you hiding?*" The question has two dimensions, striking first at *denial*, the essence of which lies not in deceiving others, but in deceiving oneself. *Denial is self-deception.* The alcoholic who swears, "I am not an alcoholic" is really convinced that he is not one, and so this first level of denial involves being cut off from the wholeness of one's self. But denying one's own identity—as "alcoholic" or as anything else—means also deceiving oneself about the steps needed to regain that wholeness, to become whole again. This second level of denial involves holding back—hiding—the denied area, refusing to make it available for healing.

And that is why stories and storytelling are so crucial in piercing denial. The practice of telling stories of "what we used to be like, what happened, and what we are like now" helps to *make whole* because it makes available one's real *identity*. In bringing us face to face with our own imperfection, stories confront us with our *self* in a way that helps us to accept the ambiguity and mixed-up-ed-ness of our human be-ing. Storytelling helps us to create a "whole," a whole that does not deny that it is made up of incongruous, fractured pieces, but *whole* nonetheless. "Healing" through storytelling involves not the elimination but the embrace of the paradox of our "both-and-ness"—the fact that we are *both* beast and angel, earthy and divine, alcoholic and sober.

It is a truism of both therapy and spirituality that one must confront self-as-feared if one is ever to find self-as-is. What an alcoholic fears most at the point of "hitting bottom" is that he or she may be "an alcoholic." The first time that identity is acknowledged, it is on a short breath and with a catch in the throat. Yet just a few months later, that same individual might be standing up at an A.A. meeting, saying easily and freely and with a sparkle in the eye, "Good evening! My name is Marilou, and I am an alcoholic." What has happened? Only when we face self-as-feared, do we find self-as-is.

This does not happen only once in a lifetime—not even in the life of an alcoholic. Life may, in a way, be understood as an on-going process in which, at each moment, we are either confronting some self-as-feared—how adequate am I as friend, lover, parent, teacher?—or integrating into our self-knowledge a recently discovered self-as-is.

In a faraway place and a long-ago time, there was once a rich man who gave all his money to the poor, joined a band of

hermits, and went to live with them in the desert and worship God.

One day the man was sent to town with another hermit to sell two donkeys that had grown old and could no longer carry their burdens. He went and stood in the marketplace, where shoppers looking for donkeys came to ask if his were worth buying. "If they were worth buying, do you think we'd be selling them?" he replied.

"And why do they have such ragged backs and tails?" he was asked.

"Because they're old and stubborn," he said. "We have to pull their tails and thrash them to make them move."

Since there were no buyers for the donkeys, the man returned with them to the desert, where his companion told the other hermits what had happened. All of them demanded to know why he had frightened the buyers away. "Do you imagine for a moment," he answered, "that I left home and gave everything away, all my camels and cattle and sheep and goats, in order to make a liar of myself for the sake of two old donkeys?"[7]

❖

One basic lesson of all religion, art, and love (not to mention the experience of addictions such as alcoholism) is that there are no shortcuts. Storytelling in and of itself conveys that there are no quick fixes. The storytelling format of "what we used to be like, what happened, and what we are like now," emphasizes a process *through time* and so points to the *healing of time*. By telling of a past at work in the present, that story-format effects a kind of re-creation of self by the self. In presenting ourselves as we were, we exercise the right to recover possession of our present-day existence. We do not recall the past for the past; story calls up the past in the present, for the present, making present that which gives meaning and value to today. "To create and in creating to be created" perfectly describes this kind of storytelling.[8]

The essential point is to live in the here and now. The *now,* of course, is a fundamental spiritual concept. All spiritual traditions lay out the themes of "daily bread" and "sufficient unto the day." The Jesus of Matthew's gospel, for example, advises: "Do not be anxious about tomorrow, for tomorrow will be anxious for itself. Let the day's own trouble be sufficient for the day." (Matt. 6:34) From the Hasidic tradition, we have this almost Zen-like story:

> **Soon after the death of Rabbi Moshe, Rabbi Mendel of Kotzk asked one of his disciples:**
> **"What was most important to your teacher?"**
> **The disciple thought and then replied:**
> **"Whatever he happened to be doing at the moment."**

And less than a hundred years later . . .

> **"What do you think of the world to come?" an admirer asked Thoreau. "One world at a time," Thoreau replied.**[9]

Time, of course, is one of the ultimate philosophical paradoxes. "What is 'the now'?" asked Augustine, who intuited a fundamental connection between the conundrum of time and the mystery of spirituality. Not by sheer accident, then, did it happen that the very first name for Alcoholics Anonymous was "The Day At A Time Program." A.A.'s earliest members recognized how the paradox of time seems singularly illuminated by the drinking alcoholic who, on the one hand, lives only in the present—for this drink, this fix—and seems incapable of learning from the past or caring about the future. The active alcoholic cannot relate to the future, to any project requiring time, and if he isn't denying the past, he's wishing either that he could wipe it out or that he had it to do all over again.[10]

On the other hand, despite that apparent alienation from past and future, active alcoholics "live only in the past or in the future . . . they have no present tense." Wanting to have it *all* "now," the addicted person has *no* "now." Those trapped in this untimely condition, whether by addiction or some other spiritual trap, live out theologian Søren Kierkegaard's description of the "aesthete."

> Because he denies his finitude and interprets himself as eternal, the aesthete has no sense of his own . . . self-development. Since for him there is no sense that he belongs to past or future, time becomes a series of now-moments which must be filled with pleasurable dis-

tractions. Although thus bound to the present, he is not satisfied with what it offers. He cannot "be here now" because he wants all future possibilities to be actualized along with the present one. There is never enough time for anything. He races through life thinking that—as each minute ticks away—he is missing out on gratification. . . . Because he is constantly fleeing from the disclosure of his own mortality . . . , [he] elects to remain locked in his own ego.[11]

Jean-Paul Sartre termed such individuals *absolutists*, offering this scathing description:

Absolutists want to exist all at once and right away. There is an original fear of oneself and a fear of truth. And what frightens them is not the content of truth which they do not even suspect, but the very form of the true—that thing of indefinite approximation. It is as if their very existence were perpetually in suspension.[12]

A half-century earlier, William James, in his "Talks to Teachers," derided that "ceaseless frenzy" in which we always feel that we "should be doing something else." The ceaseless frenzy, the race through life, are symptomatic of the numbing of spirituality. *Holding to the now*, as Barsanuphius urged, is the classic antidote for this poison, the "way" that heals the human tendency to want to fix things "once and for all."

Less philosophically and more concretely, we live "a day at a time" because we *have* only this day; the future is ahead of us, the past behind us, only the present is here with us. But "this day" has meaning only insofar as it unites *my* past with *my* future. I can "live this day" only if I understand it as part of my *whole* story—the part that I can live this day, "now."

To be human is to be "a history-making creature who can neither repeat the past nor leave it behind," noted W. H. Auden in a brief biographical sketch of D. H. Lawrence. In Kierkegaard's most famous words: "Life must be lived forwards, but it can be understood only backwards." And as Mark Twain put it in his inimitable style, "Although the past may not repeat itself, it does rhyme."[13]

All spiritualities touch on time, for time is as pervasive as spirituality. A less than five-century-old Native American tale tells of this connection.

> Long ago, the People had no light. It was hard for them to move around in the darkness and they were always cold. Mink took pity on them. He heard that on the other side of the world there was something called the Sun. It was being kept there by those on the other side of the world. So Mink decided to steal the Sun for the People. It was not an easy job, but Mink was a great thief. He stole the Sun and placed it in the sky so that it would share its light equally with the People on both sides of the world. Now it was no longer dark and cold all the time. Now there was day and night because of the Sun. The People were very happy and they praised Mink. He grew proud of himself because of that praise.
>
> "Perhaps," he said, "there is something else I can steal for the People."
>
> A long time passed and Mink saw nothing that was worth stealing. Then the Europeans came. They were new people with a lot of power.
>
> "What is it that these new people have that we do not have?" Mink said.
>
> Then he saw what it was. The Europeans had something they called Time. They used it to give them their power. So Mink decided he would steal Time. He waited until it was dark and sneaked into their house. There, in the biggest room, they kept Time up on a shelf. They kept it in a shiny box which made noises. As it made noises, two small arrows on the front of that box moved in circles. Mink could see it was a powerful thing. So he carried it off.
>
> Now Mink and the People had Time. But Mink soon found that it was not easy to have Time. He had to watch the hands of that shiny box all of the time to see what the time was. He had to keep three keys tied around his neck so that he could use them to wind up that box full of time so it would keep on ticking. Now that Mink had Time, he no longer had the time to do the things he used to do. There was no time for him to fish and hunt as he had done before. He had to get up

THE DISCOVERIES OF ALCOHOLICS ANONYMOUS

at a certain time and go to bed at a certain time. He had to go
to meetings and work when the box full of Time told him it
was time. He and the People were no longer free.

Because Mink stole Time, it now owned him and the People. It has been that way ever since then. Time owns us the
way we used to own the Sun.[14]

To ask what *story* has to do with "time" is to ask why people tell
stories. Those familiar with the rabbinic tradition, especially those
frustrated by its practice of avoiding answers by replying to questions
with another question (or, at best, a story), may appreciate this answer
to that question:

Once some disciples of the Baal Shem Tov approached him
and asked: "Why do you answer all questions by telling a
story? Why do you always tell stories?"

The disciples then steeled themselves, certain that, true to
the tradition, the Baal Shem Tov would necessarily answer
such questions about story with a story.

But the Baal Shem Tov, after a loving, lingering pause,
responded: "Salvation lies in remembrance."[15]

"Salvation lies in remembrance," the Baal Shem Tov taught, because "in the process of reminiscence, we regain the present." The
Besht knew the fundamental spiritual truth: *Those who have no past,
have no future.* Our past continues to live in our present, and the way
we live this day, the way we live this moment determines our future.
Spirituality's "pervasiveness" embraces both the past and the future in
the present moment.

Part Three

EXPERIENCING SPIRITUALITY

❖

Experience is not what happens to a man. It is what a man does with what happens to him.

Aldous Huxley[1]

The young salesman approached the farmer and began to talk excitedly about the book he was carrying. "This book will tell you everything you need to know about farming," the young man said enthusiastically. "It tells you when to sow and when to reap. It tells you about weather, what to expect and when to expect it. This book tells you all you need to know."

"Young man," the farmer said, "that's not the problem. I know everything that is in that book. My problem is doing it."[2]

Spirituality involves not just talking about something, not just reading about or considering something, not even just doing something: it involves actually *experiencing* life in a new way. Spirituality makes possible—makes one capable of—specific kinds of experience.

The *primacy of experience* may be the most profound spiritual truth demonstrated by Alcoholics Anonymous. At meetings, in the process of telling their own stories and listening to the stories of others, A.A. members begin to live out the discoveries explored in Part Two, and in living out those discoveries, they find that certain experiences flow from them—*Release, Gratitude, Humility, Tolerance, Forgiveness,* and *Being-at-home.*

These experiences share this in common—they cannot be commanded. We do not call them forth when we want them: they become available to us when we need them, *if we are available to them.* They happen and we experience them, if we are open to them, but we cannot control when or how they happen, nor can we control when or how we experience them. Once again, we find ourselves locked in paradox: We cannot command precisely those realities that we most crave.

But we can tell stories about them; and our paradox unlocks with the discovery that storytelling (and storylistening) opens us to the experiencing of those realities that we seek. The A.A. storytelling style —the general format describing "what we used to be like, what happened, and what we are like now"—shapes a *language of recovery* that acts as the key that opens the door to the experiences that are spirituality. In telling our stories and in listening to the stories of others, we actually come to experience the powerful spiritual realities of *Release, Gratitude, Humility, Tolerance, Forgiveness,* and *Being-at-home.*

The *language of recovery* that is storytelling involves not dogma or commandment, not things to be done or truths to be believed, not theory, conjecture, argument, analysis, or explanation, but a *way* of conversation shared by those who accept and identify with their own imperfection. Following the tradition of Western spirituality, Alcoholics Anonymous aims to convey experience rather than to "teach" concepts. Always truthful to experience, the language of recovery makes it possible to *see*—and thus to *understand*—reality differently. And it is in this different vision that spirituality begins.

The "language of recovery" works not because those telling their stories *describe* experiences of Release, Gratitude, and so on, but because, in the very telling of their stories they actually *experience* those realities. Those who undergo profound change, those who make the *discoveries* we explored in Part Two, enter what has been termed a new "universe of discourse." It is less that they speak differently, in new terms, than that they *see* differently, in new categories, coming to understand reality in new ways. How we speak shapes how we think, and therefore what we see, and then in turn what and how we experience. Language thus fashions experience: It is how we make it "our own." Because there is a constant back-and-forth flow between language and vision, between how we speak and what we see, spirituality influences how we live by shaping what we experience.[3]

This truth is itself beyond words, which is one reason why we have artists. Perhaps a story about an artist—indeed, about the particular vision of an artist's naive spirituality—will help.

For thirty-five years Paul Cézanne lived in obscurity, producing masterpieces that he gave away to unsuspecting neighbors. So great was his love for his work that he never gave a thought to achieving recognition, nor did he suspect that someday he would be looked upon as the father of modern painting.

Cézanne owes his first fame to a Paris dealer who chanced upon his paintings, put some of them together, and presented the world of art with the first Cézanne exhibition. The world was astonished to discover the presence of a master.

The master was just as astonished. Shortly after the exhibition opened, Cézanne, arriving at the gallery leaning on the arm of his son, could not contain his amazement when he saw his paintings on display. Turning to his son he exclaimed, "Look, they have framed them!"[4]

Chapter 11

RELEASE

❖

"COME TO THE EDGE."
"No, we will fall."
"COME TO THE EDGE."
"No, we will fall."
They came to the edge.
He pushed them, and they flew.

Apollinaire

*Everything terrifying is, in its deepest being, something helpless that
wants our help.*

Rainer Maria Rilke[1]

Many readers will be familiar with a marginally humorous story of
antique vintage.

> Clifford was leaning against the fence, enjoying a beautiful
> view from the top of the Grand Canyon, when the wooden
> posts suddenly ripped from their cement moorings. Seconds
> later, Clifford was plunging down into the abyss.
>
> Halfway to the bottom his desperate arm-waving helped
> Clifford catch and clutch the branch of a scrubby tree that
> grew from the canyon wall. Grasping, gasping, he looked both
> up and down. No way could he climb that sheer cliff, even if
> he could swing his body toward the wall. But below yawned
> the chasm, unbroken by any other tree or holding place. To
> fall would be to die, horribly crushed on the rocks below. No
> one had seen him fall, and he hung there out of sight, know-

ing that the wind would scatter his weak voice no matter how loudly he shouted.

Desperate, Clifford cried out to the heavens: "God help me!" Hearing his own trembling voice, he wailed again, "Please, God, help me."

To Clifford's amazement, he heard an immediate answer. "All right," came the voice. The initial warmth Clifford felt turned to a chill wind gripping his body as the voice continued: "Let go."

Looking down, Clifford saw the huge boulders waiting below, and he knew again that if he let go he would surely die. *Let go?* he thought. "But God, you don't understand!" he yelled up. "I'm too far up, I'll . . ."

"Let go," the voice repeated.

Silence filled the canyon. Then, in a weak, terrified voice Clifford called out, "Is there anyone else up there?"[2]

The story is corny, except that it is true; true of every one of us in the sense that it conveys a powerful spiritual truth: *So long as we cling, we are bound.* The alcoholic knows that truth as well as anyone on this earth, for it is the very essence of addiction to cling to some fixed, repetitive, once-meaningful but now self-destructive pattern. Yet the alcoholic—and the rest of us, in one way or another—hang on. "Let go," the voice calls out. "Let go of the bottle (or the pills, the possessions, the power, the pride) and you shall be free." But the insistent whine refuses. "Please, anything but that . . . take anything but that."

We crave release, but we refuse to release—and *so long as we cling, we are bound.*

❖

Spirituality is experienced, *first,* as Release. But Release, although it involves a true *free-ing,* is not the same as "freedom." Freedom cannot be given; it must be won. Release, on the contrary, is experienced rather than "gotten," received rather than attained. And so it does not work to tell one's story in order to "attain" Release; yet Release does emerge from the practice of telling one's story. "When we let the truth about ourselves be revealed, we experience a kind of release," wrote

Michael Zimmerman in his study of Martin Heidegger. Note the wording—we "let" the truth "be revealed"—implying an openness rather than some kind of exhibitionism, conveying a sense of wonder rather than of triumph.[3]

The experience of Release has been described as "the chains falling away," "a light going on," "a weight lifted," "something giving way." The very language attests that the experience is not one of triumph ("I did it!") but one of awe and wonder ("I somehow see what I never saw before!"). The awareness that we do not earn this experience, but are given it, reveals life itself and the experiences within it as gift.

In the experience of Release, as just about everywhere else in the realm of spirituality, the fundamental truth of mutuality holds. We are able to "get" only what we are willing to give. Thus it is that we can experience *release* only if we have released—only if we have *let go*. We do not find Release *by* letting go, for that would still involve the manipulative attempt to control. When we truly release, when we really *let go*, we abdicate control, and it is this surrender of control that is so terrifying. What gets in the way here is the old danger of taking ourselves too seriously, of feeling that we have "got it," and therefore have to "hold it." The reasoning seems sound: Why take a chance and let go of something valuable when it might not come back?

"Pious pigheadedness" were the words used by the seventeenth-century spiritual teacher Jean-Pierre Caussade to describe this circular and self-destructive reasoning. His admonitions not to "fuss too much about yourself" were rooted in his conviction that we take ourselves too seriously, clinging to our own self-interest and selfish needs, when our real need is the giving of self that he termed *abandonment:* "I wish I could cry out everywhere, 'Abandonment! Abandonment!' And then what? Abandonment again, abandonment without limit and without reserve."[4]

The need to let go—even to let go, totally and completely, of our most prized "spiritual" possessions—is found in all ages and all spiritual traditions.

The Rozdoler Rabbi was asked: "Wherein does the desire to become a Rebbe differ from other desires?"

He replied: "Before one attains the desire to become a Rebbe, he must break himself of every other desire."[5]

And the Christian Desert Fathers have left us this gem:

Abbot Anastasius had a book of very fine parchment, which was worth twenty shekels. It contained both the Old and the New Testaments in full, and Anastasius read from it daily as he meditated. Once a certain monk came to visit him and, seeing the book, made off with it. The next day, when Anastasius went to his Scripture reading and found that it was missing, he knew at once that the monk had taken it. Yet he did not send after him, for fear that he might add the sin of perjury to that of theft.

Now the monk went into the city to sell the book. He wanted eighteen shekels for it. The buyer said, "Give me the book so that I may find out if it is worth that much money." With that, he took the book to the holy Anastasius and said, "Father, take a look at this and tell me if you think it is worth as much as eighteen shekels." Anastasius said, "Yes, it is a fine book. And at eighteen shekels it is a bargain."

So the buyer went back to the monk and said, "Here is your money. I showed the book to Father Anastasius and he said it was worth eighteen shekels."

The monk was stunned. "Was that all he said? Did he say nothing else?"

"No, he did not say a word more than that."

"Well, I have changed my mind and don't want to sell the book after all."

Then he went back to Anastasius and begged him with many tears to take the book back, but Anastasius said gently, "No, brother, keep it. It is my present to you."

But the monk said, "If you do not take it back, I shall have no peace."

After that the monk dwelt with Anastasius for the rest of his life.[6]

❖

To listen to members of Alcoholics Anonymous telling their stories is to hear described—but more importantly to witness and even perhaps to experience—three levels of the experience of release. First and most obviously comes release from the addiction itself, from the obsession with the chemical and its effects. Lives centered on a chemical —how to find, get, and keep it (and its effects)—begin to focus on other realities. Second comes release from what Alcoholics Anonymous refers to as *the root of our troubles:* self-centeredness. Lives centered wholly on the self begin to shift perspective and look outward, reaching out to other people with genuine generosity. And third comes release from *denial,* from the fear and dishonesty of self-deception, from the dire realization that one does not even know who one is. Lives dominated by self-deception begin to discover the reality of a *self* that is real but limited, limited but real.

Alcoholics and addicts are not the only people who experience release, nor are they the only ones who need this experience. "Just plain human beings" are as susceptible to obsessions, self-centeredness, and self-deception; when we open ourselves to *release,* we, too, can experience similar moments of free-ing. A child tugging at our sleeve, begging for attention while we sit with eyes glued on the television, can reveal in a twinkling the hollowness of our habits. A spouse's gentle touch can scatter the gloom of self-pity. A character in a short story can penetrate that part of self we had been hiding even from self. Saying "I'm sorry" and having the apology immediately accepted; listening to another speak of pain and seeing your own pain for the first time; hearing the words, "I love you," when you have just done something unforgiveable—these are universal experiences. As so often in the realm of spirituality and its antithesis, addiction, "alcoholic" means simply *human being* writ large.

Release begins to happen when we lay aside the idea that we can *plan* spirituality—for ourselves or for anyone else.

Not so very many years ago, a man named Patrick wanted to visit the Holy Land. He knew that planes were being hijacked and blown up because of tensions in the region, and being a careful, extremely organized man, he did everything in his power to assure the safety of his journey.

But lo and behold, just minutes after takeoff, a bomb exploded under his seat and Patrick was blown out the side of the plane. As he fell, the panic-stricken Patrick thought back on the choices he had made—all his efforts, now apparently so worthless. He had chosen to fly Pan Am rather than TWA; he had decided to change flights in Switzerland rather than the more troubled airports in Germany or Italy; he had chosen to travel on a Saturday rather than midweek; and just a few minutes before the flight took off, he'd asked the cabin attendant to switch him from the aisle to a window seat.

By this time, Patrick was somewhere around eight thousand feet, and his situation seemed grim indeed. From the depth of his faith, Patrick called out for assistance. "Saint Francis," he cried, "help me!"

Suddenly, amazingly, a hand reached down from the heavens, grabbed Patrick by the scruff of his jacket, and held him there, suspended in midair, thousands of feet above the earth. And then, as he caught his breath, Patrick became aware that there was a voice attached to the hand, and that the voice was asking: "*Which* Saint Francis?"

Alcoholism and addiction, characterized as they are by the rigid clinging of obsession and compulsion, help us to understand the experience of release. Perhaps the greatest paradox in the story of spirituality is the mystical insight that we are able to experience release only if we ourselves *let go*. This is the paradox of *surrender*. Surrender begins with the acceptance that we are not in control of the matter at hand—in fact, we are not in absolute control of anything. Thus the experience of surrender involves the "letting in" of reality that becomes possible when we are ready to let go of our illusions and pretensions (our "unreality").[7]

If *surrender* is the act of "letting go," the experience of *conversion* can be understood as the hinge on which that act swings—it is the turning point, the turning from "denial" as a way of seeing things to acceptance of the reality revealed in surrender. The self-centeredness that undermines spirituality is rooted in a self-deception that reflects a false relationship with reality, and that false relationship begins with distorted seeing, with some kind of false understanding about the nature of reality and our relationship with it. Breaking through that *denial* and confronting reality is what members of Alcoholics Anonymous mean by "hitting bottom."

The experiencing of *release* most frequently comes at the point of exhaustion, at the moment when we "give up" our efforts and thus permit ourselves to just *be*. William James memorably described the importance of Release in his study of *The Varieties of Religious Experience*.

> . . . the way to success, as vouched by innumerable authentic personal narrations, is . . . by . . . "surrender." . . . Passivity, not activity; relaxation, not intentness, should be now the rule. Give up the feeling of responsibility, let go your hold, resign the care of your destiny to higher powers, be genuinely indifferent as to what becomes of it all, and you will find not only that you gain a perfect inward relief, but often also, in addition, the particular goods you sincerely thought you were renouncing. . . . Something must give way, a native hardness must break down and liquefy; and this event . . . is frequently sudden and automatic, and leaves on the Subject an impression that he has been wrought on by an external power.
>
> . . . a form of regeneration by relaxing, by letting go. . . . It is but giving your little private convulsive self a rest, and finding that a greater Self is there.[8]

What blocks *Release* more than anything else is the refusal to "let go" that comes from the demand for security, for certainty, for assured results. Release, like spirituality itself, requires risk.

> A very learned man who had heard of the rabbi of Berditchev —one of those who boasted of being enlightened—looked him up in order to debate with him as he was in the habit of doing with others, and refuting his old-fashioned proofs for the truth of his faith. When he entered the zaddik's room, he saw him walking up and down, immersed in ecstatic thought. The rabbi took no notice of his visitor. After a time, however, he stopped, gave him a brief glance and said: "But perhaps it is true after all!"

In vain did the learned man try to rally his self-confidence. His knees shook, for the zaddik was terrible to behold and his simple words were terrible to hear. But now Rabbi Levi Yitzhak turned to him and calmly addressed him: "My son, the great Torah scholars with whom you have debated, wasted their words on you. When you left them you only laughed at what they had said. They could not set God and his kingdom on the table before you, and I cannot do this either. But, my son, only think! Perhaps it is true. Perhaps it is true after all!" The enlightened man made the utmost effort to reply, but the terrible "perhaps" beat on his ears again and again and broke down his resistance.[9]

"Letting go" involves a breaking down of resistance to reality, a surrender of the demand for certitude; it can be pictured as a letting fall of fetters, a shucking of bonds of fear and possessiveness now experienced as no longer binding. We "wake up" to discover that the locks on our chains have been removed, and realizing this, we lift our arms and let the chains just drop away. But—the chains cannot drop if *we* have become so *attached to them* that we fear being without them. While the chains may no longer be attached to us, we may still be attached to them. The deeper *release*, then, is of *our* attachment to the chains that bind us.

The trap of attachment and the need for detachment form a consistent theme in the history of spirituality. "Attachment" is usually depicted as a clinging to material objects, but in the more profound spiritual traditions, material reality serves mainly as metaphor. Francis of Assisi, for example, focused on spiritual rather than material poverty: his poverty, his "detachment," involved the giving up of claims to "rights" and of his own will more than the surrender of material possessions. In "surrendering" property and possessions, Francis also "surrendered" his right to insist on his own will and thus was able to become, in James's words, "genuinely indifferent as to what becomes of it all."

Such detachment forms the heart and soul of Buddhist insight.

The great Buddhist saint Nagarjuna moved around naked except for a loincloth and, incongruously, a golden begging bowl gifted to him by the King, who was his disciple.

EXPERIENCING SPIRITUALITY

One night he was about to lie down to sleep among the ruins of an ancient monastery when he noticed a thief lurking behind one of the columns. "Here, take this," said Nagarjuna, holding out the golden begging bowl. "That way you won't disturb me once I have fallen asleep."

The thief eagerly grabbed the bowl and made off—only to return next morning with the bowl and a request. He said, "When you gave away this bowl so freely last night, you made me feel very poor. Teach me how to acquire the riches that make this kind of lighthearted detachment possible."[10]

All spiritual traditions emphasize *detachment,* but that emphasis does not imply that material reality should be held in contempt. The object itself is not the problem—the golden begging bowl is not bad in and of itself. Difficulties arise not because we have things, but when our relationship with our possessions becomes "attachment"—when we make them into more than "objects" by interpreting them as in some way an essential part of our very *self.*

Ibrahim Adham, a great spiritual leader of the Sufis, was wont to live in much pomp and splendor, surrounded by a large number of servants. Even his tents were pitched with golden pegs.

A wandering dervish once happened to pass by his tents, and was enormously surprised at this display of wealth by a Sufi. So he went, begging-cup in hand, to Ibrahim and questioned him thus: "It is strange that you call yourself a Sufi, and yet you are surrounded by luxury and material wealth of a kind, that even your tents are fixed with golden pegs."

Ibrahim welcomed him, and bade him to rest awhile and asked his servants to feed him well. After some time he asked the dervish if he would like to go along with him to Mecca, and the dervish readily agreed. They both set out on their pilgrimage, the princely Sufi leaving all his wealth and luxury behind him without a thought. They had not walked far, when the dervish suddenly remembered that he had left his wooden cup in Ibrahim's tent and wanted to go back to fetch it. Ibrahim smiled and said, "My friend, I left all my wealth behind without the least worry. Yet you are so much attached to a cup of practically no value that you cannot proceed to Mecca without it. The golden pegs which so much surprised you were driven into the earth, not into my heart."[11]

Nor does spirituality's wariness of "attachment" imply rejection of human relationships. Part of our human be-ing involves a profound need for other human beings; thus, spiritual teachers have always been alert to questions concerning the nature of "community" and our attachment to others. Their consistent message has been that here, as elsewhere, there is both a "right" and a "wrong" *way of joining oneself to what is.* The fourth-century Eastern father, Gregory of Nyssa, for example, distinguished between "the participation proper to virtue and the attachment proper to vice." Modern vocabulary differs, but Gregory's point remains valid: Any human relationship requires alertness to the difference between the *attachment* that becomes the claim to *possession* and the *detachment* sufficient to allow true *participation.* The first and essential "detachment" must be from the attempt and the claim to control others.[12]

In his description of the "triple abyss" into which human nature is prone to fall, the seventeenth-century mathematician and mystic Blaise Pascal offered another perspective on the theme of "attachment" and "detachment." Each "abyss" involves a different kind of libidinal enslavement to the egotistical self: (1) the *libido dominandi,* or lust for power over others and over nature; (2) the *libido sentiendi,* or lust for intense sensation; and (3) the *libido sciendi,* or lust for manipulative knowledge, knowledge that is primarily used to increase our own power, profit, and pleasure.[13]

Two more recent writers, theologian Mary Reuter and the spiritual director Richard Rohr, echo Pascal's triple abyss in their analyses of the "attachments" that undermine our spirituality. Both Rohr and Reuter emphasize the psychological and emotional attachments that can devastate our spiritual lives, making the point that "attachment" does not have to be to material things to be spiritually destructive.

Reuter suggests three layers of attachment that need to be peeled back sequentially, like an onion. First, we need to become detached from material gain, second from self-importance, and third from the urge to dominate others. Only through this process of stripping away these attachments, she writes, can we lay claim to spiritual progress.[14]

Rohr uses a language more familiar to those steeped in Twelve-Step spirituality. In an article on A.A.'s Third Step, he counsels that spirituality involves the "letting go" of three needs: the need to be in control, the need to be effective, and the need to be right. For alcoholics in early sobriety the last point may be the most important, for detachment from the need to be right, surrender of the "demand to have the last word," seems a prerequisite to the kind of listening that allows participation in the healing power of storytelling.

A folktale that can be found in many traditions captures the essence of these points.

A rich man who owned much property fell seriously ill, and though the doctors came to him from all over, none of them was able to cure him. His situation grew worse and worse, and all hope had been given up for him when one day a traveling dervish saw him and said, "Put a truly happy man's shirt on his back and he will get well."

The sick man's family and servants went looking for a truly happy man in town and could not find one, because there is no man whose happiness is complete. The sick man's favorite son, however, was determined to save his father's life by finding such a person, and so he left town and went looking elsewhere. He walked and walked until he reached the desert. By then it was nighttime, and tired from his journey, he wished to sleep. Seeing a cave, he decided to seek shelter there, and when he reached it he heard a voice say from within, "How happy I am! What a wonderful day I had! And now I think I'll go to sleep."

Hearing this, the son was delighted to have accomplished his mission so soon. He entered the cave, strode quickly to the man inside it, and was about to strip off his shirt when he realized that the fellow was naked and had none. At a loss, he stood there dismayed. "What is it?" asked the man. "What do you want?"

"I heard you say you were a happy man," said the son, "and so I wanted to take your shirt, because it alone can save my father's life."

"But if I had a shirt," said the happy man, "I wouldn't be happy!"[15]

Release flows from the understanding that all absolute attempts to control our own destiny—like all attempts to do anything "absolutely"—are ultimately doomed, for inevitably we will come up against something that we cannot control. The attempt to control the future and the demand to be in charge of everything in our lives sentences us to a daily existence obsessed with life-numbing worry.

A *Zen Comics* saying helps us to laugh at our pretensions by standing one of life's classic assumptions on its head:

I feel so much better since I gave up hope.[16]

Chapter 12

GRATITUDE

❖

Thinking is a kind of thanking. In thanking, we accept the gift of existence. In accepting ourselves, we become ourselves. As released, we gratefully enter into the play of which we are already a part. Release-ment means "homecoming." Thinking as thanking means loving.

Michael Zimmerman

Gratitude is heaven itself.

William Blake[1]

A blind man was begging in a city park. Someone approached and asked him whether people were giving generously. The blind man shook a nearly empty tin.

His visitor said to him, "Let me write something on your card." The blind man agreed. That evening the visitor returned. "Well, how were things today?"

The blind man showed him a tin full of money and asked, "What on earth did you write on that card?"

"Oh," said the other, "I merely wrote 'Today is a spring day, and I am blind.' "[2]

Because Release is a *gift*—a reality not earned, not merited, not attained in any way—there flows naturally from the experience of release, the experiencing of Gratitude. *Gratitude* can best be defined and understood as the only possible response to a gift, to something recognized as utterly, freely given. Gratitude *is* the vision—the way of seeing—that recognizes "gift."

Our culture seems on the verge of losing the meaning of the experience of gratitude, in part because we have lost all sense of "gift." Our ritual occasions of giving, from the traditional birthdays and anniversaries to the industry-created special days for everyone from grandparents to secretaries, mean that there is always handy some occasion to give "a gift"—with the result that a true *gift* is never given. For a gift is something freely and spontaneously given. A true gift is inspired rather than occasioned.

> After attending a conference, a man walked down the streets of a strange city, whiling away the hours before his plane left. Enjoying the stroll and the window shopping, he spotted a singularly attractive cashmere sweater. Thinking affectionately of his wife (who loved cashmere), the man walked into the shop, purchased the sweater, and asked the salesperson to giftwrap it.
>
> When he arrived home, he handed the gift to his wife who looked at him at first in surprise but then with something approaching suspicion. Opening the gift, she examined it appreciatively, but then looked up to ask, "And what is this *for*?"

The experience of gratitude has been lost, too, because we tend to think of it primarily as some kind of "feeling." "Do you want a shivery-warm feeling that makes you tingle all the way through your body?" Linus asks Charlie Brown in a famous cartoon parody. "Well, go pee in your pants."

Feelings are fine, but they are also transient and ephemeral; gratitude is not a feeling but an ongoing vision of thank-full-ness that recognizes the gifts constantly being received. A feeling is fleeting, an emotion for the moment; gratitude is a mind-set, a way of seeing and thinking that is rooted in a remembrance—the remembrance of being without the gift. As the philosopher William Barrett reminds: " 'Think' and 'thank' are kindred roots, and the German word *andenken*—literally 'to think on'—means to *remember;* hence, think, thank, and remembrance are related notions. Real thinking, thinking that is rooted in Being, is at once an act of thanking and remembrance."[3]

Gratitude is the vision that "sees" gift and recognizes how *gift-ed* we are. This vision has always been recognized as a core experience of "spirituality." The early American theologian Jonathan Edwards described in his *Treatise Concerning Religious Affections* how "the saints" were characterized by "a new inward perception or sensation of their minds, entirely different in its nature and kind from anything that ever their minds were the subjects of before they were sanctified." Those who seek spirituality, that is to say, *see* reality differently. It is not that they see things that others cannot see, but rather that they see what everyone else sees, but in seeing *recognize* in all reality its aspect of *gift*.[4]

Said Rabbi Bunam: "I find among the Selihot a prayer which reads: 'May He who answered Abraham on Mount Moriah answer me.' Had I been the author of this Selihah I would have worded it thus: 'May He who has answered me until now answer me at present as well.' There exists no person whom the Lord had not answered many times."[5]

Within a spirituality of imperfection, the truly holy, like the truly wise, have never thought wisdom or sanctity to be rare. As Edwards was careful to point out, all can be "saints" in the sense that all can gain this new vision of the world. But what does the vision of gratitude look like? What is this "sense of the heart," the kind of third eye that perceives gifts and giftedness at every turn? It is, in the first place, the opposite of the stubborn conviction that sees all goods as *winnings*.

Consider, for example, a teacher . . . a professor. On the one hand, she could be filled with an arrogant sense of triumph: "I hold this position because I am smart; and, by God, I worked for it! And so I am here because I *deserve* to be here, and don't you forget it!" We have all met such individuals—if we are lucky, rarely. But then there are those teachers who exult in terms of "How fortunate I am to be here, to be able to do what I love doing—thinking and researching and sharing what I find! So many people went out of their way to help or to encourage me . . . as woman, as scholar, as teacher. Without them, so many of them, I would not be here. And the only way I have to say 'Thank you' is to 'pass it on'—to give to my students as I have been given to."

All spiritual teachers have asked, in one form or another, "What do you have that you have not received?" That question can lead in two directions. Gratitude responds, "Thank you." Greed demands, "More." Although these appear to be opposite responses, the twain do meet, for each of us always expresses both. Children live this duality of greed and gratitude most openly, as a delightful vignette in the novel *The Joy Luck Club* captures in telling the story of a young Chinese girl whose Amah (nursemaid) has just informed her that they are taking a trip to see the Moon Lady.

"The Moon Lady! The Moon Lady!" I said, jumping up and down with great delight. And then, after I ceased to be amazed with the pleasant sounds of my voice saying new words, I tugged Amah's sleeve and asked: "Who is the Moon Lady?"

"Chang-o. She lives on the moon and today is the only day you can see her and have a secret wish fulfilled."

"What is a secret wish?"

"It is what you want but cannot ask," said Amah.

"Why can't I ask?"

"This is because . . . because if you ask it . . . it is no longer a wish but a selfish desire," said Amah. "Haven't I taught you that it is wrong to think of your own needs? A child can never ask, only listen."

"Then how will the Moon Lady know my wish?"

"Ai! You ask too much already! You can ask her because she is not an ordinary person."

Satisfied at last, I immediately said, "Then I will tell her I don't want to wear these clothes anymore."

"Ah! Did I not just explain?" said Amah. "Now that you have mentioned this to me, it is not a secret wish anymore."[6]

Distinguishing between secret wishes and selfish desires is difficult not only for children. Because of our human mixedness, greed and gratitude will always be connected. But we can work on that distinc-

EXPERIENCING SPIRITUALITY

tion—the difference between "Thanks" and "Gimme," between admiration and "wannabe," between the wonder of awe and the avarice of "gotta have it." And we might "work on" it by pondering the insight that one reason why we remain narrow and pinched and grasping is that we *do* have very little if we are not grateful.

Some find scandalous the saying of many spiritual teachers: "To those who have, more will be given." But that is a virtual truism, a self-fulfilling prophecy, because only the grateful are able truly to receive. There is little risk of greed in that realization because the insight is applied in the only way possible—not to material goods, but to the spiritual realities of Release, Serenity, Miracle, Tolerance, Friendship, Community, and Love. As we come to *see* the gift of these realities in our lives, the realities themselves become more present, more "experienced," more *real*.

Vision is central to gratitude—the vision that perceives gift in all reality—but gratitude as "seeing" is not the whole story. Conjoined with gratitude as vision comes gratitude as attitude: "the attitude of gratitude." An *attitude* is a posture, a way of positioning not only our body but our selves. Standing, sitting, and lying down are attitudes, each of which makes something possible. When I stand, I can see farther, I can walk, I can run; when I sit, I can lean back, relax, read; when I lie down, I can doze or sleep. *And when I am grateful, I can receive.* For "attitudes"—postures—can be spiritual as well as physical, and those who are greedy are not only not able to receive: they are primed to lose.

There was a man who coveted his neighbors' silver lamp. One day he went to them, asked to borrow an earthen mug, and was given it. The next day he returned it with a little mug inside.

"Why bring us two mugs when you borrowed one?" they asked.

"In the middle of the night I heard a groan," replied the man. "I went to see what it was and found that your mug had given birth to a baby, so I'm only returning what is yours."

The astonished neighbors said nothing and took the two mugs in silence.

The next day, the man asked for the loan of a tin plate. He

179

THE SPIRITUALITY OF IMPERFECTION

returned two tin plates and again told his neighbors that the bigger one had given birth. Delighted, they took both.

The next day he came to borrow a glass pitcher, which the neighbors were only too happy to lend him. Nor did he disappoint them, for he brought them back two pitchers, a mother and a child. They were thrilled to have such a good neighbor, who kept bringing them more and more things.

One day the man came, asked to borrow his neighbor's silver lamp, and was given it with alacrity. When several days passed without any sign of him, they knocked on his door and said, "Neighbor, why haven't you returned the silver lamp that we lent you?"

"I'm terribly sorry," replied the man, "but what can I do? In the middle of the night I heard a groan, and when I went to see what it was I found that your lamp had passed away."

"What?" said the neighbors, dumbfounded. "How can a lamp die?"

"If a cup, a plate, and pitcher can give birth," replied the man, "what's to keep a lamp from dying?"[7]

Gratitude's opposite—greed—is the vision that everything is to be "gotten." The vision that is spirituality warns that greed and misery go hand in hand. Misery arises inevitably from the belief that we are in control, that we can control everything and that anything we have, we deserve. Misery is the mind-set that we must get and get and get; it is the yearning for more, the push to acquire more, win more, own more, have more. Misery is misery because it does not know the meaning of *enough*. Those who lack gratitude's vision do not possess things; things possess them. And *that* is misery. As Eric Hoffer observed decades ago: "You can never get enough of what you don't really want."[8]

Happiness—the joy of living—comes in the experience of *gratitude* that flows from a vision of one's life as a reality received, a gift given freely and spontaneously. Such a vision removes self from the center, thus healing self-centeredness by revealing the folly of the illusion of control.

A woman came to the Maggid of Koznitz asking him to pray for her that she have a child.

180

"My mother too was unhappy as you are," said the Maggid. "Then one day she met the Baal Shem Tov and presented him with a beautiful cape. One year later I was born."

The woman's eyes brightened. "I will make you the most beautiful cape in the world!" she said.

The Maggid smiled and shook his head. "I am afraid that will not work," he said. "You see, my mother did not know this story."[9]

As the example of Alcoholics Anonymous attests, it is in the giving up of claims and demands to *control* that serenity and peace of mind begin. The "First Step" of the A.A. program reads: "We admitted that we were powerless over alcohol, that our lives had become unmanageable." Only then is the first part of A.A.'s Second Step possible: "[We] came to believe. . . ."[10]

The program and fellowship of Alcoholics Anonymous emphasize *gratitude* because A.A. members experience their sobriety as a *gift*. Each had tried, promised, struggled to "never drink alcohol again," or at least never to get sickeningly, obnoxiously drunk again. And they had meant it. But all their will, all their effort and sincerity had gone for naught, had achieved nothing. And so they gave up, gave in, in one way or another *surrendered* and came to Alcoholics Anonymous. And there, in A.A., the first thing that they heard was that they *could not* stop drinking . . . on their own or by themselves. Some resisted that truth and kept up the struggle, now against A.A. as well as against booze. And so long as they fought, they lost. So long as they tried to gain and to get—even to get sobriety—they lost. Finally, they gave up. Then, and only then, was sobriety given to them.[11]

That story, although a maddening mystery to control-oriented moderns, repeats the most familiar plot in the history of spirituality. Those who long for *freedom* attain it only after experiencing *release*— and release is a *gift*. For those who discover that in the only way possible (by experiencing it), gratitude becomes the cornerstone of spirituality, the enduring vision that undercuts the miseries of failure with the serenity that recognizes in failure itself the grounds for gift— so long as that failure, that *imperfection*, is accepted.

For the issue here is not strictly "misery" and "happiness" and their relationship to "failure." Once again, thinking in terms of "either-or" can lead astray. The essential point has to do with *control*, with its demand not only for "all at once and right away," but for *all the time*. "The addict," critic Stanton Peele observed in his study of *Love and Addiction*, "wishes to escape from the realization that it is impossible to be 'all together' all the time. He thinks there must be some way, if only he can find it, to make things perfect always."[12]

This tendency resides not only in Peele's "addict" but in all human beings: we want to do away with all misery and be happy all the time. Perhaps one source of our tendency to think in terms of either-or is our choice of words, for happiness and misery *are* "either-or." The traditional terms *joy* and *sorrow* better express our essential paradox, for we recognize *both* joy and sorrow as normal experiences; both, then, have a part in any spirituality. The attempt or the claim to experience only one will always be false—fortunately—for the person "in control" of everything is incapable of receiving a *gift*. It is worth repeating, in this context, an Hasidic story.

> Said the Porissover: "Some Hasidim are so proud of their piety that they cannot believe the Lord sends them hardships in order to awaken in them penitence for their sins. They affirm: I am a perfect Jew, and I will accept these hardships as 'afflictions from love.' But afflictions from love are not sent in vain; they are intended as a means to arouse penitence. When the Riziner was imprisoned, he wept. He was asked: 'Why do you not accept this affliction as intended in love?' He answered: 'When God sends bitterness, we ought to feel it.' "[13]

"Joy" *and* "sorrow" . . . their relationship to *control*, and therefore their relationship to *spirituality*, was once brilliantly elucidated by a woman who trains alcoholism counselors.

> Speaking to a group of nuns who were seeking deeper understanding of the realities of addiction in their own communities, Bonnie noted their concern about the pressures placed on them to constantly radiate "joy."
>
> "It's too much," one participant inserted, almost angrily. "There is sorrow in our lives, as in all lives. How can we be 'always joyful'?"

Discussion moved around the group, each participant adding a thought or a vignette that seemed only to deepen the quandary.

The pauses grew lengthier. Finally Bonnie spoke, attempting to sum up what she knew of both the tragic results of confusing *vision* with "feeling" and the treachery of the trap of control: "We *can* experience both joy and sorrow, even at the same time, for joy and sorrow are not opposites," she began. "It is not joy and sorrow, but *their* opposites, that cause damage—for the opposite of joy is cynicism and the opposite of sorrow is callousness.

"Cynicism," she continued, "is rooted in the assumption that everyone is always in control. Callousness is the *inability* to feel that follows from the fear of losing control."[14]

❖

Spirituality itself is a gift. No one "earns" spirituality, no one can acquire it or possess it, for spirituality is a reality spontaneously, freely given, and *gratitude* is the only possible response to that *gift*. In that gratitude, from that understanding of how much has been given us and how gift-ed we are, we become able to *see* at work some reality higher, larger, greater than ourselves. That vision, which comes only to those who in some way have given up trying to control, makes possible a further giving up of claims and demands to control. We give up control because we finally understand that we are not in control. And yet . . .

"Where is the dwelling of God?"

This was the question with which the rabbi of Kotzk surprised a number of learned men who happened to be visiting him.

They laughed at him: "What a thing to ask! Is not the whole world full of his glory!"

Then he answered his own question:

"God dwells wherever man lets him in."[15]

❖

THE SPIRITUALITY OF IMPERFECTION

The vision of "giftedness" is transmitted through stories. Stories speak the language of the heart, giving us the means to express our gratitude. Among the greatest of modern spiritual storytellers is Elie Wiesel. A survivor of the Holocaust, Wiesel received the Nobel Peace Prize for his writings, which speak so profoundly to the experience and the spirituality of the Jewish people. Words that Wiesel spoke on the occasion of accepting that award sum up the experience of gratitude as eloquently as is humanly possible.

No one is as capable of gratitude as one who has emerged from the kingdom of night.

We know that every moment is a moment of grace, every hour an offering; not to share them would mean to betray them. Our lives no longer belong to us alone; they belong to all those who need us desperately.

. . . And that is why I swore never to be silent whenever and wherever human beings endure suffering and humiliation. We must always take sides. Neutrality helps the oppressor, never the victim. Silence encourages the tormentor, never the tormented.[16]

And that is why we tell stories.

Chapter 13

HUMILITY

❖

St. Bernard, asked to list the four cardinal virtues, answered: "Humility, humility, humility and humility."

"You alone can do it, but you cannot do it alone."

O. Hobart Mowrer[1]

A man went to Wahab Imri and said:

"Teach me humility."

Wahab answered: "I cannot do that, because humility is a teacher of itself. It is learnt by means of its practice. If you cannot practice it, you cannot learn it."[2]

Many scholars point to the *Gesta Romanorum,* a compilation of 181 medieval morality tales, as our most ancient storybook. The twenty-sixth tale runs as follows:

There was a queen who dishonoured herself with a servant, and bore him a son. This son, on arriving at years of maturity, practised every description of wickedness, and conducted himself with the greatest insolence toward the prince, his reputed father. The prince, unable to account for such perversion of mind, interrogated the mother as to the legitimacy of her child; and finding, by her reluctant confession, that he was not his son, though loath to deprive him of the kingdom, he ordained that his dress for the time to come, should be of different texture and colour; one side to be composed of the most ordinary materials, and the other of the most valuable: so that when he looked upon the baser portion, his pride might be abated, and the vicious propensities, in which he had indulged, relinquished; on the other hand, when he surveyed the more gorgeous part, his hopes might be raised, and his spirit animated to goodness. By this judicious device, he became remarkable for humility, and ever after abandoned his dishonest life.[3]

In an era that fawns on "the rich and famous" and adopts as its rallying cry, "Me First," *humility* is a concept scorned or, worse, neglected. We know it (or fail to know it) mainly in its caricatures: the fictional Casper Milquetoast, the cringing spouse, or the spineless employee. The ancient, favorable sense of the word—connoting mildness, modesty, patience of spirit, and the willingness to remove oneself from the center of the universe—has been eroded in the modern era by unfavorable interpretations in which "lowly" calls to mind servility and self-abasement, "meek" is equated with cowardly submissiveness, and "mildness" is interpreted as blandness—plain vanilla ice cream in a freezer crowded with Chocolate Raspberry Truffle and Swiss Almond Praline.[4]

Humility as *earthiness* may be less a distortion than humility as *groveling* or *timidity*, but each of these modern interpretations misses the essence of this ancient, classic virtue. For *humility* signifies, simply, the acceptance of being human, the acceptance of one's human being. It is the embrace of the both-and-ness, *both* saint *and* sinner, *both* beast *and* angel, that constitutes our very be-ing as human. Beginning with the acceptance that being human—being mixed (and therefore sometimes mixed-up)—is *good enough*, humility involves learning how to live with and take joy in that reality.

As a spiritual *experience*, humility contains its own unique paradox: Those possessed by it do not realize that they do participate in it! And those who think they possess it most often have no idea what "it" is. As a Sufi saying suggests: "A saint is a saint unless he knows that he is one."[5]

One day a rabbi, in a frenzy of religious passion, rushed in before the ark, fell to his knees, and started beating his breast, crying, "I'm nobody! I'm nobody!"

The cantor of the synagogue, impressed by this example of spiritual humility, joined the rabbi on his knees, saying, "I'm nobody! I'm nobody!"

The shamus (custodian) watching from the corner, couldn't restrain himself either. He joined the other two on his knees, calling out, "I'm nobody! I'm nobody!"

At which point the rabbi, nudging the cantor with his elbow, pointed at the custodian and said, "Look who thinks he's nobody!"[6]

Humility is, above all, *honesty*. True humility neither exaggerates nor minimizes but accepts. As Dag Hammarskjöld put it in *Markings:*

Humility is just as much the opposite of self-abasement as it is of self-exultation. To be humble is *not to make comparisons.* Secure in its reality, the self is neither better nor worse, bigger nor smaller, than anything else in the universe. It *is*—is nothing, yet at the same time one with everything.[7]

"To be humble is not to make comparisons."

The story is told that the humble Rabbi Akiba Eyger once sent a note to his shoemaker asking him to return the boots he had been given for repair. He addressed the shoemaker as follows: "To the Most Holy Revered Great Scholar . . ." The shoemaker, thinking the rabbi was mocking him, was offended and hurried to him to complain. The rabbi's reply was of the utmost simplicity: "How can you think I meant to mock you? Letters to me are addressed that way all the time."[8]

"To be humble is not to make comparisons."

Certain Greek fishermen once netted a magnificent golden tripod from the deep. Its ownership became a matter of intense international concern. The quarrel was referred to Delphi. "Whoever is first of all in wisdom," hissed Pythia, "to him the tripod belongs." So peace was declared and the tripod presented to Thales of Miletus, a philosopher who enjoyed everyone's respect. But Thales passed it on to a second sage, whom he considered wiser than himself. The second sage passed it to a third, and so forth, until finally the tripod circled back to Thales, who discreetly gave it to Delphi.[9]

"To be humble is not to make comparisons." In response to modern narcissism's extolling of "Me First" and "Number One," humility does not necessarily suggest an attitude of *"Me Last"* (although that would provide a more appropriate starting-point for spirituality). What humility does counsel is that such comparisons are dangerous and foolish; the problem with both "first" and "last" as goals is that both are extremes. As A.A. co-founder Bill W. advised literally thousands of alcoholics: "Our problem is that we try, even demand, to be 'all-or-nothing.'" Human be-ing—being in the middle—is to be *neither* all nor nothing.

According to ancient Christian legend, God created the angels to worship and to serve Him. Then, after he had begun the creation of our world but before the creation of human beings, God granted the angels a vision not only of humankind but of the Christ. And God commanded the angels to serve humans and to worship the Christ.

To the angels, this was a strange command—that they, pure spirits, should so defer to beings lesser than themselves, creatures mingled with matter.

Now it happened that of all the angels God created, the most beautiful and most brilliant was Lucifer, the "light-bearer." This greatest of the angels, immersed in his own brilliance and enamored of his own beauty, refused God's command, declaring: "I will not serve!"

And so Lucifer and the angels who followed him were cast out from Heaven, becoming "the bad angels" termed "devils."

"It was pride that changed angels into devils; it is humility that makes men as angels," observed Saint Augustine in commenting on this popular early Christian story. The ancient mythic story of Lucifer's rebellion reminds that the tradition of spiritual wisdom sees in "Me First" the original source of all "sin"—the root of all deviation and distortion of our true being.[10]

❖

Within Alcoholics Anonymous the term used to signify the opposite of humility is *grandiosity,* and A.A. meetings glitter with stories—humorous, perhaps, only to those who can identify with them—illustrating the pitfalls of high-flown pomposity.

> There I was, the brilliant market analyst who was going to make a million bucks by the age of thirty, only I didn't have the time to put my scheme into practice, because I was lying on the bathroom floor in my own drunken vomit.

> With my background, and schooling, and connections, not to mention my brilliant diplomatic skills, I knew that I was destined to be the greatest statesman of the twentieth century—but as time went on, all that I seemed capable of doing was sitting in my darkened living room and reaching out, time and time again, for the bottle.

> I knew, without any doubt whatsoever, that I was God's greatest gift to women, this age's greatest lover, if only I could remove my arms from their embrace around the toilet bowl.

So common is this acceptance of "grandiosity" as a chief failing of alcoholics that it led one of the authors, then a graduate student researching Alcoholics Anonymous, into a trap. Puzzled about the tendency for even intelligent alcoholics to get mired in the self-deceit of denial, he approached one of the field's leading figures, Dr. Dan Anderson, then-president of the Hazelden Foundation.

> "Why is it," I asked, "that even intelligent alcoholics can get so trapped in denial of their alcoholism? Is it because of grandiosity—they think that they can do anything to their bodies and survive, they think that they are 'too smart' to be 'alco-

holic'? Or is it because of self-loathing—they despise themselves and feel they deserve to die, if they are alcoholics?"

"Ernie, Ernie, Ernie," Dan groaned with a patient smile.
"The alcoholic's problem is not that he thinks, 'I am very
special.' Nor is the alcoholic's problem that he thinks, 'I am a
worm.' The alcoholic's problem is that he is *convinced: "I am
a very special worm."*

The problem with "very special worm," of course, is comparison;
such a vision is not the kind of *mixed* that underlies humility, which
begins with the acceptance that we are neither uniquely "very special"
nor absolutely "worm." The humility of *both/and* refuses precisely the
kind of uniqueness, the claim to be exceptional, that "either-or" demands. Humility—the acceptance that being human is good enough
—is the embrace of ordinariness. That is not to say that humility sees
ordinariness as "good enough"; humility rather sees *us* as good
enough, even in our ordinariness.

Humility, as A.A. co-founder Bill Wilson understood so well, begins with rejection of the demand to be *"all-or-nothing."* Human
be-ing—existing and carrying out our lives in the middle—is to be
neither all nor nothing. Humility involves learning how to live with
(and even rejoice in) that reality, the reality of our mixed-up-ed-ness,
our being both saint and sinner, both beast and angel. *Live with and
rejoice in*—for humor, humorously defined as "the juxtaposition of
incongruities," is the placing together of two things that do not "belong" together. And what could be more incongruous than the
strange mixture of beast and angel that we are, this spark of divinity
encased in a hunk of nothingness?

When we come face to face with the reality of our own imperfection, which *is* the reality of our very be-ing, we can either laugh or cry;
comedy and tragedy, as the masks we see in theaters suggest, inter-
twine. At certain moments in our lives, in fact, it seems that the most
fundamental choice each of us has is between *fighting* ourselves and
laughing at ourselves.

An earlier chapter introduced Ernest Becker's vivid formulation:
"Man is a god who shits." Faced with the incongruous image of a
defecating divinity, we can either howl in outrage or laugh out loud.
When confronting our own incongruities, humor is usually the

healthier choice, as the wisdom of word-origins hints. For the words *human, humor,* and *humility* all have the same root—the ancient Indo-European *ghôm,* best translated by the English *humus.* A classroom incident that occurred at the Rutgers University Summer School of Alcohol Studies several years ago helps clarify these connections.

> **The instructor wrote the words *human, humor,* and *humility* on the blackboard and then turned to the class—a motley mixture of degreed professionals and would-be alcoholism counselors who were mainly recovering individuals from all imaginable walks of life—and challenged: "You all know what *humus* is, don't you?"**
>
> **In the back of the room, draped over various parts of three chairs, sprawled a rangy man, about six-and-a-half feet tall, weighing approximately 250 very solid pounds. An observer might have guessed that this student hailed from the great state of Texas, dressed as he was in cowboy boots and a ten-gallon hat and wearing a name-tag cut in the shape of a large star that read, "Tex."**
>
> **In a deep drawl Tex rumbled his answer: "Yeah, Doc— worm-shit!"**

Tex had a point. The dictionary describes *humus* as "a brown or black substance resulting from the partial decay of plant and animal matter." Although the role of worms (and their excrement) in facilitating the activities of soil micro-organisms is a disputed point in the agricultural sciences, Tex's spontaneous outburst helped his classmates and his teacher grasp the connections between Becker's "god who shits" and Anderson's "very special worm."

Humor, humility, humanity . . . we cannot work on one without working on the others. We cannot *have* one without *having the others.* To attend to any one of the three begins the process of bringing us *home*—home to ourselves, to the mixed-up-ed-ness of our human be-ing. Home is the place where we can be ourselves and accept ourselves as both good and bad, beast and angel, saint and sinner. Home is the place where we can laugh *and* cry, where we can find some peace within all the chaos and confusion, where we are accepted and, indeed, cherished by others precisely because of our very mixed-up-edness. Home is that place where we *belong*, where we *fit* precisely because of our very unfittingness. Humility allows us to find the fittingness in our own imperfection.

Because the acceptance of both-and-ness implies the acceptance of our imperfection *as* imperfection rather than the claim to find in it some "very specialness," *humility* is the foundation and keystone of any spirituality of imperfection. Such a spirituality is first and foremost free-ing, as a joyous Hasidic tale reminds us.

> **The king visited a prison and talked to the prisoners. Each asserted his innocence, except one who confessed to theft. "Throw this scoundrel out," exclaimed the king. "He will corrupt the innocents."[11]**

❖

A spirituality of imperfection is a spirituality of the unspectacular. An American spiritual giant, Abraham Lincoln, is reputed to have observed that "God must like ordinary folk—he made so many of us." A generation after Lincoln, the French Carmelite nun Thérèse of Lisieux (whose spirituality was named the "little way") encouraged a correspondent with these words: "Ordinary folk, like you and me, must be greatly loved by God since there are so many of us, always have been, most likely always will be."[12]

These very different nineteenth-century spiritual geniuses, the tragic American president and the simple French contemplative, both rested in the confidence that, in Thérèse's words, "our faults cannot hurt God. Nor will our failures interfere with our own holiness" for "genuine holiness is precisely a matter of enduring our own imperfections patiently." This perspective, a recent commentator notes in words that echo Lincoln's own mournful observations, leaves "no room . . . for the moral narcissism which so often besets religious people."

To any who know its fellowship, and especially its wariness of "grandiosity," this is the same spirituality that infuses Alcoholics Anonymous. In this spirituality—Lincoln's rustic humility, Thérèse's "little way," A.A.'s embrace of identity as *alcoholic*—it makes no difference whether we are "good" in any conventional sense. The key point is that, however "good" we may think we are (or are not), we cannot afford to take any kind of stand on our own "goodness." It is equally dangerous to think of ourselves as *having* goodness as to think of ourselves as *lacking* goodness. Both are distortions, for it is precisely the *weakness* in whatever goodness we *do* have a share in that gives us our claim on reality and on the help of a Higher Power.

The message resounds, as always, in all traditions, loud and clear: Mistakes are part of being human. The real meaning of "sin" has to do not with committing evil deeds, not with willfully breaking laws, not even with the *act* of "falling short." The term *sin* classically signifies not an action but the *state* of falling short, a situation of alienation from reality. One brilliance of Alcoholics Anonymous is that it never uses the term *sin*, a word hopelessly overloaded with convoluted meanings, but talks instead of the "defects of character" and the "shortcomings" of those who *are* "alcoholics." For sin has become a word of religion, of absolutes; *shortcomings* is a word of humanity, a concept in tune with the understanding that we are imperfect.

And if we do "fall short"? That very awareness of "falling short" implies two related realities: First, we are trying, and second, we need to try again. There is no *failure* here, for spirituality, as the ancients reminded over and over again, involves a continual falling down and getting back up again. That is why humility—the knowledge of our own imperfections—is so important, and that is why spirituality goes on and on and on, a never-ending adventure of coming to know ourselves, seeing ourselves clearly, learning to be at home with ourselves. The great need is for *balance*—when we are down, we need to get up; and when we are up, we need to remember that we have been, and certainly will be again, "down."

It was a large meeting, well over two hundred people. At one end of the room stood the canister of regular coffee; at the other end, the pot of decaf. Conversation around the first coffeepot centered on a man who was clearly depressed and afraid.

"I just feel like I'm at the end of my rope," he admitted. "It's one damned thing after another. Nothing seems to be

THE SPIRITUALITY OF IMPERFECTION

going right. This week my dog died, my kids came down with strep throat, I can't keep my mind on my work, my wife and I are fighting constantly. I just don't know how I'm going to make it."

"Well, son," an oldtimer said gently, "at least you didn't take a drink today."

The conversation at the other end of the room centered on a man who exuded good cheer. "I just feel so wonderful," he was saying. "What a week this has been! I got a promotion at work; my daughter is graduating from college with honors; my wife and I are like newly married lovers. And just yesterday I had the best golf game of my life!"

"It all sounds great," another oldtimer said gently. "But remember . . . you're an alcoholic. Just one drink will destroy it all."

A cynical onlooker might think, "Well, isn't that just great—once you're in A.A., you can't do *anything* right!" And in a sense that's accurate. As one A.A. member once put it: "This is a screwy place, because we are all screwy!" Phrased another way, once you adopt a spirituality of imperfection, you know that you can't do anything— good *or* bad—perfectly. Or, in the words of Austin MacCurtain in his review of the autobiographical thoughts of novelist John Updike: "The world punishes us for taking it too seriously as well as for not taking it seriously enough."[13]

The point of Humility is to find a *balance*, that place in the middle of life's teeter-totter that allows one foot to reside on the side of "god/ saint/angel" and the other on the side of "worm/sinner/beast." From this perspective, A.A.'s most significant contribution to the tradition of a spirituality of imperfection can be summed up in two words: *sober alcoholic*. Placed together, by themselves, those words demand disbelief and ridicule; the greatest tribute to Alcoholics Anonymous is that people do not break into paroxysms of laughter on hearing that weird combination of concepts. Instead, those two bonded words— *sober alcoholic*—have come to form a cohesive unity that has become a part of our modern vocabulary.

It is true, of course, that alcoholics got well before Alcoholics Anonymous; back then they called themselves "ex-alcoholics." That term, in fact, crept into the first ten printings of the A.A. Big Book, which borrowed its vocabulary from earlier sources.[14] But after the end of World War II, when the early members had more time to examine their text before its eleventh printing, they realized that the term *ex-alcoholic* did not accurately portray how they viewed themselves; indeed, the word contradicted their whole insight, which *was* that they would always be "alcoholic" even as they struggled to stay sober. And so, in 1946, they made the only substantive change of words in the first 164 pages of their Big Book, substituting *ex-problem drinker* for *ex-alcoholic*. That change in wording ratified A.A.'s essence —each member's acceptance of the human condition as paradoxically *mixed*. And it is in such embrace of one's own human be-ing as *mixed* that Humility consists.

But Humility connotes not only *balance* but *right ordering*. For within the acceptance of "mixed," there is a choosing of priorities, a putting into practice of "First Things First." And so, in the tradition, one accepts "beast" but that does not exclude cherishing and fostering those attitudes and activities that flow from "angel." In the more concrete example of Alcoholics Anonymous, members learn to live with being alcoholic, even as they rejoice in being sober. Accepting the reality of "both/and" does not mean that beast and angel, alcoholic and sober, are valued equally; the two ever-present opposites are rather seen as balancing, in a way stabilizing, each other. "First Things First," then, not only repudiates the demand for "all or nothing" but affirms that although "both" are present, they are not the same.

Humility's "right ordering," like humility's balance, has to do *first* with oneself. One fruit of such "right ordering" and balance is the refusal to "order" among people. A humility that begins with the acceptance of self as imperfect will not be interested in judging others: "To be humble is not to make comparisons." And so it is that because Humility chooses to look first, and indeed *only,* at one's own defects and shortcomings, it serves as the foundation for another powerful spiritual reality: Tolerance.

A preacher came to Tiktin on the Sabbath of the Penitential Period, the Sabbath of Repentance . . . and reproved the congregants for being great sinners. Afterwards, Rabbi Meyer Hurwitz, Rabbi of the city, said to him:

"Why did you not reprove me among ourselves, instead of shaming me in public?"

The preacher replied: "I meant no one in particular. I spoke in general terms."

"Nay," retorted the Rabbi. "All your hearers are good folk. You could have had in mind only my sins."[15]

And from the Sufi tradition.

I remember, being pious in my childhood, rising in the night, addicted to devotion and abstinence. One night I was sitting with my father, remaining awake and holding the beloved Koran in my lap, whilst the people around us were asleep. I said: "Not one of these persons lifts up his head, or makes a genuflection. They are as fast asleep as if they were dead."

He replied: "Darling of thy father! Would that thou wert also asleep, rather than disparaging people."[16]

Seeing first one's own defects and shortcomings is Humility; the fruit of that vision is Tolerance.

Chapter 14

TOLERANCE

❖

The way our "worthy" alcoholics have sometimes tried to judge the "less worthy" is, as we look back on it, rather comical. Imagine, if you can, one alcoholic judging another.

Bill Wilson[1]

Innocently unaware of the prejudices held against him, an old black man, staunchly religious, some years ago applied for membership in an exclusive church. The pastor attempted to put him off with all sorts of evasive remarks. The old man, becoming aware that he was not wanted, said finally that he would pray on it and perhaps the Lord would tell him just what to do.

Several days later he returned. "Well," asked the minister, "did the Lord send you a message?"

"Yes sir, he did," was the answer. "He told me it wasn't any use. He said, 'I've been trying to get in that same church myself for ten years, and I still can't make it.' "[2]

"Honesty gets us sober," Bill Wilson once observed, "but tolerance keeps us sober." Such tolerance, A.A. members know, is not a grudging putting-up-with but a loving identification with—the *Tolerance* that is the antechamber to *Forgiveness,* the tolerance that is the flowering of a spirituality of imperfection. When we accept ourselves in all our weakness, flaws, and failings, we can begin to fulfill an even more challenging responsibility: accepting the weakness, limitations, and mixed-up-ed-ness of those we love and respect. Then and only then, it seems, do we become able to accept the weakness, defects, and short-comings of those we find it difficult to love.[3]

Learning how to live with other human beings is one of the grand, classic problems of human be-ing. Most of us "tolerate" each other by identifying with and seeking out those with whom we share strengths; most of the time, we ignore or avoid those whose strong points are not ours. Thus, when we join groups, we usually do so on the basis of shared strengths. Those who enjoy competing in sports seek out other sports enthusiasts, professors are most comfortable with other academics, coin and stamp collectors, automotive buffs, art apprecia-tors . . . all look for and socialize with those whose interests and skills make possible shared enthusiasms.

But Alcoholics Anonymous and other Twelve-Step groups are founded on a different truth: Human beings connect with each other most healingly, most healthily, not on the basis of common strengths, but in the very reality of their shared weaknesses. *Among those who accept their imperfection* there seems to be a special sense of likeness or oneness in their very mutual flawedness—in "torn-to-pieces-hood" somehow shared. In such a context of *shared weakness*, qualities in other people that might, in different circumstances, irritate or anger instead elicit compassion and identification.

Shared weakness: *the shared honesty of mutual vulnerability openly acknowledged*.[4] That's where we connect. At the most fundamental level of our very human-ness, it is our weakness that makes us alike; it is our strengths that make us different. Acknowledging *shared weakness* thus creates a rooted connectedness, a sense of common begin-nings. We will grow in our different directions, with our different strengths, but our roots remain in the same soil as everyone else's—the earthy *humus* of our own imperfection.

There was once a man who had desecrated the sabbath against his will because his carriage had broken down, and although he ran, he did not reach the town before the begin-ning of the holy hours. For this, young Rabbi Mikhal imposed a very harsh and long penance on him. The man tried to do as he had been told, but he soon found that his body could not endure it. He began to feel ill, and even his mind became affected. About this time he learned that the Baal Shem Tov was visiting a place nearby. He went to him, mustered his courage, and begged the master to rid him of the sin he had committed. "Carry a pound of candles to the House of Prayer," said the Baal Shem, "and have them lit for the sabbath. Let that be your penance."

The man at first thought the zaddik had not quite understood what he had told him, but when the Baal Shem insisted on his incredibly mild dictum, the man told him how heavy a penance had been imposed. "You just do as I said," the master replied. "And tell Rabbi Mikhal to come to Chvostov where I shall hold the coming sabbath."

The man did as the Baal Shem had asked. Now on the way to Chvostov, a wheel broke on Rabbi Mikhal's carriage and he had to continue on foot. Although he hurried all he could, it was dark when he entered the town, and when he crossed the Baal Shem's threshold, he saw he had already risen, his hand on the cup, to say the blessing over the wine to introduce the day of rest. The master paused and said to Rabbi Mikhal who was standing before him numb and speechless: "Good sabbath, my sinless friend! You had never tasted the sorrow of the sinner, your heart had never throbbed with his despair—and so it was easy for your hand to deal out penance."[5]

This sense of *shared weakness* creates what is truly a *community*. Participants in such a setting learn to appreciate rather than resent the strengths in others because they know that, at bottom, they are the same—flawed and imperfect. Those who do not share weakness find in others' strengths a threat. But those who recognize shared weakness see in others' strengths a *hope:* the hope that *your* strengths might also support *me*. With shared weakness as our common bond, we can rejoice in another person's strengths rather than be threatened by them.

Spirituality begins with this first insight: We are all imperfect. Such a vision not only invites but requires Tolerance: active appreciation of the richness and variety of human beings on this earth, along with the understanding that we all struggle with the same demons, we all share the same fears and sorrows, we all do the best we can with what we have.

A man who took great pride in his lawn found himself with large and recurring crops of dandelions. Although he tried every method he knew to get rid of them, they continued to plague him. Finally, in desperation, he wrote the Extension Service of the Agriculture Department of the State University, enumerating all the things he had tried and concluding with the question: "What shall I do now?"

After a somewhat prolonged time even for such correspondence, the reply finally came: "We suggest you learn to love them."[6]

"Honesty gets us sober, but tolerance keeps us sober." Alcoholics learn tolerance quickly, from their own experience. It is simply unimaginable that a recovering alcoholic would say to a fellow alcoholic, "Come on, now, buck up, and take command of yourself! Have a drink now and then—you can do it, you're in control!" The alcoholic knows that she herself could not do that, and so she knows that other alcoholics cannot do it either. What unites alcoholics, what makes it possible for one alcoholic to learn from another, is that the foundation they share is not a strength but a *weakness;* each knows what he or she *cannot* do.

❖

As in most matters of spirituality, tolerance begins with *vision*—the ability to see the world in a way that is somehow "different." Tolerance requires that special kind of vision that "sees" helplessness, for if we can see our own helplessness, then we can understand that others are helpless, too. In the same vision, of course, tolerance "sees" strengths—not only the capabilities and virtues of ourselves and our friends, but also the strengths of others whom we do not especially like or even those who have, in some way, wronged us. If we can see our own mixed-up-ed-ness and accept it, if we can see and accept the mixed-up-ed-ness of people we love and respect, then we can eventually move toward an acceptance of the mixed-up-ed-ness of even those we find it difficult to love.

This vision, of course, goes beyond the grudging *mere* "tolerance" or "putting-up-with-because-I-have-no-choice" of a non-spiritual vocabulary. The essence of tolerance lies in its openness to *difference.*

Some time after Rabbi Shalom had died, two of his disciples came to Lublin to study with Rabbi Jacob Yitzhak, called "the Seer." They found him out in the open, saying the blessing of the New Moon. Now, because he did this a little differently in some details from what their teacher had accustomed them to, they did not promise themselves much from Lublin and decided to leave the town the very next day. When they entered the rabbi's house, shortly after, he spoke words of greeting to them and immediately added: "A God whom one could serve only in one set way—what kind of God would that be!"[7]

Tolerance abides at the heart of Eastern spiritualities. The *bodhisattva* is one who has achieved immortality but who chooses to participate in the sufferings of the world and in the sorrows of others. The nature of the bodhisattva is endless, boundless compassion, understood as the healing process that allows life to continue. Sensitivity to the tolerance rooted in the compassion that comes only from shared weakness is also honored in the Muslim tradition.

A devout aged woman once asked the Holy Prophet Muhammad to speak to her son, who spent all his wages on dates, leaving her penniless. The Prophet promised to do so after five weeks' interval.

On the appointed day the boy was brought before the Prophet, who spoke to him very kindly, saying, "You are such a sensible young man that you ought to remember that your mother has endured much suffering for your sake, sacrificing all that she had and earned in order to bring you up. Yet now that she is so old and you are in a position to support her, you squander your money on dates. Is this just or right? I hope, by the grace and mercy of Allah, you will give up this habit." The boy listened very attentively and profited by what he heard.

Afterwards, the Prophet's disciples wondered among themselves and finally asked the Prophet himself why the reproof had been delayed for thirty-five days. The Holy Prophet replied in explanation: "I am myself fond of dates, and I knew

THE SPIRITUALITY OF IMPERFECTION

I had no right to advise the lad to abstain from them until I had myself refrained from eating them for five weeks."[8]

A favorite monastic story demonstrates early Christian insight into the connection between tolerance and the recognition of one's own weakness.

There was a desert father who each day ate just three biscuits. A brother came to him and when they sat down to eat the old man set three biscuits before the brother. The old man saw that the brother needed more food and brought him three more biscuits. After they had their fill and got up, the old man condemned the brother and said to him, "It is not right, brother, to serve the flesh." The brother asked pardon and left.

The next time the old man ate, he placed before himself three biscuits, as was his custom. He ate them and was still hungry although he restrained himself. Again the next day he withstood his hunger. The old man began to weaken and he knew that God had abandoned him. Prostrating himself before God with tears, he begged that he not be abandoned. Then he saw an angel who said to him, "Because you condemned the brother, this has happened to you. Know therefore that the ability to deny the flesh or to do any good work is not within your power; rather, it is the goodness of God which strengthens you."[9]

In the postmodern era, we have learned tolerance at least in part from technology. The term *postmodern* means, simply, the change in consciousness that occurred (in the United States) between the Crash of 1929 and the end of the Second World War, when it was discovered that human beings were not only *not* in control of the world but even could destroy it.[10] Until 1945, most humans assumed their task was to perfect the world; the experiences of Auschwitz and Hiroshima brought the awesome, humbling discovery that we are as likely to annihilate it.

It is neither accident nor coincidence that Alcoholics Anonymous originated in the 1930s and flourished at the dawn of the postmodern, nuclear age. A.A.'s vision of *tolerance* derived in part from the changing worldview—the understanding that unless we learn to tolerate each other, we might destroy ourselves—and in part from its members' vast experience with tolerance's opposites: pride and conceit. Drinking alcoholics tend to think that they know everything and that everybody else knows nothing. And so, partly as a repudiation of the intolerance that they recognized as a part of their disease, partly also as a rejection of other programs, medical and religious, that seemed to them to claim too much certainty, the earliest A.A. members were determined to live an open-mindedness that encouraged variety and cultivated tolerance.[11]

The letters and writings of co-founder Bill Wilson are replete with this vision of tolerance, born of humility, open-mindedness, and especially, experience.

But as for the A.A. therapy itself, that could be practiced in any fashion that the group wished to practice it, and the same went for every individual. We took the position that A.A. was not the final word on treatment; that it might be only the first word. For us, it became perfectly safe to tell people they could experiment with our therapy in any way they liked.

In the early days of A.A. I spent a lot of time trying to get people to agree with me, to practice A.A. principles as I did, and so forth. For so long as I did this . . . A.A. grew very slowly.

Alcoholics Anonymous is a terribly imperfect society because it is made up of very imperfect people. We are all dedicated to an . . . ideal of which, because we are very human and very sick, we often fall short. I know because I constantly fall short myself.

Nobody can cause more grief than a power-driven guy who thinks he has got it straight from God. These people cause [the world] more trouble than the harlots and drunkards. . . . I have had spells of that very thing and [so I] ought to know.[12]

"Honesty gets us sober, but tolerance keeps us sober." When alcoholics stand up at A.A. meetings and tell their stories, the experi-

ence of tolerance is almost palpable. Stories invite tolerance because they sensitize both hearers and tellers to the richness and complexity of our diverse possibilities: Each human being has his or her own story, and every story is unique. But the telling and hearing of those unique stories takes place in a setting where each participant is conscious of an *identity rooted in limitation*. This foundation of shared weakness invites an attitude that allows differences to be seen as strengths and therefore as enriching rather than threatening. Stories founded in an identity defined by limitation and shared with others who acknowledge that same limitation involve less the "discussion of weaknesses" than the acceptance that one has much to learn from others. Such storytelling testifies that one is "teachable."

For in the setting of A.A. storytelling and storylistening, two paradoxical things happen. First, participants discover their shared story; and second, they come to realize that each of their stories is unique. But the discovery of shared story must precede the realization of uniqueness and difference: for only the foundation of shared weakness, shared limitation, and shared flawedness can sustain the openness to difference, the attitude of "teachableness," and the vision that undergirds tolerance.

❖

The Spanish philosopher Miguel de Unamuno, in his study translated as *The Tragic Sense of Life*, set himself the task of defining what he termed *amor spiritualis* ("spiritual love")—that relationship between two people that makes both of them more whole, more fully human.

> Spiritual love is born of sorrow. . . . For men love one another with a spiritual love only when they have suffered the same sorrow together, when through long days they have ploughed the stony ground buried beneath the common yoke of a common grief. It is then that they know one another and feel one another and feel with one another in their common anguish, and so thus they pity one another and love one another. For to love is to pity; and if bodies are united by pleasure, souls are united by pain. . . . To love with the spirit is to pity, and he who pities most loves most.[13]

Unamuno's vision was shared by his contemporary, writer James Joyce, for whom "pity is the feeling which arrests the mind in the presence of whatever is grave and constant in human suffering and unites it with the human sufferer."[14] The term *pity* invites misunderstanding in an age that assumes a condescension in all compassion, but the word means simply the *unity* that comes from shared suffering —the *identification* that alone can sustain true Tolerance. "Identify, don't compare," A.A. advises. Comparing has to do with quantifying, weighing one thing against another, which has to do with the "material"; the *spiritual,* of course, cannot be compared. Thus, the chief danger of comparison is that it locks us into the not-spiritual, the material.

A psychiatrist has called *identification* "the halfway house between self-love and other love."[15] From a spiritual perspective, identification is that aspect of spirituality's *vision* that allows us to "see" that as human beings, we are all standing under the same tragedy, that we are all united in not being "God." It takes time and practice to learn to "see" in this way, for through the years we have learned another way of seeing: If someone isn't like me, then there is something wrong with him.

But if we learn to "see"—*first*—ourselves as limited, then everything shifts, the whole world turns upside down. For how can I fixate on the thought that there is something wrong with someone else if I am looking at the world from the framework that there's definitely something wrong with me? Looked at in this way, the other person isn't weird or pathetic, but a brother or sister in weakness and imperfection. Looked at from this perspective, another person's strengths become reason for hope: "If he could climb above his imperfection, if she could find a way to be strong, then there is hope for me, too. In fact, having found their way, perhaps they can help me find my way."

In such a vision and in such a place, we can stop trying to conceal our imperfection and therefore our very essence. We can stop *hiding.* For what is there to hide or hide from when it is our very weaknesses that give us strength? In such a setting, others, listening, *identify* and in the process of identifying, come to discover their own identities.

A man who lived in the same town as Rabbi Zusya saw that he was very poor. So each day he put twenty coins into the little bag in which Zusya kept his phylacteries, so that he and his

family might buy the necessities of life. From that time on, the man grew richer and richer. The more he had, the more he gave Zusya, and the more he gave Zusya, the more he had.

But once he recalled that Zusya was the disciple of a great maggid, and it occurred to him that if what he gave the disciple was so lavishly rewarded, he might become even more prosperous if he made presents to the master himself. So he traveled to Mezritch and induced Rabbi Baer to accept a substantial gift from him. From this time on, his means shrank until he had lost all the profits he had made during the more fortunate period. He took his trouble to Rabbi Zusya, told him the whole story, and asked him what his present predicament was due to. For had not the rabbi himself told him that his master was immeasurably greater than he?

Zusya replied: "Look! As long as you gave and did not bother to whom, whether to Zusya or another, God gave to you and did not bother to whom. But when you began to seek out especially noble and distinguished recipients, God did exactly the same."[16]

"Identify, don't compare." Tolerance involves the acceptance of both likeness and difference. And so discovering one's own *identity*— who one is—requires not only "identification" but *differentiation*, which comes only by recognizing and respecting differences. Through the knowledge of those things about us that make us different from others, we come to know who we are; but, equally important, *we also come to know who we are not.* Recognition and acceptance of who we are *not* is essential to experiencing ourselves as fully separate individuals. Separation is as central to the process of human development as identification; they are the twin poles of our nature.[17]

How can differentiation take place without becoming comparison? Alcoholics Anonymous had two co-founders, William Griffith Wilson and Dr. Robert Holbrook Smith, and they were very different. Although both were Vermont-born, Wilson became almost a caricature of the go-getting New Yorker, while Smith settled into the amiable routines of midwestern life. Bill became the operator, who enjoyed adulation and thrived on the company of "the important"; Dr. Bob, the classic surgeon, was most at home working one-on-one, most comfortable with "the nobodies."

Even in their disease they were different. Except for the one occasion that led to his first meeting with Dr. Bob in 1935, Wilson never suffered any temptation to drink alcohol after his spiritual experience of December 1934. Dr. Smith fought that urge to drink every day of his sober life, until his final year when the painful ravages of the cancer that would kill him afforded strong distraction. Had they met in a bar, it is unlikely Bill and Bob would have struck up even a conversation; meeting in common need, they found a way of melding their differences that gave new meaning to the term *fellowship*. For in their incomparable differences, the only "pattern" they set was of the Tolerance that is basic to Alcoholics Anonymous, a tolerance founded precisely in the *variety* of available models.

"The variety of available models": within Alcoholics Anonymous, within any A.A. group, members find not one but *many* sources of identification. There is no "one best, most sober, A.A. member"—not in the world, not in this city, not in an individual A.A. group, not even in that smaller group sipping coffee together after a meeting. Looking around a particular group, one is struck by Ann's patience, Ben's humor, Charlie's cheerfulness, Dorothy's ability to listen, Ed's serenity, Fran's open-mindedness, George's gratitude . . . and it goes on and on and on. Each and every A.A. member offers something uniquely attractive, but no one member ever has it all.

Bill Wilson understood the need for such a variety of models, as his own practice with "sponsors" attests. The recollections of Bill's widow, Lois, and the stories of some other old-time members of the fellowship suggest this description of this aspect of Wilson's sobriety:

> "Who was Bill's sponsor?" Well, on the one hand, Bill always considered his "sponsors" to be Ebby T., who had originally brought him the message that became A.A., and the Jesuit priest, Father Edward Dowling, with whom Bill had taken his first full Fifth Step.
>
> But on a more practical daily basis, it was Bill's habit to choose as "sponsor" some individual who demonstrated a particular quality that Bill knew, from his own personal in-

ventory, that he needed to work on. For example, if Bill detected in himself, as he often did, a deficit in patience, he would approach Peter, who showed that quality in outstanding fashion, and Bill would ask Peter to serve as his sponsor.

That relationship would last for between four and eight months. It ended not because Bill attained "perfect patience," but rather because his continuing inventory revealed the need to work on some other shortcoming—for example, resoluteness. For all Peter's patience, he was not very much of an achiever, and so Bill would look again among his acquaintances for someone who demonstrated perseverance and determination, and he'd find such an attractive quality in, say, Richard. Bill would then approach Richard as he had Peter, and ask him to serve for a time as his sponsor.[18]

This "variety of models" not only served Bill's different growth needs as they changed through time, it also meant tolerating both Peter's lack of resoluteness and Richard's deficits in patience. A variety of models encourages looking to others' strengths rather than focusing on their weaknesses. It invites tolerance.

Some have accused Alcoholics Anonymous of "brainwashing" and especially of forcing "religion" upon its adherents. But careful observers remain constantly amazed at the variety of beliefs that one finds among its members and at its meetings. "Unlike Tolstoy's families," observed psychologist Patricia Kearns, "all drinking alcoholics are alike; each sober alcoholic develops a sobriety that is unique."[19]

The use of the phrase *Higher Power*—his, hers, yours, or mine—rather than the word *God*, reminds members of A.A.'s tolerance of individual differences in religious belief and spiritual inclination. The most basic understanding of the concept "Higher Power" within Alcoholics Anonymous is that it is *that which keeps me sober*. In a sense, this is to out-James William James; it is the ultimate pragmatic concept of God. For alcoholics who have tried and failed time after time to stay sober by themselves, for alcoholics who have tried and failed after using any one of innumerable techniques, that which finally *does* keep one sober becomes "God."

Dr. Abraham Twerski, psychiatrist and orthodox rabbi, tells this story:

A recovered alcoholic was telling a friend that on awakening each morning he prays to G–d* for another day of sobriety, and that each night before retiring he thanks G–d for having granted him a day of sobriety.

"How do you know it was G–d who gave you the day of sobriety?" the friend asked.

"It had to be," the man responded. "He was the only one whom I had asked."[20]

❖

Tolerance. Perhaps the best evidence for A.A.'s claim that its fellowship and program are "spiritual rather than religious" is that Alcoholics Anonymous spreads by heresy. A true story about intolerance within Alcoholics Anonymous may help to illustrate both this point and how A.A.'s tolerance works.

Some years ago, an A.A. group that met near a prestigious university in a large city developed a problem. The group had been accustomed to begin its meetings with the reading of the A.A. Preamble and of "How It Works" from the Big Book, and also a reading from the quasi-devotional non-A.A. book, *Twenty-Four Hours a Day*.

Consciousness having been raised, some members began to complain about the implicit sexism of some of the meditative readings. Their solution was to select yet another reading from yet another devotional book, *Each Day a New Beginning*. Still other members found those readings also deficient, and in time, the group was beginning its meetings with readings from six different meditation books! Finally, this situation became too much for still other members of the group, who began to complain that there was insufficient time left for story and discussion. With typical, true alcoholic open-mindedness came one response to their concerned complaint: "That's the trouble with you pointy-head academics! All you want to do is hear yourselves talk!"

* Again, out of respect for Rabbi Twerski and Orthodox tradition, in borrowing his story we follow his practice of omitting the vowel in the divine name.

And so the battle was joined in earnest, the disagreements heated up, and soon it became clear that this group was in deep trouble—it began holding "group conscience meetings" every week after the regular A.A. meeting. Finally, the differences were declared irreconcilable, and it was determined that the two factions—the readers and the talkers—would have to go their separate ways.

In the process of dividing up, every item imaginable was debated. The splinter faction found a new location in a nearby church, but because there was limited on-street parking available, a problem arose about the exact time the new group would meet. The group's treasury didn't cause much trouble—it's fairly easy to split fourteen dollars—but the "group conscience" meeting almost descended into a riot when it came time to divide up the coffee. This was a self-consciously sophisticated group, and instead of canned, brand-name coffee, these members ground their own beans and had several different flavors of both caffeinated and decaffeinated beans. These were finally portioned out scoop by aluminum scoop.

All of the difficulties overcome and the divisions equitably made, the two groups agreed on their separate meeting times and places—still Wednesday night, but one half-hour apart.

The first few weeks of the new arrangement found latecomers to one meeting glaring at earlygoers to the other. But then, after about six weeks, an amazing thing occurred—amazing, however, only to those unfamiliar with A.A. history. A newcomer approached the first group and after the meeting observed: "Gee, you people sure do a lot of reading around here!"

"Well, yes," came the response. "You know, others felt the same way, and so they started their own group. Why don't you come around a little bit early next week, and I'll take you over to our *daughter group*."

Roughly three weeks later, another occurrence transpired. A newcomer came to the "daughter group" and after the meeting commented: "I heard there was a lot of good meditation literature in A.A., but you people don't seem to read any of it."

"Well, as a matter of fact, there is a lot of that literature around," came the response, "and some of the groups around here use it at their meetings. Look, one of those groups is meeting tonight, so why don't I walk over there with you—it's just a couple of blocks."

Six months after the beginning of the original dissension, when one A.A. group of 21 core members had split into two, there now existed two A.A. groups—one with 18, the other with 15 core members. As one of the original members observed to another while drinking one of those delicious cups of specialty coffee, "Alcoholics Anonymous doesn't have to spread by 'heresy,' but it sure can help!"

Occasionally, the question is asked: "How long will Alcoholics Anonymous last?" All institutions degenerate, and so it is conceivable that someday those who claim to follow the A.A. program will allow their practice to degenerate into formalism, imposing membership "requirements," insisting on rigid adherence to certain "rules," conducting meetings according to some inflexible pattern, and stringently applying various theories and doctrines about "disease" or "codependence" or whatever. In such a setting, the Twelve Steps will likely be scorned or, worse, given only lip service.

But should that happen in some cold and distant future, we can also be sure that somewhere, perhaps under a battered bridge or in a dingy alcove, perhaps even in an atmosphere free of cigarette smoke and without the requisite coffeepot, some alcoholic who is trying to stay sober will sidle up to some other alcoholic who may even be drinking and say: "Psst, buddy. You must be awfully thirsty, but let me tell you how it was with me when I used to need a drink."

And in that moment of acknowledged shared weakness, an A.A. meeting will begin, and the story of Alcoholics Anonymous will continue, and nothing that any of A.A.'s individual groups, or those who borrow its Steps, or those who run treatment programs, or those who write books, or the wider culture itself might do will ever be able to prevent that from happening.

Whenever, wherever, one alcoholic meets another alcoholic and sees in that person first and foremost *not* that he or she is male or female, or black or white, or Baptist or Catholic or Jew, or gay or straight, or *whatever,* but sees rather another alcoholic to whom he or she *must* reach out for the sake of his or her own sobriety—so long, in other words, as one alcoholic recognizes in another alcoholic first and foremost that he or she *is* alcoholic and that therefore *both* of them need each other—there will be not only *an* Alcoholics Anonymous, but there will be *the* Alcoholics Anonymous that you and I love so much and respect so deeply.[21]

Chapter 15

FORGIVENESS

❖

The memory of things past is indeed a worm that does not die. Whether it continues to grow by gnawing away at our hearts or is metamorphosed into a brightly colored winged creature depends . . . on whether we can find a forgiveness we cannot bestow on ourselves.

Dominic Maruca

Forgiveness is an answer, the divine answer, to the question implied in our existence. An answer is answer only for him who has asked, who is aware of the question.

Paul Tillich[1]

A former inmate of a Nazi concentration camp was visiting a friend who had shared the ordeal with him.

"Have you forgiven the Nazis?" he asked his friend.

"Yes."

"Well, I haven't. I'm still consumed with hatred for them."

"In that case," said his friend gently, "they still have you in prison."[2]

The book *Alcoholics Anonymous* makes an astounding statement: "Resentment is the 'number one' offender. It destroys more alcoholics than anything else." "Surely," the casual reader thinks, "that must be a mistake: surely it is *alcohol* that destroys alcoholics." But the Big Book means what it says, and in the very next sentence explains why: "From [resentment] stem all forms of spiritual disease."[3]

Resentment is the poison of the spiritual life. The word means, literally, "feeling again," in the sense of "feeling *backward*": the emphasis is on a *clinging* to the past, a harping on it that becomes mired in it. Resentment goes over and over an old injury: revisiting the hurt, the powerlessness, the rage, the fear, the feeling of being wronged. Scraping the scab off the wound, resentment relishes anew its pain; it is the particular kind of memory that reinforces the vision of *self-as-victim*. This vision is the antithesis of spirituality, for spirituality begins with the recognition of *our own* imperfection. Focusing on the past faults and failings of others blinds us to the reality of our own present defects and shortcomings.

It was this peril—the danger of cutting ourselves off from the spiritual resources that offer the only possible healing of our own imperfection—that the desert genius Evagrius Ponticus cautioned against in explaining the proper use of *anger*. Evagrius noted that resentment—clinging to misdirected anger—stifled spiritual life by stealing the very tools of virtue:

> We need to reclaim anger for its proper purpose. It is always a waste of good anger to get annoyed with other human beings. . . . What the ascetic needs to do is to focus his attention . . . on the fact that he is annoyed. Instead of seeing some other human being angrily, he tries to see his own anger. He can then begin to fight against it.[4]

Anger can be an important part of the process, the journey, that is the construction and discovery of our spiritual home. But resentment has the capacity to stop that process, to abort that journey. The anger that metamorphoses into *resentment* isolates us, creating the illusion that the world has stopped in its tracks and has come to focus entirely upon *our* hurts, *our* desires, *our* victimhood. In resentment there is no chance of release but only imprisonment in a painful past and the gradual stifling of all serenity, indeed, of all humanity. "If a man removes his bitterness, he becomes human; otherwise he becomes an animal," observed one Sufi teacher.[5]

Resentment unites anger, fear, and sadness in a kind of closed-circle, scissors-paper-rock game.[6] In the absence of resentment, anger, fear, and sadness tend to heal each other. Anger can act like a scissors, cutting through fear—the fear that like an enveloping shroud wraps itself around and threatens to smother the rock that is sadness. But

that very sadness, which rises from the realization of our own tran-
sience and the ultimate futility of our human efforts to control, is the
only tool we have to blunt anger—to forestall the resentment that
anger becomes if it is nourished even after our fears have been quelled.

Anger and sadness butt against each other, steel against stone. But
just as scissors "take" paper and rock "takes" scissors, sadness will
finally take anger—if we let that sadness through. For sadness, shared,
can heal. Anger storms in the hard passage between fear and sadness;
cultivated, it turns into a jagged resentment that tears rather than
trims and that resists healing. Denying fear and scorning the sadness
that is shared, resentment refuses the possibility of going through and
beyond anger into forgiveness.

The danger of anger—the reason why the "wrath" that is Evagrius'
ira has been classically listed as "sinful"—lies not in anger itself, but in
resentment, the clinging to and prolonged attachment to anger. Resentment is the refusal, out of fear, to cross the bridge of sadness and
let ourselves back into the impermanent world of relationship. Anger
as resentment refuses relationship, slashing at everything and everyone that comes close. But our pain can be healed only by some kind of
closeness, some kind of connection with others. Sadness opens us to
the need for unity and community.

❖

In his book *Is Human Forgiveness Possible?*, theologian John Patton
examines the New Testament story in which Peter asks Jesus of Nazareth, "Lord, when my brother wrongs me, how often must I forgive
him? Seven times?" And Jesus answers: "No, not seven times; I say
seventy times seven times." (Matt. 18:21–22) Patton comments:

> Peter's question seems to say, "Please give me a rule so I don't have
> to keep dealing with this. How can I know when enough is enough? I
> want to know what to do instead of having to come to terms with the
> whole history of our relationship." Jesus' response to the question
> says in effect, "I am unwilling to give you a way out of a continuing
> relationship to your brother."[7]

For the opposite of "resentment" is *forgiveness,* recognized by centuries of spiritual thinkers as "the endpoint of human life." Forgive-

ness is "given," and not only in English; the French say "par-*donner*," the Spanish "per-*donar*." That is because, in the words of D. M. Dooling, a student of mythic spirituality: "Forgiveness belongs to the divine. It is God's act: something *other*, something that is not ours; and unless we can acknowledge this, the word is only 'a noise we make with our mouths.' "

Forgiveness is not ours to give, but ours to receive. We cannot create it; we can be certain only that it is beyond us, in the sense of beyond our control, beyond our ability to will it into existence.[8]

❖

In ancient times, people thought, discussed, wrote, and agonized about the meaning of experiences like forgiveness; in modern times, investigators conduct research. Thus it is that forgiveness has become a topic of inquiry for a group of Seattle University scholars. Beginning with blatantly victimized people whose stories had appeared in newspapers, and then extending the process to more ordinary individuals (including the investigators themselves), the project explores how attitudes toward the victimizer change or fail to change over time.[9]

Preliminary research findings echo ancient understandings of forgiveness and shed intriguing light on the ongoing story of a spirituality of imperfection. Forgiveness, the investigators rediscovered, does not come easily, but it does, apparently, come suddenly. "Serene" persons—those who had suffered victimization but who now harbored no resentments—described not a specific act of forgiving, but rather a *discovery* of themselves as *having forgiven*. These individuals reported the failure of their direct efforts to forgive—they couldn't force the experience. "The harder I tried to forgive, the more I seemed to resent," was a frequent description. Realizing this, they stopped "trying to forgive" and instead "just sort of let go"; and then, after varying intervals of time, came the astonishing discovery that the resentment had disappeared, that they somehow already *had* forgiven.

That's Phase One of the process, and perhaps we could pause here for a bit of analysis. The research verifies that forgiveness is *spiritual:* it is one of those realities that cannot be "willed," that becomes more impossible the harder one tries to will it. Forgiveness, in fact, becomes possible only when *will* is replaced by *willingness;* it results less from *effort* than from *openness*.

Within Alcoholics Anonymous, this understanding of forgiveness is conveyed in typically straightforward fashion.

When some hurting person approaches an A.A. sponsor or friend to complain of being victimized or to moan that he cannot get rid of a resentment because he feels "unable to forgive," the usual advice, judiciously offered, runs: "Well, I'd say, Pray for the son of a bitch!"

And astounding as it may sound to the outsider, it works! Time after time at meetings of Alcoholics Anonymous, experiences of forgiveness are detailed in just such stories. "I just *couldn't* forgive the *&%#, but my sponsor said 'Pray for the s.o.b.,' and I did, and would you believe it, one day I realized that I no longer felt resentful . . . somehow, the whole thing just didn't bother me anymore!"

The "prayer" that most usually works is the only prayer often possible: "God, please give that s.o.b. what he deserves!" And so long as one does not presume to suggest "what he deserves," amazingly, it works. The surrender of the claim to control, implicit in all real prayer, is of course one part of what is going on here, but we can push further; and that is what Phase Two of the research project attempted, as the interviewers asked more questions, probing more deeply into the actual experience of forgiveness. Although assembled from several interviewers and constructed from even more interviews, the following exchange captures the flavor as well as the findings of this phase of the research.

"When we spoke a year ago," the interviewer started off, "you said that you 'just couldn't forgive.' And you said the same thing just six months ago, when we last spoke. So tell me, what else happened to you, with you, during these last six months, the period of time when somehow you forgave? Please detail the events in your life over this time."

Almost invariably, the response began: "Oh, nothing special—just the usual." And then the continuation would run: "Well, yeah, but wait a minute—it's not really connected much, but I guess I should mention it, especially because it

sort of does have to do with forgiving, even though it's sort of the other way around. You see, I got involved in this thing at work, an affair with a guy in the office—oh, I love my husband, this was really just playing around, it wasn't serious and I didn't intend it to last, but . . . well, my husband found out about it, and he was really hurt and really angry. I can't say I blame him—I mean, I felt like . . . well, I thought, 'There it all goes, I've really blown it. I'll probably lose not only him but even the kids . . . and you know what? I mean, you probably won't believe this, but *he forgave me!* We were sitting there one night, after the kids were in bed, and I saw this determination on his face, and I figured, 'Here it comes—now I hear about the divorce lawyer.' But instead he came over and put his arms around me and started crying and saying he hurt like hell, but he didn't want to lose me forever, and could we just close the door on that thing at work and try to be lovers ourselves again?!

"Well, I could hardly believe it. I just couldn't believe it! But somehow, that's how it's been working out. Oh, we still have our ups and downs and our spats about the kids and all, but, hey, we're making it! And it's so good to know that he loves me even though I did that, to know that he's forgiven me."[10]

Almost invariably in these interviews, the respondent makes no direct, explicit connection between the described experience of *being forgiven* and the fact that he or she *had* forgiven; and yet, even more invariably, *the experience of being able to forgive was preceded by some experience of being forgiven.*

These interviews confirm the enduring spiritual insight that forgiveness is not a willed act ("I'm going to forgive") but a profound, internal transformation involving two discoveries. The first discovery is that we *have been* forgiven, which somehow makes possible the second discovery: that we already *have* forgiven. Uniting these experiences is the discovery of commonality—the sense of having rejoined the human community—for both revelations involve finding a new relationship with some "other." Our need *for* forgiveness is thus profound, for it is *the experience of being forgiven* that pulls us out of the

EXPERIENCING SPIRITUALITY

stagnating mire of a self-centered focus on our own pain and pushes us back into the not-necessarily-pure but at least circulating stream of community and commonality.

We connect to each other by our imperfections, through contact with our own flaws and failings. And herein lies the significance of an ancient penitential practice too readily rejected as "negative" and "medieval" but recaptured by the positive spirituality offered by Alcoholics Anonymous. Many alcoholics, on first hearing it, balk at A.A.'s Ninth Step: "Made direct amends to such people wherever possible, except when to do so would injure them or others." Yet countless more alcoholics have had the experience of finally making an amend they had dreaded—acknowledging the "exact nature" of their wrongs to someone they had injured—and finding their admission met by the almost casual assurance, "Thanks for coming around to tell me that: I do appreciate it, but please know that I forgave you a long time ago. Today, I'm just glad that you're sober."

Let's not fool ourselves that such sweet forgiveness happens every time an amend is made, or even that it happens often. *But it does happen*, and once is all that it takes. The power of A.A.'s Ninth Step is that it permits the possibility of experiencing forgiveness—the experience, first, of being forgiven that then makes it possible for the alcoholic to forgive and thus to become free of the "number one offender" of resentment.

❖

Like all spiritual realities, Forgiveness cannot be commanded—cannot be either demanded of others or required of ourselves. It is no accident, then, that A.A.'s Ninth Step, the "amends step," is followed by the Tenth Step, which begins: "Sought through prayer and meditation . . ." The classic A.A. advice to "pray for the son of a bitch" underlines the fact that we are forgiven only if we are willing, first, to forgive. How does one become "willing"? Spiritual tradition suggests through prayer, for all agree that the main effect of prayer is upon the pray-er—the one who does the praying.

All "spirituality" implies prayer, but what does that word mean? Theologian Margaret Miles has described prayer as "a habit of interior attentiveness, an activity that creates a formerly unknown self." The nature of that "unknown self" is suggested by another theologian,

Lawrence Cunningham, who finds in prayer "a counterbalance to the nakedness of autonomy." The first prayer, as Cassian established in the fifth century when he adopted the words of Psalm 70 as the introduction to each monastic Hour, is a scream, a cry for help. "O God, come to my assistance: O Lord, make haste to help me!" Prayer is the response to the realization, the discovery, that we are not in charge, not in control, *not God*. As Thérèse of Lisieux recognized, "prayer arises, if at all, from incompetence, otherwise there is no need for it."[11]

"Incompetence" . . . *imperfection*. The A.A. shibboleth—"pray for the son of a bitch"—rankles some at first hearing, but its singular aptness becomes evident in an insight offered by university president Dennis O'Brien in his musings on *God and the New Haven Railway, and Why Neither One Is Doing Very Well*. O'Brien notes "the affinity between cursing and praying"—they are related, he remarks, because "both forms of discourse address what is out of human control: one with a destructive and the other with a creative purpose." Both praying and cursing flow from frustration.[12]

All prayer, then, is *petition;* but petition for what? The practice of prayer has its own story, and this story answers: "Reconciliation, forgiveness." In the early days of Christianity, during times of persecution, some new believers committed the "unforgivable sin" of denying the Christian faith by sacrificing to the pagan gods. Many who did this later repented and longed to be readmitted to the Christian community. But the leaders of that community disclaimed the power to reconcile the apostates—*unless their pardon was asked by someone who had refused to deny the faith, someone about to be martyred for it.* And so the former apostates sought out the imprisoned Christians marked for martyrdom, begging their intercession. After the death of the martyr, her or his intercessory requests were granted, and thus some apostates were reconciled, and thus the early Christians learned from experience the power of the prayers of the saints: their prayers healed *Zerrissenheit*, "torn-to-pieces-hood"—prayer restored community.[13]

Prayer heals brokenness—not only the broken community, but the brokenness within that is unforgiveness, the inability to forgive. Such healing prayer, the tradition insists, requires faith. What kind of "faith"? Hasidic rabbi Abraham Twerski tells this story from his own experience:

At the Western Wall in Jerusalem I saw a blind man being led to the wall. He felt the stones with his fingertips, applied a gentle kiss to the sacred stones, and began speaking to G–d. Although he spoke very rapidly, I could catch some of the words. He was relating to G–d various things that had happened to him, and some of his requests.

At one point he stopped abruptly. "Oh, I'm sorry," he said. "I already told You that yesterday."

The sincerity of the man's prayer was electrifying. He had no doubt whatever that what he had said yesterday had been heard.[14]

From the same tradition, and the same source, another story speaks to the question: "What kind of faith?"

When Rabbi Menachem Mendel was a small child, his grandfather, Rabbi Shneur Zalman, held him on his lap and asked the child, "Where is *Zeide* (grandfather)?"

The child touched the grandfather's nose. "No," the rabbi said, "that is *Zeide*'s nose. But where is *Zeide*?"

The child touched the grandfather's beard. "No, that is *Zeide*'s beard. But where is *Zeide*?"

The child descended, ran to the next room and shouted, "*Zeide*!" and Rabbi Shneur Zalman went into the room.

Gleefully the child pointed, "There is *Zeide*!"

The message is a powerful one. *Zeide* is the one who responds when called.

We know that G–d is our Father. He responds.[15]

The core *attitude* of all prayer is perhaps best summed up by a story from a related but very different tradition. Most know that Muslims pray five times daily; few remember that the word *Islam* means "submission."

Sa'ad son of Wakas was a companion of the Prophet. In his last years he became blind and settled in Mecca, where he was always surrounded by people seeking his blessing. He did not bless everyone, but those whom he did always found their way smoothed for them.

Abdallah Ibn-Sa'ad reports:

"I went to see him, and he was good to me and gave me his blessing. As I was only a curious child, I asked him: 'Your prayers for others always seem to be answered. Why, then, do you not pray for your blindness to be removed?'

"The ancient replied: 'Submission to the Will of God is far better than the personal pleasure of being able to see.' "[16]

❖

To forgive, truly to forgive, involves letting go of the feeling of resentment *and* of the vision that underlies that feeling—the vision in which we see ourselves as being offended against, the vision of *self-as-victim*. As in all matters relating to the spiritual, focusing on *feeling* distracts from the more profound and truly important issue—the actuality of *be-ing*. The core of resentment is less a "feeling" than the *"seeing"* of one's self as being a victim. To see "self-as-victim" is to adopt a worldview in which forgiveness becomes impossible.

The main spiritual shift that takes place in the event of being-forgiven/forgiving is thus a new experiencing of self; blaming others falls away, and we begin to accept primary responsibility for who we *are*. Forgiveness comes when we let go of the feeling of resentment *by* surrendering the vision of self-as-victim. If we have been injured, we no longer experience the injury as a barrier to relationship. Instead, we see the injury in the perspective of our own imperfection: How can we expect anyone else to be perfect if we ourselves are imperfect? Within that understanding comes the profound realization that we have been forgiven for our own imperfections. And then there follows, in time, a second and equally profound internal transformation: we understand that we have already forgiven others.

Thus it is that we do not *forgive*; instead, we *discover* forgiveness in both its forms—both that we have been forgiven and that we have forgiven. Spirituality's *mutuality* holds true here as everywhere: We are forgiven only if we are open to forgiving, but we are able to forgive only in being forgiven—we get only by giving, and we give only by getting.

✧

Modern culture, with its tendency to "absolutize fulfillment as the basic truth and the final goal of human existence" has lost all sense of the experience known as forgiveness.[17] The competitive mind-set fostered by untempered market economies mistrusts such giving with no assurance of getting, seeing it as foolishness in a world that lives less "on" the edge than "by" the edge. But there is another source for our loss of faith in forgiveness: the confusion of forgiveness with other phenomena. And so it may be helpful to travel once again down the path of the *via negativa,* exploring what forgiveness is *not* in order to understand better what it is.

Forgiveness is not explanation. Remember the story about the Episcopal priest who went to her confessor and discussed with him her tendency to control and other troublesome behaviors? When she began to explore possible psychological facets of her behaviors, the confessor interrupted to ask: "Do you want forgiveness or an explanation?"

Explanations have to do with exploring causes, with digging down into the past in an effort to exert whatever control is still possible over the past. Forgiveness, on the other hand, has to do with letting go of the past—giving up the claim to control the past and refusing to be controlled by it.

But forgiving is not the same thing as forgetting. "Letting go" of the past is not some kind of erasure; forgiveness is not an attempt to obliterate the past or wipe the slate clean. "The stupid neither forgive nor forget; the naive forgive and forget; the wise forgive, but they do not forget," commented radical psychiatrist Thomas Szasz, echoing the nineteenth-century German philosopher Arthur Schopenhauer, who phrased this core insight in another way: "To *forgive and forget* means to throw away dearly bought experience."[18]

For-GIVE-ness, recall, connotes *gift;* to confuse forgiving with forgetting would lose—even violate—that reality. If forgiving were the same as forgetting, then forgiving would be an act in some way under our human control. But we are capable of forgiveness only if we are acted on by some reality outside of, beyond, and in some way greater than ourselves. *We cannot bestow forgiveness either by or on ourselves.*[19]

Confusing forgiving with forgetting sets another trap: We become convinced that mistakes and wrongdoings not only can, but *should*, be forgotten. Spiritual tradition sees it as a strange delusion that our problems have to be gotten rid of; instead, the sages and saints suggest, such difficulties are best put to use. The offense is precisely what must *not* be forgotten, since it is through the act of facing what has happened and fitting it into a whole by re-membering it that the possibility of atonement (making at-one) occurs and forgiveness comes to fruition. "Salvation lies in remembrance."

And so, finally, because the past is important, *there can be no "unconditional forgiveness."* Because we are human, and therefore limited, there can be no unconditional anything. We are *not God*. Forgetting that, as is our all-too-human tendency, we commit idolatry by assuming that since God loves and forgives unconditionally, we can be like God and do the same. But all "idolatry" has ironic consequences, producing the opposite of the goal intended. Thus the claim to "forgive unconditionally" is the antithesis of benign, for it devalues the one we are supposedly forgiving by implying that he is not responsible for his choices.[20]

Any understanding of forgiveness must include some notion of responsibility. Forgiveness, divine *or* human, does not remove responsibility for our actions. If we ignore the consequences of irresponsible actions by claiming or asking for unconditional forgiveness, then forgiveness loses its significance—it comes to be interpreted as *not caring*. Every human being is responsible for his or her choices: which means, quite simply, that each of us has a need to matter—somehow, to someone. We especially need to know that our actions have an effect on the people we love.

When behavior, no matter how selfish or bizarre or hurtful, is repeatedly met with what is intended to be unconditional forgiveness, one must wonder whether "who I am" or "what I do" matters at all. What is needed in such instances is not unconditional forgiveness but confrontation—the kind of confrontation that every alcoholic fortunate enough to be truly loved eventually encounters. Until we are ready to accept our own responsibility and stop blaming someone else for our problems, change and healing will not occur. That does not mean that people who have been victimized by others are to blame themselves for their hurt and their pain. But as A.A.'s first spinoff, Al-

Anon, rediscovered, even victims are responsible for what they do *now*. And one thing they must do now, if healing is to occur, is to stop looking for explanations, to stop seeing themselves as victims and to start "cleaning themselves up." In short, to forgive.

> Rabbi Elimelech of Lizensk was asked by a disciple how one should pray for forgiveness. He told him to observe the behavior of a certain innkeeper before Yom Kippur.
>
> The disciple took lodging at the inn and observed the proprietor for several days, but could see nothing relevant to his quest.
>
> Then, on the night before Yom Kippur, he saw the innkeeper open two large ledgers. From the first book he read off a list of all the sins he had committed throughout the past year. When he was finished, he opened the second book and proceeded to recite all the bad things that had occurred to him during the past year.
>
> When he had finished reading both books, he lifted his eyes to heaven and said, "Dear G–d, it is true I have sinned against You. But You have done many distressful things to me too.
>
> "However, we are now beginning a new year. Let us wipe the slate clean. I will forgive You, and You forgive me."[21]

❖

For devout Muslims, the first of the divine names is *the All-Merciful— the All-Compassionate.*

> A Sufi saint, on pilgrimage to Mecca, having completed the prescribed religious practices, knelt down and touched his forehead to the ground and prayed: "Allah! I have only one desire in life. Give me the grace of never offending you again."
>
> When the All-Merciful heard this he laughed aloud and said, "That's what they all ask for. But if I granted everyone this grace, tell me, whom would I forgive?"[22]

Life, as every alcoholic knows, is unfair. Sometimes it hurts, but it is often in the depth and agony of the hurt that we find our "way." All spiritualities, but especially those that urge some kind of "perfection," emphasize finding part of that "way" in God's—reality's—forgiveness of humans, of us. But a spirituality of imperfection raises the perhaps more difficult topic of another kind of forgiveness, the need we humans occasionally have to forgive God. A story told by a volunteer who works with terminally ill children connects many of these ideas.

My idea was pretty simple at the beginning. I started to volunteer in wards with terminally ill children or burn victims—just go in there to cheer them up a little, spread around some giggles. Gradually, it developed that I was going to come in as a clown.

First, somebody gave me a red rubber nose, and I put that to work. Then I started doing some elementary makeup. Then I got a yellow, red, and green clown suit. Finally, some nifty, tremendous wing-tip shoes, about two and a half feet long, with green tips and heels, white in the middle. They came from a clown who was retiring and wanted his feet to keep on walking.

It's a little tricky coming in. Some kids, when they see a clown, they think they're going to be eaten alive. And kids in hospitals and burn units, of course, are pretty shaky. . . .

Burnt skin or bald heads on little kids—what do you do? I guess you just face it. When the kids are really hurting so bad, and so afraid, and probably dying, and everybody's heart is breaking. Face it and see what happens after that, see what to do next.

I got the idea of traveling with popcorn. When a kid is crying, I dab up the tears with the popcorn and pop it into my mouth or into his or hers. We sit around together and eat the tears.[23]

". . . and eat the tears." Sometimes, that is all that we can do. But somehow, when we do that "together," healing and forgiveness—not only by "God" but even of "God"—can happen.

Chapter 16

BEING-AT-HOME

❖

The mistake we make is to turn upon our past with angry wholesale negation. . . . The way of wisdom is to treat it airily, lightly, wantonly, and in a spirit of poetry; and above all to use its symbols, which are its spiritual essence, giving them a new connotation, a fresh meaning.

John Cowper Powys

It is difficult to be a saint in the midst of one's family.

Anatole France[1]

A boy with a rare disease had to live his entire life in a sterile plastic bubble, for a single germ, an unsterilized touch, could be fatal. Anyone reaching to him through the hermetically sealed opening in the bubble had to wear sterilized gloves, and everything that came to him—books, food, utensils, gifts —had to be decontaminated before passing through that opening. He was sealed off, isolated, in permanent quarantine.

But even the airtight, sterile bubble couldn't save him. When the boy understood that he was dying, he asked for only one thing—to reach outside the bubble and touch his father. Doomed, knowing that this encounter was death itself, the boy reached out and touched his father's hand.[2]

The boy in the bubble can serve as a metaphor for us all. Suffering begins in the bubble that is our family, our first home. Touching each other brings pain and even involves danger—the risk of being

THE SPIRITUALITY OF IMPERFECTION

wounded by someone we love. But life is sterile, lonely, and not worth living in the kind of bubble that precludes touch. For that touching, even if it hurts, is life itself.

Our pain and sorrow begin at the very beginning, when we begin —within our family. Family contains its own paradox, serving on the one hand as shield and protection against newborn vulnerability and, on the other hand, as the setting within which we suffer our first wounds. As infants we are dependent upon our parents to defend and shelter us, and yet it is inevitably also our parents who first wound us. Given our prolonged physical immaturity and the complex dangers of our modern, technologized world, those who love us must forbid, "No," as often as they affirm "Yes."

Soon enough, we are also confronted with the sad but undeniable fact that our parents are imperfect beings who make mistakes—they are not God. We discover that we have been born into a kind of paradoxical "4-H Club." If I get close enough to *hug* someone, then I am close enough also to *be hugged* by that person; but I am also close enough to *hit* or to *be hit*—even if, as often happens, the blow is accidental. In a less physical image of the same 4-H's, if I let people close enough to *heal* me, then they are also close enough for me to heal them; but in coming that close, we can not only heal but we can also *hurt* each other—again, perhaps, unintentionally.

The 4-H's, understood either way—the more physical image of hugging and being hugged, hitting and being hit; or the more abstract conception of healing and hurting, being hurt and being healed—are present in *every* relationship, including (and perhaps, most important) family. It is, after all, within our families that we learn "relationship." Perhaps that is why the ultimate act of maturity is presented in both literature and psychology as the forgiveness of one's forebears.[3]

Yet if we are to believe the pop-therapy literature that has become epidemic in modern American culture, the issue is not *forgiveness* but the need to free ourselves from our familial past, to find release from our parents' chains. "Growing up" is presented as a process of looking to the past in order to finger forebears who should have loved us more, protected us more, praised us more, given us more. We are encouraged to think of ourselves as victims—victims of our own families.

According to this literature (which "lines the shelves in bookstores like different brands of aspirin in a drugstore," as Wendy Kaminer put it in her *New York Times* analysis of the new "disease" of codependence), *all* our unhappiness begins at home, in the family. There, in our first "home," we are inevitably subjected to a varying range of physical and emotional abuse, resulting in injury and insult to our "inner child," that innocent and pure, even "divine" entity that exists within us all. The goal of adulthood and recovery, we are told, is to heal that inner child, to recover the innocence and purity of our original self—the identity that existed before our parents got their hands on it, molding, mangling, twisting, deforming. Because our families are (almost by definition) "dysfunctional," we too become dysfunctional, adopting "types" and "roles" instead of forming our own unique, integrated identities. And so instead of truly "actualized" human beings, we become "women who love too much," "enablers," "heros," "mascots," "lost children" and a host of other such "survival roles." Having been diagnosed as "improperly individuated," we cling to these labels for dear life, for they seem the only source of identity available in the modern family.[4]

The literature of pop therapy and pop spirituality seems to make the assumption that along with the divine child within us there is a "divine" way of interacting with each other—a method free of mistakes, flaws, and imperfections. Parents can be taught how to raise their children without wounding the holy child within; adults whose inner child has been wounded can recover, in recovery, their primary, pure essence. But for anyone familiar with the long tradition of a spirituality of imperfection, this worldview is inherently flawed. As John Garvey noted in his study of *The Prematurely Saved:* "When Saint Anthony went into the desert to face himself and God, he did not find in himself a poor self-image. He found demons."[5]

The presentation of good (health/recovery) and evil (sickness/addiction) as polar opposites, absolutely black and absolutely white, ignores the fundamental truth, the basic significant reality, of the human being: We are inherently and intrinsically imperfect and therefore any relationship we enter into—voluntarily or involuntarily, familial or otherwise—will necessarily be flawed.[6]

To be related to *any* other human being is to be *both* healed and hurt, *both* wounded and made whole. Our choice is not between whether we will be healed or hurt but, rather, to which of those always-present realities we shall attend. The relative presence of healing and hurting varies over time; but if the balance within our parental families did not tip toward the side of hurt, would we ever set off to begin families of our own? As A.A. co-founder Bill W. reminded so often: "Pain is the touchstone of all growth." We may not like that, but the tradition of spiritual wisdom suggests that that is the way it is. "Reality," a popular sidewalk scrawl of recent decades reminds, "is for those who can't handle drugs."[7]

❖

William James's gloriously vivid image of *Zerrissenheit* extends beyond the perception of a fractured, broken self. We can apply it also to the sense of broken links between self and others, between self and larger reality, between self and *family*, between self and the very concept of *home*. Modern humankind feels homeless in the deepest meaning of the word: not in the transient sense of having no place to sleep for the night, not even in the wider sense of poverty's homelessness, but in a monstrous, universal sense of having no place wherein we *fit*. James's *Zerrissenheit* thus comes full circle; those broken within, also cut off from what is without, find themselves fundamentally estranged —not at home with self, not at home with family, not at home with the world.

This is a terrible feeling, a terrible be-ing—this *dukkha* sense of a bone ripped out of its socket. The experience is of lost souls circling endlessly, seeking the place where they "fit." For only in finding that "fit" is the bone re-healed into its socket, and only thus does one find a place to rest, a place to hide, a place to *be* one's-self . . . a *home*.

A spirituality of imperfection helps us find that experience, that *fit*. First, by accepting ourselves as imperfect and essentially *mixed*, we fit into our own being. And second, by applying the spirituality of imperfection to our relationships with others, and especially to *family*, we learn to "see" all relationships, and most important *family* in a different way, and so learn how to *fit* with others, how to find a real *home*.

Seeing family in a different way involves *gratitude:* being grateful for what we *do* have instead of moaning and groaning about what we *do not* have. A spirituality of imperfection helps us to see family itself as a gift, for it is in our families that we learn our first and most important lessons. We learn to value differences, to let go of resentments, to forgive transgressions, to think of others before we think of ourselves. We learn that what we do affects others, that what others do affects us, and that we are related to each other through need and through love—through sweat and tears—as well as through blood.

Rabbi Moshe Leib of Sasov learned to love when he went to an inn and heard one drunken peasant ask another, "Do you love me?" "Certainly I love you," replied the second. "I love you like a brother." But the first shook his head and insisted, "You don't love me. You don't know what I lack. You don't know what I need." The second peasant fell into sullen silence, but Rabbi Moshe Leib understood: "To know the need of men and to bear the burden of their sorrow, that is the true love of men."[8]

❖

Master Shaku Soen liked to take an evening stroll through a nearby village. One day he heard loud lamentations from a house and, on entering quietly, realized that the householder had died and the family and neighbors were crying. He sat down and cried with them. An old man noticed him and remarked, rather shaken on seeing the famous master crying with them: "I would have thought that you at least were beyond such things." "But it is this which puts me beyond it," replied the master with a sob.[9]

Life hurts—where is there growth without suffering? Pain is not without its reasons, for it serves the purpose of telling us that "something is wrong," something does not fit. Pain, with its intense message of "unfittingness," moves us to move on in our pilgrimage, to seek new ways of fitting into our own being and into the community of other (imperfect) beings.

Life hurts, but in the hurt there is the potential for healing. The healing of events, the release from victimhood and therefore from resentment, is attained by *gratitude*—gratitude understood not as some warm, transitory feeling but rather as the vision, the understanding, that allows one to see how truly gifted each of us has been and continues to be, not least in our *family*. Gratitude, Milton Mayeroff suggests, is the "natural expression of being in place."[10]

❖

Being-at-home involves, first, coming home to ourselves—being able to accept our own imperfect humanness. This is the first and, really, the only coherent meaning of another concept: *self-forgiveness*. Self-forgiveness, as a spiritual act, is quite simply the opening of one's self to "experiencing forgiveness," which begins with allowing another to forgive us. It is in letting some other that close—close enough that his or her forgiveness matters to us—that we find ourselves released from fundamental estrangement from self and the world. We discover that we can and do *fit*, that we can be-at-home with both self and the world. Self-forgiveness requires the kind of openness that is first of all *trust*. There is a letting go of the *fears* connected with one's old identity, expectations, and beliefs—and not least the belief that one can do this by oneself.

The total experience of forgiveness—being forgiven and forgiving —is a reclaiming of one's true self. In *own*-ing (making one's *own*) the part of self that had been split off—because it was seen as imperfect, flawed and therefore, in this perfectionist world, somehow shameful—that "dark side" becomes less threatening. There is less to fear in the vision of self as ordinary, imperfect, and limited—*neither* devil *nor* angel, but *both*. And this acceptance flows into and involves an awareness of connection with others who are also, inevitably, imperfect, and with the world, which, because it is made up of imperfect beings, does not demand perfection of us. In accepting this vision of self, others and the world, we let go of the feeling that we have to betray our true self in order to become a part of humanity.[11]

Home is, ultimately, that place where we find the peace and harmony that comes from learning to live with the knowledge of our own imperfections and from learning to accept the imperfections of others. Such a place, such a *home*, can exist in various settings, but its ultimate foundation rests jointly within self and within some group of trusted others. Some places are more conducive to this experience than others. But wherever and whenever we do attain that sense of "being-at-home," we experience a falling away of tensions, a degree of balance between the pushing and pulling forces of our lives. In such a *place,* we can cease fighting—most important, we can cease fighting with ourselves. We find the *space* to be the imperfect beings that we are, and we discover that in such a space, we also become able to let others be who they are.

Scholars have found in this experience of *home*—the longing and the searching for it—a sensitivity exquisitely developed in most alcoholics. The anthropologist Gregory Bateson, in his essay on Alcoholics Anonymous, "The Cybernetics of 'Self,' " pointed out how the lonely drinker at the bar, as he gets more and more lubricated, becomes either maudlin or pugnacious. It makes little difference, Bateson observed: whether weeping or fighting, he has at least become *engaged with* someone else. Psychiatrist Edward Khantzian, following a lead suggested by analyst Michael Balint in his study of *The Basic Fault,* notes how "alcoholics seek the effects of alcohol to establish a feeling of 'harmony'—a feeling that everything is now well between them and their environment." The alcoholic's "sense of incompleteness" combines with "the yearning for this feeling of harmony" to become "the most important cause of alcoholism or, for that matter, any form of addiction."[12]

❖

But what kind of place is this *home*—this space of harmony and balance that not only alcoholics but all of us seek? And *how* is it created? Home is, first, the "kind of place" where we "fit in" *because of*—indeed *by*—our limitations. It is that setting where our inabilities and incongruities fit and therefore belong. And thus it is a place where "feeling bad" can be turned into *"being* good."

Visiting a strange city, a newly sober A.A. member sets out to find an A.A. meeting. Following directions received on the telephone, he walks into a hall that is part of a large church-complex and begins to search for the room where the meeting is being held. The first door he opens reveals a group of children in choir robes, getting ready to sing. He closes the door rather quickly . . . no, that's not it. He looks in another door . . . no, half a dozen women are sewing and talk-ing. That's not it.

Approaching panic, for he has never felt comfortable in a

church, he walks quickly down the hallway, feeling a little lost, thinking that if he sees an exit he will take it, but still hoping to find what he came for. Suddenly a cloud of cigarette smoke wafts down the hallway, and he smells the bitter, burnt aroma of strong coffee. He hears voices, and the welcoming sound of people laughing. Walking faster, he finds a room with the familiar blue-jacketed books on the table and the oh-so-trite but now-so-welcome framed mottoes on the wall. Entering the room, greeted by a dozen smiles, he sighs deeply and smiles back. He's found *home*.

Home is the place where we fit in precisely because of our limitations, where we fit in not because of what we have but because of what we lack.

A man was looking for a good church to attend and he happened to enter one in which the congregation and the preacher were reading from their prayer book. They were saying, "We have left undone those things which we ought to have done, and we have done those things which we ought not to have done."

The man dropped into a seat and sighed with relief as he said to himself, "Thank goodness, I've found my crowd at last."[13]

Our first "home" is our parents' home, and our first stories begin there. Sigmund Freud once observed his grandson playing a game— the lost/found game of *"fort-da."* The toddler, sitting in his playpen, developed a way of demonstrating a kind of mastery. When someone entered the room, he would pick up a ball or other toy and, throwing it away from himself, look at the visitor and exclaim *"Fort!"*— "Gone!" As soon as the visitor acknowledged "gone" and showed the requisite sadness and anxiety, the child would triumphantly produce the "lost" object, exclaiming *"da!"*—"Here it is!"

This is perhaps the shortest story we can imagine: An object is lost and then regained. A child's story, enacted by himself, told in just two words and yet containing the requisite beginning (an object exists), middle (it is lost), and end (it is found). In this child's story, as in all

stories, something must be lost or absent for the narrative to unfold—
after all, if everything stayed in place, there would be no story to tell!
If we were only evil, or only good, there could be no stories. "Lost has
meaning only in relation to found," literary critic Terry Eagleton commented in his discussion of the *fort-da* game. "But, of course, found
has meaning only when the thing is first lost." Once we become aware
of the essential limitation of our own humanity, we cannot think of
any reality without thinking also of its possible absence, without
knowing that its presence is in some way arbitrary and provisional.[14]

Yet if *we ourselves* are to be found, another familiar truth comes
into play: We are all looking for, but we find what we are looking for
only by *being* looked for.

Some years ago on a sunny Sunday afternoon in Seattle, a
young priest stopped to talk to a parishioner and her five-
year-old daughter, Carmine. The little girl had a new jump
rope, and the priest began to demonstrate the intricacies of
jumping rope to her.

After a while Carmine began to jump, first once, then
twice. Mother and priest clapped loudly for her skill. Eventually, the little girl was able to jump quite well on her own and
wandered off with her new-found skill. Priest and mother
chatted a few moments until Carmine, with the saddest, wis-
est eyes imaginable, returned dragging her rope. "Mommy,"
she lamented, "I can do it, but I need lots of clapping."[15]

As children learn (and not least from stories), reality comes with
suffering; everything contains within itself its own paradox. Those
who applaud can also ignore, what is found can be lost, what hurts
can also heal, what is loved can inflict pain. For the essence of *suffering*, as the very word signifies, is *to be done to*. Thus it is that, in a very
literal sense, suffering makes us *real*, for it defines our boundaries.[16]

Most of the time, we tend to think of *boundaries* as only negative
—that which *keeps* us "out" or "in." But boundaries are important
for their positive function: They *define* us. By setting limits in a way
that gives *identity*, telling us who we are and are not, they make it
possible to *fit*, to *belong*, and so to feel—and be—*good*. Without

boundaries we would not exist, any more than we can be present in any place other than in the skin that is in a way our "home."

For this is the main meaning of *home:* It is the place where we fit, where we belong, and where we can *hide.* The word *hide* has a poor reputation among modern men and women, for it suggests concealment and dishonesty, even shame. Yet the words *hide* and *home* have the same root—the Indo-European source-word, *KEI,* which signifies a bounded space. For *hide* is not only a verb meaning "conceal," it is also a noun signifying "skin" or "pelt." A football is a "pigskin"; a baseball is "the horsehide."

In one extended meaning, the word *hide* served as a synonym for "home," signifying "land enough for one free family and dependents." That early English usage was based on an interesting story.

> **When Queen Dido and her people, fleeing the city of Tyre and the treacherous wrath of her greedy brother Pygmalion, came to what the Romans knew as Carthage in northern Africa, they were greeted by warlike native-traders eager for the riches that the emigres had brought with them. Knowing that her people were too exhausted to fight, that they needed time and a place to recoup their strengths, the queen set out to bargain with the canny inhabitants, who could hardly conceal their scorn for a nation led by a woman.**
>
> **After a short period of sharp haggling, Dido contracted to exchange the wealth they had brought with them for "enough land to be encompassed by a bull's hide." The sellers, thinking they had struck a very good deal, encouraged the queen to find the largest bull she could, even assisting her in that search.**
>
> **Having found the bull and had it slain, Dido proceeded to cut its hide into very thin strips. Those strips, laid end to end, encompassed almost 120 acres—enough land to hold a citadel, which she called *Byrsa* (Greek for: "the skin stripped off, hide"); it grew to be the city of Carthage.[17]**

Home and *hide* both have to do with boundaries, with limits. Boundaries establish *space,* that internal quality that is the capacity of letting some reality be present to us and for us. By defining who we *are* and *are not,* our boundaries establish our *identity.* The space within the boundary is cleared out, made free. In this ancient under-standing, the boundary is not that through which something ceases to be, but rather that from which something *begins to be what it is,* is *free* to be what it is. *Home,* then, is the place that is like our pelt, our skin, our *hide,* in that it is that which covers us less in a concealing than in a protective way.[18]

Where would we be—*what* would we be—without our skin, our hide? My *hide* defines me; it establishes the limits, the boundaries, between the "me" and the not-me. *Home* is the place where one's very "hide"—limited and bounded almost by definition—*fits.* It is the place where I can be naked, which is to say *vulnerable*—undefended against being wounded because of confidence that there I will not be wounded. Or if I am wounded, that I will also be healed. In every sense of both terms, *home* is the place where I can *hide.*

Home is always there, in a sense, but it needs to be dis-covered, somehow brought into our experience. How do we do this—how do we find *home*? The tradition of a spirituality of imperfection teaches that of all the tools at our command, the surest way to touch the human spirit—to find home, to find the place where we fit—is in and by and through the practice of telling and listening to stories. This is why the great spiritual teachers have always been storytellers, and why we retell, over and over and over again, the stories of those teachers. All stories convey how human beings like us sought and found or failed to find "home," the experience of "fitting in" to some reality. Stories thus bring us both home to ourselves and into fellowship with others.

Core to the failure of "home"—the feeling of *Zerissenheit,* of not fitting in, even to our own being—is the sense of not even knowing our own story. We do not know our story when we cannot *own* our own story because we have internalized others' versions of who we are and who we "should" be. Each of us carries around within ourselves not only a storyteller but also a *critic,* an inner tyrant and constant commentator who judges and scolds, reprimands and censures. This critical tyrant is not *conscience,* which in true inventory-mode praises as well as chides, but rather represents both "superego" and "ego-ideal," for neither of whom can we ever do—or be—"good enough."[19]

Some try to silence that commentator, that critic, even to get rid of it, through the use of alcohol or drugs, or through immersion in sexuality, food, gambling or the amassing of material possessions; but always, inevitably, these are doomed efforts, for we destroy ourselves rather than destroying the critical voice, which is, indeed, an essential part of us. But if we cannot rid ourselves of that voice, we can, at least, *balance* its effects, purge its power and its sting. We disarm the inner critic by enlarging our frame of reference so that the critical voice no longer takes up *all* of our inner space. That enlargement takes place most tellingly, most fittingly, by immersion in story—by the telling and hearing of the experience, strength, and hope of others who describe "what we used to be like, what happened, and what we are like now."

In such a setting "a new presence" is discovered, one that is more *witness* than judge. And as more and more is told and heard, a new kind of *community* is born and grows. When we enter a new place together, when we show each other the things we usually hide, a special kind of connecting occurs: Telling our story to someone, we enter into trust.[20]

Whenever the rabbi of Sasov saw anyone's suffering, either of spirit or of body, he shared it so earnestly that the other's suffering became his own. Once someone expressed his astonishment at this capacity to share in another's troubles.

"What do you mean 'share'?" said the rabbi. "It is my own sorrow; how can I help but suffer it?"[21]

❖

A Beduin set out one day with his son to graze his camel and look for wild herbs to bring back for his wife to cook. On their way home, a herd of gazelles appeared in their path. Quickly the father stopped the camel and slid from her back. Warning the boy not to stray, he moved toward the gazelles, which streaked off as soon as he stepped toward them. But the Beduin was a keen hunter, and he eagerly followed on their trail.

As the child waited alone, a She-Ghoul, that monster of

the wilderness who feeds on human flesh, spied him and with one leap sprang upon and greedily devoured him.

The father hunted long but could not catch a single deer. Resigning himself, he returned to his camel to find that his son was gone. On the ground he found dark drops of blood. "My son! My son is killed!" he shrieked. And in sadness he led his camel home.

On the way he passed a cave, where he saw the She-Ghoul dancing, fresh from her feast. Taking careful aim, the Beduin shot the She-Ghoul dead. He slashed open her belly, and in it he found his dead son. He laid the boy upon his cloak, pulled the woolen cloth around him tight, and so carried him home.

When he reached his tent the Beduin said to his wife, "I have brought you back a gazelle, dear wife, but as God is my witness, it can be cooked only in a cauldron that has never been used for a meal of sorrow."

The woman went from tent to tent for the loan of such a pot. But one neighbor said, "Sister, we used the large cauldron to cook the rice for the people who came to weep with us when my husband died." And another told her, "We last heated our big cooking pot on the day of my son's funeral." She knocked at every door but did not find what she sought. So she returned to her husband empty-handed.

"Haven't you found the right kind of cauldron?" asked the Beduin. "There is no household but has seen misfortune," she answered. "There is no cauldron but has cooked a meal of mourning." Only then did the Beduin fold back his woolen cloak and say to her, "They have all tasted their share of sorrow. Today the turn is ours. This is my gazelle."[22]

❖

The word *witness* means "one who knows the truth." In an environment of storytelling and storylistening, where each person is at different times both teller and listener, the hearers do know "the truth"— about the tellers—in a special way. For unlike seeing, where one can look away, listeners cannot "hear away" but must listen. As the philosopher Hans-Georg Gadamer pointed out: "Hearing implies *already*

THE SPIRITUALITY OF IMPERFECTION

belonging together in such a manner that one is claimed by what is being said."[23]

The *hearing* that happens when people "belong together" fashions a narrative *home*—a place where our anomalies of behavior, our ambivalences of thought and feeling, the ambiguities of our human being all *fit in.* In such a place we look not for explanations or causes of our behavior: We discover, instead, forgiveness. Here again is *mutuality*—storytelling calls into being the place, the setting, where one can "Be at Home"—and "Home" is that place or setting where one can tell one's story.[24]

Such a place, the kind of community we call *home,* is discovered rather than created, found rather than made. Too many speak too glibly about creating a community by "sharing" thoughts, feelings, stories. But *community* requires more than the sharing of stories—true community requires the *discovery of a story that is shared.* People "sharing" their separate stories, no matter how similar those stories may be, is not the same as *shared story.* In this context, "sharing" is not something that we can create and control—it is something that *happens,* an experience serendipitous and unbidden; and when it happens, we experience gratitude for the dis-covering of a shared story. In the words of theologian Mary Daly: "The deepest possible community [is] the community that is discovered rather than 'formed,' when we meet others who are on the same voyage."[25]

That, after all, is what happens at meetings of Alcoholics Anonymous—the discovery of a shared story. Such meetings bear out the theological truism, "There is no *koinonia* without *kenosis*": there can be no "community" without the "emptying out" that springs from the *gratitude,* the generosity, that undergirds all "humility." A story may help us "see" both points.

About noon one working day, an itinerant clown stood at the edge of New York City's Central Park, juggling and engaging the passersby by calling out questions, inviting them to sit down, making them laugh. Little by little a crowd gathered. After a while, a man in a three-piece suit looked at his watch and realized that he had to return to work. Moved by the performance, he went to drop a twenty-dollar bill into the hat at the clown's feet.

"Don't give me twenty dollars!" the clown called out. "Buy us all some apples instead!"

The man in the three-piece suit was startled but receptive; within ten minutes he returned with a bag of apples for the group.

And with those apples a little community was created in Central Park—twenty people surrounding a juggler, eating apples. When others came by to watch, the only way the newcomers could be transformed from confused outsiders to members of the group would be if somebody told them "the story of the apples."[26]

✧

In *The Power of Myth*, Joseph Campbell tells of an event that happened in Hawaii in a place called the Pali, where the winds come rushing through a great ridge of mountains.

One day, two policemen were driving up the Pali road when they saw, just beyond the railing that keeps the cars from rolling over, a young man preparing to jump. The police car stopped, and the policeman on the right jumped out to grab the man but caught him just as he jumped, and he was himself being pulled over when the second officer arrived just in time to pull the two of them back.

Do you realize what had suddenly happened to that policeman who had given himself to death with that unknown youth? Everything else in his life had dropped off—his duty to his family, his duty to his job, his duty to his own life—all of his wishes and hopes for his lifetime had just disappeared. He was about to die.

Later, a newspaper reporter asked him, "Why didn't you let go? You would have been killed." And his reported answer was, "I couldn't let go. If I had let that young man go, I couldn't have lived another day of my life."[27]

The message of all spirituality is that, in some mysterious way, we are all one—that therefore the joy and the sorrow of any one of us is the joy and the sorrow of all of us. Recognizing and living that reality is not "codependence": it is *love*. "It is not judgment or discussion of sins, excuses or understanding of allievating circumstances that break the heart, but mercy and love," wrote desert spirituality scholar Benedicta Ward. An oft-quoted saying of Hillel reminds: *"If I am not for myself, who will be? And if I am only for myself, what am I?"*[28]

A final favorite story may perhaps suggest new insight into the nature of that careworn word, *love*.

An old Jewish woman was dying of rectal cancer. Her husband sat at her bedside, holding her hand, talking to her, crying with her.

A nurse came into the room. "Excuse me, sir," she said, gently touching his shoulder. "It's time to change the bandages. If you'd leave the room, I'll be done in just a few minutes."

"Excuse *me*," the man replied with a gentle but determined smile, "but I'll stay right here. This *tush* and I have had a lot of good times together. I'm not going to turn my back on it now."

Ending a book on spirituality with a reference to a *tush* may seem ill-advised. But paradox will have its way, however much we might try to pretty things up. Dr. Bob Smith, after all, was a proctologist. When one of his colleagues heard that the surgeon was devoting his life to helping alcoholics, he commented, "Well, I guess Smitty's still working with assholes."

And so, through the humor that signals not the hiding but the embrace of pain, we circle back to humility and our common humanity. If we can accept the reality of our imperfection, the fact that we are put together funny, that we are, by our very nature, limited and thus do not have absolute control over our lives, we are taking the tentative steps that are all that we can take on the pilgrimage that is spirituality. Once we accept the common denominator of our own imperfection, once we begin to put into practice the belief that imperfection *is* the reality we have most in common with all other people, then the defenses that deceive us begin to fall away, and we can begin to see ourselves and others as we all really are.

A passage often referred to as "the promises" appears on pages 83 and 84 of the book *Alcoholics Anonymous,* shortly after the reminder: "The spiritual life is not a theory. *We have to live it.*" Because so much of this book has been inspired by A.A.'s spirituality, it seems fitting to conclude with that paragraph, for we believe that it applies to all who seek a spiritual way of life.

> If we are painstaking about this phase of our development, we will be amazed before we are half way through. We are going to know a new freedom and a new happiness. We will not regret the past nor wish to shut the door on it. We will comprehend the word serenity and we will know peace. No matter how far down the scale we have gone, we will see how our experience can benefit others. That feeling of use-lessness and self-pity will disappear. We will lose interest in selfish things and gain interest in our fellows. Self-seeking will slip away. Our whole attitude and outlook upon life will change. Fear of people and of economic insecurity will leave us. We will intuitively know how to handle situations which used to baffle us. We will suddenly realize that God is doing for us what we could not do for ourselves.[29]

To those "promises" we would add: If we learn to accept our imperfection with humor, as the reflection of our very humanity, we will experience humility and tolerance, we will understand that we are already filled with forgiveness, we will see the gift of our lives, the chains will fall away, and we will be free—free not so much *from* fear or "dependence," but free *for* love, for life itself.

NOTES

❖

All wisdom is plagiarism; only stupidity is original.

Hugh Kerr, "Preacher, Professor, Editor,"
Theology Today 45:1 (April 1988), 1.

Introduction *The Story of Spirituality*

1. Francis Vincent's observation is taken from a speech he gave at Fairfield University, as reported under the title "Education and Baseball," *America* 164:13 (6 April 1991), 372–73.

2. The "If a thing is worth doing, it is worth doing badly" quotation is from Gilbert Keith Chesterton, *The Paradoxes of Mr. Pond* (Philadelphia: Dufor Editions, 1963; orig. 1937), p. 55.

   The Rabbi Zusya story, which is often retold, may be found most conveniently in Martin Buber, *Tales of the Hasidim: The Early Masters* (New York: Schocken Books, 1947), p. 251.

3. On the connection between perfectionism and the "modern," see Leszek Kolakowski, *Modernity on Endless Trial* (Chicago: University of Chicago, 1990), and Stephen Toulmin, *Cosmopolis: The Hidden Agenda of Modernity* (New York: Macmillan-Free Press, 1990). For a brief summary of the overall point, see the review of Isaiah Berlin's *The Crooked Timber of Humanity* by Conor Cruise O'Brien in *The New York Review of Books* of 25 April 1991, "Paradise Lost."

4. The context here is well set by Sydney E. Ahlstrom, *A Religious History of the American People* (Garden City, NY: Doubleday-Image, 1975), vol. 2, pp. 437–38.

5. This story, often retold, is based on details drawn from many sources, as reported in Ernest Kurtz's research study, *Not-God: A History of Alcoholics Anonymous* (Center City, MN.: Hazelden Educational Services, 1991).

6. The best-known statement of this perception appears in the wording of the American Public Health Association's Lasker Award, awarded to Alcoholics Anonymous in 1951, which may be found reprinted in *Alcoholics Anonymous Comes of Age* (New York: Alcoholics Anonymous World Services, 1957), p. 301. Other early statements were offered by the philosopher Gerald Heard, "The Ad Hoc Religions," *Fortnight,* December 15, 1954; and the psychologist O. Hobart Mowrer, "Alcoholics Anonymous and the 'Third Reformation,' " *Religion in Life* 34 (1964), 383–97. More recently, the idea can be found in several articles in a special issue of *Journal of Psychoactive Drugs* 19:3 (July–September 1987).

7. Because such detailing seems useless as well as unnecessary, we choose not to offer specific citations to the Wilson correspondence.

8. This story is retold in many versions. Perhaps the most accessible source is its appearance as the frontispiece of Elie Wiesel, *The Gates of the Forest* (New York: Holt, Rinehart and Winston, 1967). This is a translation (by Frances Frenaye) from the French, *Les portes de la forêt.* In *Souls on Fire* (New York: Summit Books, 1972), pp. 167–68, Wiesel ends this story more somberly; instead of the concluding "God made man because he loves stories," there appears this italicized paragraph: *"It no longer is. The proof is that the threat has not been averted. Perhaps we are no longer able to tell the story. Could all of us be guilty? Even the survivors? Especially the survivors."*

9. Joseph Campbell, *The Power of Myth* (New York: Doubleday, 1988), p. 3. Those interested in the power of Campbell's thought will find most useful his first large work, *The Hero With a Thousand Faces* (Princeton: Princeton University Press, 1949). For a fuller perspective on the great myth teacher, see also Fred Siegel, "Blissed Out & Loving It: The Eighties & the Decline of Public Life," *Commonweal* 117:3 (9 February 1990), pp. 75–77, and perhaps especially Brendan Gill, "The Faces of Joseph Campbell," *The New York Review of Books* (28 September 1989), pp. 16–19.

10. This story appears in several slightly varying versions; we rely here especially on Frederick Franck, "The Mirrors of Mahayana," *Parabola* 11:2 (May 1986), p. 66.

11. We borrow this version from Wilkie Au, *By Way of the Heart* (New York: Paulist Press, 1989), p. 46, who cites Belden C. Lane, "Rabbinical Stories: A Primer on Theological Method," *Christian Century* 98:41 (16 December 1981), pp. 1307–8. Versions of the story also appear in William Bausch, *Storytelling: Imagination and Faith* (Mystic, CT: Twenty-Third Publications, 1984), pp. 68–69, and Anthony de Mello, *Taking Flight* (New York: Doubleday-Image, 1990), p. 60.

Part One
The Roots of Wisdom

1. Viktor Frankl uses these words to close his book *The Unconscious God: Psychotherapy and Theology* (New York: Simon and Schuster, 1975 [orig. 1948]), p. 142.

2. Quoted by Jon Winokur, ed., *Zen to Go* (New York: New American Library, 1989), p. 52.

Chapter 1 *The Fragrance of a Rose*

1. A related idea is captured by Rollo May, *The Cry for Myth* (New York: W.W. Norton, 1991) p. 166: *"Human beings can reach heaven only through hell."*

2. Retold by Anthony de Mello, *One Minute Wisdom* (New York: Doubleday-Image, 1988), p. 137.

3. For this telling of the story, see Maurice S. Friedman, *A Dialogue with Hasidic Tales: Hallowing the Everyday* (New York: Insight Books, 1988), p. 41. See also Louis I. Newman, *The Hasidic Anthology: Tales and Teachings of the Hasidim* (New York, London: Scribner, 1934), p. 344. The definition of *zaddik* as "an imperfect holy man" is by Harold W. Polsky and Yaella Wozner, *Everyday Miracles: The Healing Wisdom of Hasidic Stories* (Northvale, NJ: Jason Aronson, 1989), pp. 9–10. See also Sister Donald Corcoran, "The Spiritual Guide: Midwife of the Higher Spiritual Self," in John R. Sommerfeldt, ed., *Abba: Guides to Wholeness and Holiness East and West* (Kalamazoo, MI: Cistercian Publications, 1982), pp. 336–59: "The guru is the backbone of Hinduism. So also the roshi in some sense IS Zen Buddhism, the sheik IS Sufism, the zaddik IS Hasidism. To find the quintessential spirit of a particular [spiritual] tradition it is best to look to its great guides, for here one finds that tradition as a *lived* experience and not merely a set of doctrines and concepts." A further discussion of the meaning of *zaddik* may be found in Louis Jacobs, *Holy Living: Saints and Saintliness in Judaism* (Northvale, NJ: Jason Aronson, 1990), pp. 9–10, 100.

4. The Conrad quotation is from *Under Western Eyes* (New York: Doubleday, Page & Co., 1926), p. 3. Many of the ideas here are inspired by suggestions offered by historian-theologian Margaret Miles in introducing her study of some of these figures of speech (tropes) in her book, *Practicing Christianity* (New York: Crossroad, 1988). The quotation in the text is from Miles, p. 19, drawing on theologian Sallie McFague on "the way language and more basically, thought, works."

5. On health and illness as metaphor, see Susan Sontag, *Illness as Metaphor* (New York: Farrar, Straus and Giroux, 1978), and further commentary on that insight not only in Sontag's later writings but in Kurtz, *Not-God: A History of Alcoholics Anonymous*, pp. 201ff. The quotation here is from Jerome Dollard, as quoted by Thomas Prugh, "Alcohol, Spirituality and Recovery," *Alcohol Health and Research World* 10:2 (Winter 1985–86), 28–31, 53, supplemented by correspondence and conversations between Dollard and Ernest Kurtz.

6. The word *abba* means literally "old man": at times it is used descriptively, as here; at other times, capitalized, it becomes a kind of honorific title—"elder" in the

NOTES TO PAGES 19-21

sense of "to be revered." The story here is "Number 8" attributed to Poemen in "The Alphabetical Collection," which can be found in various formats. For this version, see Simon Tugwell, *Ways of Imperfection* (Springfield, IL: Templegate, 1985), p. 20. The full story may be found in *The Sayings of the Desert Fathers: The Alphabetical Collection*, trans. Benedicta Ward (Kalamazoo, MI: Cistercian Publications, 1975), p. 167. See also *The Wit and Wisdom of the Christian Fathers of Egypt*, trans. Ernest A. Wallis Budge (London: Oxford University Press, 1934); *Les Sentences des Peres du Desert: serie des anonymes*, trans. Dom Lucien Regnault (Solesmes: Bellefontaine, 1985); on the desert experience as a testing of what it means to be human, see Derwas J. Chitty, *The Desert A City* (Oxford: Basil Blackwell, 1966) pp. xvi, 4, 11.

7. Chesterton, *The Paradoxes of Mr. Pond*, p. 55.

8. Newman, *Hasidic Anthology*, p. 315.

9. It might be of interest especially to alcoholics that the second of the two inscriptions over the building that housed the Delphic oracle counseled, "Nothing to excess." Sartre's insight can be best explored in his *Being and Nothingness;* many readers may find useful for context Thomas M. King, *Sartre and the Sacred* (Chicago: The University of Chicago Press, 1974).

10. Newman, *Hasidic Anthology*, p. 167.

11. Thomas à Kempis's *The Imitation of Christ,* for so long an object of mockery, may find new readers in the postmodern age. See also Gary R. Sattler, *Nobler than the Angels, Lower than a Worm* (Lanham, MD: University Press of America, 1989), subtitled *The Pietist View of the Individual in the Writings of Heinrich Muller and August Hermann Francke*. Thérèse is well introduced by Tugwell, *Ways of Imperfection*, pp. 219–29. There has been a recent rebirth of interest in Saint Thérèse, "the Little Flower," a rebirth perhaps not unrelated to self-conscious postmodernism: see, for example, Margaret Dorgan, "Thérèse of Lisieux: Mystic of the Ordinary," *Spiritual Life* 35:4 (Winter 1989), 201–17, and Barbara Corrado Pope, "A Heroine Without Heroics: The Little Flower of Jesus and Her Times," *Church History* 75:1 (March 1988), 46–60.

12. Cf. Margaret Dorgan, "Thérèse of Lisieux: Mystic of the Ordinary," quoting Thérèse, who well understood this aspect: "Sanctity does not consist in saying beautiful things. It does not even consist in thinking them, feeling them! It consists in suffering and suffering everything."

13. The quotation is from Tugwell, *Ways of Imperfection*, p. 50, analyzing the Macarian Homilies.

14. Hasidism dates from the eighteenth century, the era of the Enlightenment that marks the dawn of the modern age—the beginning of the belief in unlimited progress and the demand for this-worldly perfection. Pietism was the spiritual response to that new faith. But because most forms of Christian Pietism rejected history, it is to the insight of Hasidic Judaism that we must turn to find the richest new-modern expression of the age-old insight of the spirituality of imper-

fection. Poor and persecuted, the Jews dispersed in the heartland of central Europe saw in increasing rationalism not hope but threat. Their wariness was not of mind, as their appreciation of literary art amply attests. Rather, fiercely true to the monotheistic insight that defines the essence of Judaism, they recognized in the demand for and the worship of *control* a form of idolatry. "Hear, O Israel, I am the Lord, your God" begins the ancient *shema,* and Hasidism defended that faith against idolatry of the human no less than against the idolatry of pagan gods.

15. Friedman, *Dialogue with Hasidic Tales,* p. 126.

16. T. S. Eliot, *Four Quartets* (New York, Harcourt Brace & Co., 1943) p. 15. This insight has been used by, for example, Kenneth Leech, in his *Soul Friend* (San Francisco: Harper & Row, 1977), p. 143, in treating of the apophatic theology: Apophasis, or negative theology, is at the heart of the spiritual tradition of Eastern Christianity, and indeed it is "the fundamental characteristic of the whole theological tradition of the Eastern Church." Another interesting use that builds on Eliot here is A.M. Allchin, *The Dynamic of Tradition* (London: Darton, Longman & Todd, 1981).

17. Usefully detailed treatment of when, how, and why Alcoholics Anonymous left the Oxford Group, a separation that occurred differently in New York and Akron, may be found in Walter Houston Clark, *The Oxford Group: Its History and Significance* (New York: Bookman Associates, 1951), and in smaller context but greater specific detail in Robert Thomsen, *Bill W.* (New York: Harper & Row, 1975); Ernest Kurtz, *Not-God: A History of Alcoholics Anonymous;* and both the A.A.-published *'Pass It On': The Story of Bill Wilson and How the A.A. Message Reached the World* (New York: Alcoholics Anonymous World Services, 1984) and the Al-Anon-published *Lois Remembers: Memoirs of the Co-Founder of Alanon and Wife of the Co-Founder of Alcoholics Anonymous* (Don Mills, Canada: T.H. Best Printing Co., 1975.)

The quotations of both Walter Houston Clark and Carl Jung may be found in Stanislav Grof, "Spirituality, Addiction, and Western Science," *ReVision* 10:2 (Fall 1987), 5–18.

18. The Pelikan quotation is taken from *The World Treasury of Modern Religious Thought* (Boston: Little, Brown, 1990), p. 8.

It also merits noting here that there is a large danger in the too glib use of "spiritual rather than religious"—the error of falling into a search for some kind of "generic spirituality." As the stories told herein illustrate, there is no generic spirituality—spirituality all comes in some sort of brand. The point is well clarified by an image of Wittgenstein recently appropriated by a modern writer:

The belief that when we peel away cultural encrustations we will arrive at the essence of a tradition or a culture assumes that whatever was there at the beginning was pure, and all later additions or amendments are corrupting, or are sidetracks. . . . To paraphrase a metaphor Wittgenstein used in another context: we may peel away the leaves to try to get at the essence of the artichoke, and find that the leaves were what the artichoke was about.

John Garvey, "Leaves of the Artichoke: The Marriage of Religion and Culture," *Commonweal* 20 (April 1990), 240–41.

19. See John Farina, "The Study of Spirituality: Some Problems and Opportunities," *U.S. Catholic Historian* 8:1, 2 (Winter/Spring 1989), 15–31. For one recent expression of this insight in specifically the American historical context, see Denise and John Carmody, "On American Religious Thought," *Religion and Intellectual Life* 5:1 (Fall 1987), 42–58; for example: p. 57, where the authors discuss "the matter of reinterpreting liberty and reliance on experience to empower a conversion from consumerism to what for lack of a better alternative we can call spirituality."

20. For Wilson's wariness, see the "We Agnostics" chapter of *Alcoholics Anonymous: The Story of How Many Thousands of Men and Women Have Recovered from Alcoholism*, 3rd ed. (New York: Alcoholics Anonymous World Services, 1976), known within Alcoholics Anonymous as "the Big Book." See also the description of his thoughts as recorded by biographer Robert Thomsen, in *Bill W.*: "He was willing to concede religious comfort might be all right for some—for the old, the hopeless, for those who had passed beyond loving, beyond any hope of really living, but, by Christ, he was different."

21. We draw here most directly from Anthony de Mello, *The Song of the Bird* (New York: Doubleday-Image, 1982), pp. 72–73. There is an almost identical ancient Sufi tale, "The Man Who Walked on Water," retold by Idries Shah, *Tales of the Dervishes* (New York: E.P. Dutton, 1970), pp. 84–85.

22. This is based on personal conversation with a friend whose generosity and example have taught me much about spirituality, the Rev. Chilton Knudsen; it is used with her kind permission.

23. As a final word on "Spirituality is not therapy," it is worth pondering the words of Siegel, "Blissed Out & Loving It: The Eighties & the Decline of Public Life":

In a society where therapy had already replaced religion as the source of solace, health has now replaced ethics as the measure of morality. It is your job to feel good about yourself, regardless . . . In the reworking of the old Protestant scheme of the self-made man and the self-saved soul, self-healing became popularized. New Age medical gurus explain that cancer is really only a form of cellular despair. If you have willed it, you can cure it. On the other hand, if you fail, you have only yourself to blame. . . . Bizarre as it may seem in a society already awash in individualism, the primary message of many of these groups has been that people suffer from an excess of selflessness. The country needed to be taught self-love. And one way to achieve the self-love is to cut yourself off entirely from your past, "by healing the child within," that is, eliminating the middleman and "reparenting" yourself. This time, of course, the job will be done right.

24. Those familiar with the history of religious thought in America will recognize the affinity between the spirituality of imperfection and the "Realistic Theology,"

more commonly called "neo-orthodoxy," associated with the names of theologians Reinhold and H. Richard Niebuhr—an American manifestation almost exactly contemporaneous with the birth and development of Alcoholics Anonymous. Those interested in this parallel will find a detailed treatment in Kurtz, *Not-God.*

25. The Sartre observation is from *Being and Nothingness;* here again, it would be useful to consult Thomas King's study, *Sartre and the Sacred.* The Meister Eckhart quotation is by way of Maurice Friedman, ed., *The Worlds of Existentialism: A Critical Reader* (Chicago: University of Chicago Press, 1964), p. 33, selected from Raymond Bernard, *Meister Eckhart: A Modern Translation* (New York: Harper Torchbooks, 1957); See also, for a deeper appreciation of the "armor" reference, Ernest Becker, *Angel in Armor* (New York: Free Press, 1969).

26. Marion Woodman, "Worshipping Illusions," *Parabola* 12:2 (May 1987), p. 64.

27. Retold by Anthony de Mello, *One Minute Wisdom* (New York: Doubleday-Image, 1988), p. 116.

Chapter 2 *Beyond the Ordinary*

1. The Camus quotation is from Albert Camus, *The Fall* (New York: Vintage, 1956 [*La Chute* 1956]), p. 84. The Gregory of Nyssa is *via* John Garvey, *The Prematurely Saved and Other Varieties of Religious Experience* (Springfield, IL: Templegate, 1986), p. 15, quoting theologian Jurgen Moltmann, in his essay, "The Unity of the Triune God" (printed in *St. Vladimir's Theological Quarterly* 3 [1984]), who in turn quotes Saint Gregory of Nyssa.

2. Retold by de Mello, *Song of the Bird,* p. 71.

3. Millicent E. Buxton, David E. Smith, and Richard B. Seymour, "Spirituality and Other Points of Resistance to the 12-Step Recovery Process," *Journal of Psychoactive Drugs* 19:3 (July–September 1987), 279–80.

4. Proverbs 31:30; Sirach 11:2–3.

5. Adapted from the retelling by Raphael Patai, *Gates to the Old City: A Book of Jewish Legends* (Detroit: Wayne State University Press, 1981), pp. 219–20.

6. Retold by Anthony de Mello, *The Heart of the Enlightened: A Book of Story Meditations* (New York: Doubleday, 1989), p. 27.

7. Mark D. Hart, "Reconciliation of Body and Soul: Gregory of Nyssa's Deeper Theology of Marriage," *Theological Studies* 51 (1990), 450–78, here quoting Gregory's *De virginitate* IV. 1, pp. 25–35.

8. This story can be found in de Mello, *Song of the Bird,* p. 137.

9. The words *proper* and *own* and *fitting* invite investigation in a large unabridged dictionary. For one exploration of these ideas informed by such depth, see David Stendl-Rast, "The Mystical Quest, Attachment, and Addiction," *ReVisions* 10:2 (Fall 1987), 37–43.

NOTES TO PAGES 34-39

10. This story is frequently retold. See, e.g., de Mello, *Song of the Bird*, p. 86; Edmund Fuller, *Thesaurus of Anecdotes* (New York: Crown Publishers, 1942), p. 41; Robert Hendrickson, *World Literary Anecdotes* (New York: Facts on File, 1990), p. 76.

11. Francis's *Admonitions* 11:3 are quoted and cited by Tugwell, *Ways of Imperfection*, pp. 129–30. For more on Francis, see especially *Scripta Leonis, Rufini et Angeli: Sociorum S. Francisci (The Writings of Leo, Rufino and Angelo—Companions of St. Francis)*, ed. and trans. Rosalind B. Brooke (Oxford: Clarendon Press, 1970), where the alternate-page availability of the Latin text helps the reader penetrate what are in other editions at times shaky translations and interpretations.

12. As the well-known student of world religions Mircea Eliade has noted, "Man becomes aware of the Sacred because it manifests itself, shows itself, as something wholly different from the Profane. . . . In his encounters with the Sacred, man experiences a reality that does not belong to our world and yet is encountered in and through objects or events that are part of the world." Mircea Eliade, *The Sacred and the Profane* (New York: Harcourt, Brace & World, 1959), pp. 10–11. For a useful interpretation, Otto Grundler, "John Calvin: Ingrafting in Christ," in E. Rozanne Elder, ed., *The Spirituality of Western Christendom* (Kalamazoo, MI: Cistercian Publications, 1976), p. 170.

13. We found this story in an otherwise unidentified clipping from the periodical, *The Utne Reader*, for May–June 1989, pp. 103–4, which cited Shawn Gosieski, *New Cyclist*, Fall 1988.

14. Belden C. Lane, "Merton as Zen Clown," *Theology Today* 46:3 (October 1989), 259–60.

15. Joseph Cardinal Ratzinger, *Seek That Which Is Above: Meditations Through the Year* (San Francisco: Ignatius Press, 1986 [orig. German, 1985]), p. 21.

16. Newman, *Hasidic Anthology*, p. 160.

17. A similar understanding is conveyed in the Russian mystical tradition that honored stuttering as the sign of a true prophet: See Anthony Ugolnik, *The Illuminating Icon;* for the scriptural references, the best place to begin would be with John L. McKenzie, *A Dictionary of the Bible* (New York: Macmillan, 1965); a more detailed discussion is offered by Leech, *Soul Friend*, p. 143.

18. Despite the unfashionableness of this idea, it is far more at the core of the spirituality of Alcoholics Anonymous than is the recent "feel-good" focus on "self-esteem." See the book *Alcoholics Anonymous*, especially its p. 62 delineation of "the root of our troubles," and also the A.A. book that develops that insight, *Twelve Steps and Twelve Traditions* (New York: Alcoholics Anonymous World Services, 1953), especially pp. 64–78, treating Steps Six and Seven of the A.A. program.

19. This story appears in many collections, but we draw from the version set down by Gregory M. Corrigan, *Disciple Story: Every Christian's Journey* (Notre Dame, IN: Ave Maria Press, 1989), p. 93.

20. Donald Nicholl, "Conversion of Heart," *The Tablet* (21 October 1989).

21. Tugwell, *Ways of Imperfection*, p. 213, quoting and citing Caussade, *Lettres Spirituelles*, vol. 1 (Paris, 1962) pp. 96, 117. See *Alcoholics Anonymous*, pp. 83–84, reproduced on p. 243 of this book.

22. Newman, *Hasidic Anthology*, p. 429.

Chapter 3 *The Reality of Limitation*

1. We found this quotation in George Seldes, comp., *The Great Quotations* (New York: Lyle Stuart, 1960), p. 238, citing *The Works of Ralph Waldo Emerson*, 1913.

2. Thomas Hopko, "Living in Communion: An Interview with Father Thomas Hopko," *Parabola* 12:3 (August 1987), 50–59.

3. *The Shepherd of Hermas* may be found in Francis X. Glimm, Joseph M.-F. Marique, and Gerald G. Walsh, eds., *The Apostolic Fathers* (Washington, DC: The Catholic University of America Press, 1947), pp. 235–352, with a useful Introduction pp. 225–32. The salient points are discussed by Tugwell, *Ways of Imperfection*, pp. 2–3, 7–8. For a modern expression of the "two angels" insight and vocabulary, see Rollo May, *The Cry for Myth* (New York: W.W. Norton, 1991), pp. 225ff., in his discussion of Marlowe's *Faust.*

4. Irenée Hausherr, *Penthos: The Doctrine of Compunction in the Christian East* (Kalamazoo, MI: Cistercian Publications, 1982), pp. 18–19.

5. Retold by de Mello, *Heart of the Enlightened*, pp. 109–10.

6. Tugwell, *Ways of Imperfection*, pp. 6–7, thus summarizes the vision of the ancient author of the *Didache*. For an accessible translation, see Glimm, Marique, and Walsh, *Apostolic Fathers*, pp. 167–84, which offers the advantages of a useful introduction and notes.

7. How Augustine is treated has become almost the sure touchstone of modern efforts to "popularize spirituality." Augustine makes a convenient whipping-boy for the fad-inclined who are by definition devoid of all sense of historical perspective. For more nuanced, sensitive, and appreciative treatments, see Margaret R. Miles, *Practicing Christianity*, passim; also Jaroslav Pelikan, *The Chrisitian Tradition: A History of the Development of Doctrine*, vol. 1: *The Emergence of the Catholic Tradition: 100–600* (Chicago: University of Chicago Press, 1971), index listings; the selections that appear in Bernard McGinn, John Meyendorff, and Jean Leclerq, eds., *Christian Spirituality: Origins to the Twelfth Century* (New York: Crossroad, 1986); Richard Woods, *Christian Spirituality* (Chicago: Thomas More Press, 1989), especially chapter 7; and the essay by Vernon J. Burke, "Augustine of Hippo: The Approach of the Soul to God," that appears in E. Rozanne Elder, ed., *The Spirituality of Western Christendom* (Kalamazoo, MI: Cistercian Publications, 1976), pp. 1–12.

A briefer and more accessible summary of the point here may be found in Garry Wills, "The Phallic Pulpit," *The New York Review of Books* (21 December 1989), 20–26—note especially p. 22:

> What intrigues Augustine is the sexual dramatization of the human being's internal disjunctions. The other desires do not have such clear and uniform early symptoms as the body's arousal by concupiscence—or its failure to be aroused. He dwells more on the body's impotence than its importunacy, since the former shows a kind of ultimate rebellion, when the soul cannot get the body to go along even with its *sinful* plans. Here "desire will no longer serve desire." The great revolutionary of Eden, grasping at god-head, cannot even find a willing recruit to lesser little rebellions of the flesh.

8. For an in-depth appreciation of Eliot's use of Julian, see A.M. Allchin, *The Dynamic of Tradition* (London: Darton, Longman & Todd, 1981), passim, as well as the useful essays in Robert Llewelyn, ed., *Julian: Woman of Our Day* (London: Darton, Longman & Todd, 1985). For a useful analysis of Julian's significance within the mystical tradition, see Thomas M. Gannon and George W. Traub, *The Desert and the City: An Interpretation of the History of Christian Spirituality* (Chicago: Loyola University Press, 1969), pp. 124ff. On *behoovely* as "necessary," see Tugwell, *Ways of Imperfection*, p. 206, note 117, an insight that is extended insightfully by Donald Macdonald, "Courtesy and Sin," *Review for Religious* 50:3 (May–June 1991), 447ff. More on Julian's attitude to "sensuality," and its historical context, may be found in Kenneth Leech, *Experiencing God: Theology as Spirituality* (San Francisco: Harper & Row, 1985), pp. 255–56.

9. Leszek Kolakowski, *Religion: If There Is No God—On God, the Devil, Sin, and Other Worries of the So-Called Philosophy of Religion* (New York: Oxford University Press, 1982), p. 199. The Pascal reference is also from this work, p. 200.

10. See Tugwell, *Ways of Imperfection*, p. 37, citing Systematic #582.

11. A.A.'s Second Step—"[We] Came to believe that a Power greater than ourselves could restore us to sanity"—well captures precisely these qualities.

12. Matthew 5:43–48, translation as in *The Jerusalem Bible* (Garden City, N.Y.: Doubleday, 1966): For a recent expression and application of the insight developed here, see William C. Spohn, "The Moral Vision of the Catechism: Thirty Years That Did Not Happen," *America* 162:8 (3 March 1990), pp. 189–92. See also the discussion of "perfect" by Cynthia Bourgeault, "The Gift of Life: The Unified Solitude of the Desert Fathers," *Parabola* 14:2 (May 1989), 28.

Especially in the context of the American ideal of equality, such a misreading of *perfect* in the sense of "embracive" or "complete" as if it meant "flawless" seems strange. But it becomes understandable if we recall the story of mainstream religious thought in America, which from the time of the Puritans remained fixated on "original sin." That doctrine's simple purpose was to capture the basic spiritual sense that "something is wrong," while suggesting an explanation that absolved the individual of responsibility for causing that flaw in herself or himself.

But when economic circumstances on the new continent led to political distortion of that understanding, those who rebelled against the distortion ended up refusing the insight itself. That rejection left a vacuum that gives rise to periodic rediscoveries, the nature of which has not changed in a secular age. The discovery runs: "I feel as though there is something wrong with me, but since I am really okay, it must be someone else's fault."

13. Bill W., personal correspondence; for further expressions and citations, see Kurtz, *Not-God*, p. 51.

14. Budge, trans., *Wit and Wisdom of the Christian Fathers of Egypt*, p. 151. The story is retold by Tugwell, *Ways of Imperfection*, p. 18.

15. We will see Evagrius in more detail, and with complete citations, in Chapter 5.

16. Often retold, for example by Tugwell, *Ways of Imperfection*, pp. 17–18, this story may be found translated in its entirety in Ward, *Sayings of the Desert Fathers*, pp. 109–10.

17. Columba Stewart, trans., *The World of the Desert Fathers: Stories and Sayings from the Anonymous Series of the Apophthegmata Patrum* (Fairacres Oxford: SLG Press, 1986), pp. 22, 36.

18. Austin Hughes, "The Spirituality of the Desert Fathers," in Maurice Couve de Murville, ed., *The Unsealed Fountain: Essays on the Christian Spiritual Tradition* (Dublin: Veritas, 1987), p. 44; also, Ward, *Sayings of the Desert Fathers*, p. 138, which Hughes also cites.

19. Austin Hughes, "The Spirituality of the Desert Fathers," in Couve de Murville, ed., *Unsealed Fountain*, p. 43; also Ward, *Sayings of the Desert Fathers*, p. 28, no. 10 of Ammonas. The story may also be found in Tugwell, *Ways of Imperfection*, p. 16, and in *Dorotheus of Gaza: Discourses and Sayings*, trans. Eric P. Wheeler (Kalamazoo, MI: Cisterican Publications, 1977), p. 137.

20. Polsky and Wozner, *Everyday Miracles*, p. 27, citing Louis I. Newman, *Maggidim and Hasidim: Their Wisdom* (New York: Bloch, 1962), p. 191, where we also found this story.

21. This story is adapted from Tugwell, *Ways of Imperfection*, pp. 89–91, with some details from Chitty, *Desert A City*, pp. 132ff.

22. Larry McMurtry, *Lonesome Dove*, (New York: Simon & Schuster, 1985), p. 625. Jeffrey A. Kottler and Diane S. Blau, *The Imperfect Therapist: Learning from Failure in Therapeutic Practice* (San Francisco: Jossey-Bass, 1989), p. 5, cite a variant edition, p. 696.

23. Raphael Simon, "The Spiritual Program—Its Importance for Mental Health," *Studies in Formative Spirituality*, 10:2 (May 1989), 163.

24. Newman, *Hasidic Anthology*, p. 354.

25. Friedman, *Dialogue with Hasidic Tales,* p. 40.

26. For greater depth here, see Margaret Miles, *Practicing Christianity* and Chitty, *The Desert A City.* We will pick up and develop this theme in Chapter 5, in our discussion of Evagrius of Pontus and his *logismos.*

27. Benedicta Ward, *Harlots of the Desert: A Study of Repentance in Early Monastic Sources* (Kalamazoo, MI: Cisterican Publications, 1987), p. 87; see also p. 102: "The good monk who relies on his own virtue, in however small a degree, falls into despair, which is the real sin of mankind."

28. Wilson, private correspondence quoted in *Not-God,* p. 121.

29. Martin Buber, *Tales of the Hasidim: The Later Masters* (New York: Schocken Books, 1948) pp. 187–88; Polsky and Wozner retell the story, citing this source in *Everyday Miracles,* p. 259.

30. Timothy Garton Ash, "Eastern Europe: The Year of Truth," *The New York Review of Books* 37:2 (15 February 1990), 18, reports Vaclav Havel's expression of this insight on the eve of his becoming the first president of post-Communist Czechoslovakia: "The crucial 'line of conflict,' he wrote earlier, did not run between the people and the State, but rather through the middle of each person, 'for everyone in his or her own way is both a victim and a supporter of the system.' A banner I saw above the altar in an East Berlin church vividly expressed the same basic thought. It said: 'I am Cain *and* Abel.'"

Chapter 4 *A Sense of Balance*

1. As quoted by Martin E. Marty, *Context* 20:9 (1 May 1989).

2. This is adapted from de Mello, *Song of the Bird,* p. 129, who—perhaps because he was a native of the Indian subcontinent—there says, "black . . . white."

3. One of the earliest statues in the Cairo Museum of Egyptian Antiquities portrays an early pharoah standing between and being supported by two such figures, one "angelic," the other a mischievous inhabitant of the nether regions. For the Titans, see E.R. Dodds, *The Greeks and the Irrational* (Berkeley: University of California Press, 1951), pp. 155–56.

4. Thomas Bulfinch, *The Age of Fable* (New York: Everyman's Library, 1908), p. 14; Edith Hamilton, *Mythology* (New York: W.W. Norton, 1983 [1930]), p. 49, and see also pp. 54–62. Also worthy of note in investigating this point is Edmund Bernard O'Reilly, *Toward Rhetorical Immunity: Narratives of Alcoholism and Recovery,* an unpublished dissertation available from University Microfilms (#88-24778), pp. 44, 46. H.J. Rose, *Gods and Heroes of the Greeks* (London: Methuen, 1957), p. 28, notes concerning Demeter: "One or two legends set forth the terrible nature of her anger; the best known is the punishment of Erysichthon, a Thessalian prince who scorned her advice to spare a sacred grove from which he wanted

to cut timber. She sent an insatiable hunger upon him, and he and his father's house were reduced to beggary." To the ancient Greek, insatiability was the ultimate curse.

5. William Barrett, *Irrational Man: A Study in Existential Philosophy* (New York: Doubleday/Image Anchor, 1958), p. 117, for this quotation; passim for many of the other references and allusions here.

6. Quoted by H. Shelton Smith, *Changing Conceptions of Original Sin: A Study in American Theology Since 1750* (New York: Charles Scribner's Sons, 1955), p. 210; Smith's citation is to Niebuhr's Gifford Lectures: *The Nature and Destiny of Man,* I, p. 182.

7. News commentator John Chancellor, in commenting on the assassination attempts on which he has reported in his career, used the "best-beast" image in telling of the death of Rahjiv Gandhi; the Santayana quotation is from *The Background of My Life,* p. 230, as cited by White, *The Intellectual Versus the City* (Cambridge, MA: Harvard University Press, 1962), p. 188; the Ernest Becker quotation may be found on p. 58 of *The Denial of Death* (New York: Macmillan-Free Press, 1973).

8. For the Barrett quotation, William Barrett, *The Illusion of Technique: A Search for Meaning in a Technological Culture* (Garden City, NY: Doubleday/Anchor, 1978), pp. 344–45. The Sufi story is from Sheikh Muzzafer Ozak al-Jerrahi, *Irshad: Wisdom of a Sufi Master,* trans. Muhtar Holland (Amity, NY: Amity House, 1988), p. 116; Rollo May, *Cry for Myth,* p. 294, records Abraham Maslow observing, after his heart attack: "I wonder if we humans could love—love passionately—if we knew we'd never die."

9. Retold by Buber, *Later Masters,* pp. 249–50.

10. As Sam Keen noted in *Fire in the Belly* (New York: Bantam, 1991), p. 136: "We all carry eternity in our hearts and yet our tenure in time is brief and, finally, tragic. Death interrupts the happiest of lives before all of its promises are fulfilled. The Greeks know what we have conspired to smother with easy smiles and false optimism—paradoxically, a tragic sense of life yields more joy than warm fuzzies."

11. See William James, *The Varieties of Religious Experience* (New York: Mentor-New American Library, 1958 [1902]), pp. 126, 135, 141; our interpretation here owes much to Don S. Browning, *Pluralism and Personality: William James and Some Contemporary Cultures of Psychology* (Lewisburg, PA: Bucknell University Press, 1980), pp. 248–49; for the final point, see also Robert L. Short, *The Gospel According to Peanuts* (Richmond: John Knox Press, 1965) and two delightful books by Abraham J. Twerski, *When Do the Good Things Start?* (New York: Topper Books, 1988) and *Waking Up Just in Time* (New York: Topper Books, 1990), which make creative, spiritually therapeutic use of "Peanuts."

12. The Unamuno quotation is from Miguel de Unamuno, *The Tragic Sense of Life,* trans. J.E. Crawford Flitch (New York: Dover, 1954 [1921]), p. 17; the Porissover story is from Newman, *Hasidic Anthology,* p. 485.

13. See Kallistos Ware, "Fathers in the Spirit," *Parabola*, special issue on "Likeness: The Radiance of Spirit-Bearing Elders," 9:4 (Summer 1989), 6–8; Sergei Hackel, "The Eastern Tradition: Russia," in Cheslyn Jones, Geoffrey Wainwright, and Edward Yarnold, eds., *The Study of Spirituality* (New York: Oxford University Press, 1986), pp. 266–68; Peggy V. Beck, "In the Company of Laughter," *Parabola* 11:3 (Fall 1986), pp. 18–25: for an expression of this idea in the Buddhist tradition, cf. M. Conrad Hyers, *Zen and the Comic Spirit* (London: Rider & Company, 1974), pp. 40, 135.

14. The tradition derived from Augustine thus accentuated dangers and complexity, the awareness of which led to emphasis on the need for discipline—the emphasis that shaped Western monasticism, which sought to institutionalize what had been learned by and from earlier teachers.

    But soon that effort oversimplified to its own "either-or." The memory of Rome's fall and the barbarian invasions in and after the fifth century moved many who sought monastic respite to increasing distrust of self, and especially of self-will. The resulting emphasis on obedience to the monastic rule in time degenerated into formalism, a focusing of attention on mere externals. Those who retained the original insight saw the rule as embodying for their practice what was known of the Christian life. The urging of obedience to the monastic rule marked that age's attempt to "act yourself into a new way of thinking instead of trying to think yourself into a new way of acting." But others made of the same monastic rule yet another either-or idol against which truer spiritual insight yet again revolted; for more on Augustine, see note 7 to Chapter 3.

15. An excellent summary of Luther's theology in context may be found in Jaroslav Pelikan, *Reformation of Church and Dogma* (Chicago: University of Chicago Press, 1984), pp. 127ff. For the point here, and especially its relationship to the core Reformation doctrine of "justification by faith," see especially pp. 154–55. This is volume 4 of Pelikan's series, "The Christian Tradition: A History of the Development of Doctrine," which is especially useful for its columnar format that makes readily available Pelikan's sources. The Maggid of Koznitz story is retold by Friedman, *Dialogue with Hasidic Tales*, p. 39.

16. Hester Goodenough Gelber, "A Theater of Virtue: The Exemplary World of St. Francis of Assisi," in John Stratton Hawley, ed., *Saints and Virtues* (Berkeley: University of California Press, 1987), pp. 15–35.

17. *Alcoholics Anonymous*, p. 58—which is of course part of the heart of the famous chapter, "How It Works."

18. The version of this story that we offer draws most from William Bausch, *Storytelling: Imagination and Faith* (Mystic, CT: Twenty-Third Books, 1984), who attributes it to a tape recording by Belden Lane. Another version, titled "The Baal Shem Tov's Servant," appears in *Jewish Folktales*, selected and retold by Pinhas Sadeh, translated by Hillel Halkin (New York: Doubleday-Anchor, 1989), pp. 357–61, who in "Notes on Sources," p. 442, says: "The text comes from a mid-nineteenth-century book published in Lemberg by Rabbi Ya'akov Kodnir." An-

other version may be found in Meyer Levin, *Classic Hasidic Tales* (New York: Dorset Press, 1931), pp. 165–76, "After the Death." Closer to Sadeh is the version offered by Patai, *Gates to the Old City*, pp. 687–95, who attributes it to *'Adat Tzaddiqim*, by Michael Levi Rodkinson-Frumkin (Lemberg, 1865).

Chapter 5 *Experiencing the Spiritual*

1. This story is retold frequently. We draw directly from Abraham J. Twerski, *Living Each Day* (Brooklyn: Mesorah Publications, 1988), p. 12, meditation for 11 Tishre. Another version may be found in Wiesel, *Souls on Fire*, pp. 89–90.

2. Ancient as is the distinction between "knowledge about" and "knowledge of," its American expression by William James remains a modern classic. See the treatment in his *Principles of Psychology* (New York: Dover, 1950 [facsimile reprint of New York: Henry Holt, 1890]), vol. 1, pp. 221 ff. The point is discussed by James M. Edie, *William James and Phenomenology* (Bloomington: Indiana University Press, 1987), pp. 31–32, and by Gerald E. Myers, *William James: His Life and Thought* (New Haven: Yale University Press, 1986), pp. 274, 314ff. Although this aspect is not directly treated in any of these places, the reader will find it useful to think also on how this distinction was related to the Jamesian interest in mystical phenomena.

3. Leech, *Soul Friend*, p. 46, details how Theophan the Recluse, a representative of the Russian Orthodox tradition, "warned of the danger of self-deception through the sense of inner warmth, and particularly of the danger of over-concern with the physical exercises."

4. Thoreau is quoted by Richard R. Niebuhr, "Looking Through the Wall: A Meditation on Vision," *Parabola* 11:1 (February 1986), 6. The Shen Hui quotation appears in Thomas Merton, *Zen and the Birds of Appetite* (New York: New Directions, 1968), p. 5.

5. Hans-Georg Gadamer, *Truth and Method* (New York: Crossroad, 1988) translation of *Wahrheit und Methode* (Tübingen: J.C.B. Mohr, 1960), pp. 419–20. The translation used here is *via* David Couzens Hoy, *The Critical Circle* (Berkeley: University of California Press, 1978), p. 66. Hoy's whole section on "Understanding and Language," pp. 61–68, will amply reward the thoughtful reader.

6. Retold by de Mello, *One Minute Wisdom*, p. 175.

7. Twerski, *Living Each Day*, p. 341 (meditation for 13 Elul); "sweetness" was also a favorite term of Jonathan Edwards: cf. Elisabeth S. Dodds, " 'My Dear Companion,' Sarah Edwards," *Christian History Magazine* 4:4 (n.d.), pp. 15–17.

8. Ari L. Goldman, *The Search for God at Harvard* (New York: Times/Random House, 1991), p. 232.

9. For a recent example of the Christian East, see "Likeness: The Radiance of Spirit-Bearing Elders," *Epiphany* 9:4 (Summer 1989), 56, 66: "It is not enough to read the lives of the saints and the teachings of the Church from an intellectual point

of view. There is a savor that must be found: the savor of Orthodoxy, the savor of Christian tradition. It is a spiritual taste for which we must cultivate a spiritual hunger."

10. Drawn from Kurtz workshop presentation, "Historical Sidelights on Alcoholics Anonymous," based on the history detailed in Kurtz, *Not-God.*

11. Richard Marius, "What is Human Nature?," *Harvard Magazine* 93:4 (March-April 1991), 121, tells this story, in his review of Richard Pipes, *The Russian Revolution* (New York: Alfred A. Knopf, 1990).

12. See Paula M. Cooey, "Eros and Intimacy in Edwards," *The Journal of Religion* 69 (October 1989), pp. 484–501, on Edwards's "sensuality"—his definition of love as "delight relishing sweetness in the qualifications of the beloved." Cooey also usefully discusses the "tactile quality" of Edwards's images. Also helpful here is Wayne Proudfoot, "From Theology to a Science of Religions: Jonathan Edwards and William James on Religious Affections," *Harvard Theological Review* 82 (April 1989), pp. 149–68. For a more contemporary expression of the sense developed here and in the following paragraph, see Michael Downey, *A Blessed Weakness: The Spirit of Jean Vanier and L'Arche* (San Francisco: Harper & Row, 1986), pp. 57–58.

13. Friedman, *Dialogue with Hasidic Tales,* p. 46.

14. For more on Evagrius Ponticus, see Elizabeth A. Clark, "New Perspectives on the Origenist Controversy: Human Embodiment and Ascetic Strategies," *Church History* 59:2 (June 1990), pp. 145–62, but especially 149ff.; also Gannon and Traub, *The Desert and the City,* pp. 39ff. Best, of course, would be to read Evagrius himself, but his writings are less available in English than in French: Évagre le Pontique, *Traité pratique ou le moine,* tm. 2, édition critique du texte grec, par Antoine et Claire Guillaumont (Paris: Éditions du Cerf, 1971), pp. 506–35. In the paragraphs that follow, we draw also on Paul Jordan-Smith, "Seven (and more) Deadly Sins," *Parabola,* 10:4 (November 1985), pp. 34–45; also on Tugwell, *Ways of Imperfection,* who devotes a full chapter to Evagrius, pp. 25–36.

15. For an early expression of this tradition, see the *Penitential* of the Irish monks: A useful treatment for comparison with the Evagrian understanding may be found in Peter O'Dwyer, *Celi De: Spiritual Reform in Ireland, 750-900* (Dublin: Editions Taillura, 1981), pp. 63–66.

16. Here especially, see Jordan-Smith, "Seven (and more) Deadly Sins," p. 37; also Hausherr, *Penthos,* p. 23, for development of the distinction between *LYPE* and *PENTHOS.*

17. *Twelve Steps and Twelve Traditions,* p. 50.

18. A more modern vocabulary recognizes all "addiction" as involving the desperate, impossible attempt to fill a spiritual void with a material reality. For an insightful exploration of several themes in the paragraph, see John Loudon, "Experiments in Truth," *Parabola* 10:4 (November 1985), pp. 19–23.

19. James, *Principles of Psychology,* vol. I, p. 402.

20. James tells this in "The Sentiment of Rationality," which may be found in John J. McDermott, ed., *The Writings of William James: A Comprehensive Edition* (Chicago: The University of Chicago Press, 1977 [orig. Random House, 1967]), p. 337.

21. James, *Principles of Psychology*, vol. II, p. 561 (italics and caps James's). This is also a main point of James's unfortunately too often overlooked *Talks to Teachers*, which may be found in several reprintings.

22. The quotation on "memory" and the interpretation of Wendell Berry, *Remembering: A Novel* (San Francisco: North Point Press, 1988) are both from Robert McAfee Brown, "Three Sides of Memory," *Christianity and Crisis*, February 20, 1989, p. 31. Just below, the quotation of the Oxford Group insight is from *Twelve Steps and Twelve Traditions*, p. 61; for commentary and context, see Kurtz, *Not-God*, p. 125, with note on p. 353.

23. Based on Ernest Kurtz's workshop presentation, "Spirituality and Storytelling," this formulation is adapted from Kolakowski, *Religion*, pp. 218–19.

24. Wiesel, *Souls on Fire*, p. 153.

25. Corrigan, *Disciple Story*, p. 99.

Chapter 6 Shared Vision, Shared Hope

1. Matina Horner is quoted by William D. Miller, "Dorothy Day and Simone Weil: Two Who Loved God," *New Oxford Review* 55:2 (March 1988), 23.

2. Retold by Buber, *Later Masters*, p. 251.

3. Also in the first century, both Barnabas and the anonymous author of the Didache emphasized that although "God has . . . shown us the 'way of life,' . . . this revelation is not a lump sum on which we can presume. The word of God has to be cultivated [by seeking] out the company of the saints every day, in order to lean on their words." See Simon Tugwell, *The Apostolic Fathers* (London: Geoffrey Chapman, 1989); Peter Brown, "The Saint as Exemplar in Late Antiquity," in John Stratton Hawley, ed., *Saints and Virtues* (Berkeley: University of California Press, 1987), p. 10, quoting Poemen: "Go and join a man who fears God: just by remaining near him you will gain instruction."

   The quotation of Poemen follows its attribution to him by Tugwell, *Ways of Imperfection*, p. 71, but Poemen is here reporting what "Abba Ammonas said": Ward, *The Alphabetical Collection*, p. 180 (Poemen #96). For other expressions of this very important, often misunderstood, early insight see also André Louf, "Spiritual Fatherhood in the Literature of the Desert," in John R. Sommerfeldt (ed.), *Abba: Guides to Wholeness and Holiness East and West* (Kalamazoo, MI: Cistercian Publications, 1982), p. 42, who has Dorotheus quoting Poemen: "The fathers say that staying in a cell is half [of monastic observance], and to see the elders the other half." Chitty, *Desert A City*, offers much detail on the tensions between the anchorite and the cenobitic styles of life.

   The quotation of Rabbi Jacob Yitzhak is drawn from Kallistos Ware, "Symeon the New Theologian," in *Study of Spirituality*, p. 237.

4. For the quotation of Basil, just above, see Andrew Louth, "The Eastern Fathers: The Cappadocians," in Jones, Wainwright, and Yarnold, *Study of Spirituality,* p. 165. The indirect quotation of Augustine is, as indicated, by a member of Alcoholics Anonymous, and out of respect for the A.A. tradition of anonymity at this level of publication, citation is withheld.

5. The final quotation is from *Alcoholics Anonymous Comes of Age,* p. 70 (emphasis Wilson's); the description of the larger context is as presented by Kurtz, "Historical Sidelights on Alcoholics Anonymous."

6. *Alcoholics Anonymous,* 2nd ed. (1955), p. 184. "The reason A.A. works," a popular theory goes, is that it "teaches alcoholics that they need other people." But as the literature of Alcoholics Anonymous makes clear, no one knows better than *drinking alcoholics* that they need others! In some of the most brilliant passages in *Twelve Steps and Twelve Traditions* (see especially the treatment of Steps Six and Seven, pp. 64–78), Wilson delineated the active alcoholic's "demands for domination and dependence." To demand domination or dependence is to need others— the alcoholic's *problem,* A.A. thought and practice make clear, is failure to recognize *how* human beings need each other. Discussion of the "demands for domination and dependence" is also a frequent theme of Wilson's correspondence with A.A. members.

7. The passage describing "the sinful woman" may be found in Luke 7:36–39. The quotation of Vanier is taken from a recording of his Harold M. Wit Lectures at Harvard University, 6 and 7 November 1988: the quotation here is from the lecture of 6 November.

8. This quotation is taken from Vanier's Harvard Harold M. Wit lecture of 7 November 1988. Added details are drawn from Downey, *A Blessed Weakness.*

9. Downey, *A Blessed Weakness,* p. 61: "Although we have been concentrating on the positive qualities of the heart, it can also be ambiguous, even disordered and unruly; a place of great darkness and sin. An encounter with the anguish and suffering of a handicapped, weak, or vulnerable person often stirs up in us a great deal of fear which can bring about hatred and anger and even the desire to harm the weaker person. We are shocked to find ourselves capable of such evil."

10. Retold by de Mello, *Heart of the Enlightened,* p. 40.

11. See Edward Sellner, *Mentoring: The Ministry of Spiritual Kinship* (Notre Dame, IN: Ave Maria Press, 1990). For the history of this practice, see Leech, *Soul Friend.*

12. For a useful discussion of this point, see John C. Raines, "Toward a Relational Theory of Justice," *Cross Currents* 39:2 (Summer 1989), 132; for greater depth of background, Andrew Feffer, "Sociability and Social Conflict in George Herbert Mead's Interactionism, 1900–1919," *Journal of the History of Ideas* 51:2 (April–June 1990), pp. 233–54.

13. For an exploration of this example connected with its source, the thought of anthropologist Clifford Geertz, see Mihaly Csikszentmihalyi, "More Ways Than One to Be Good," review of Carol Gilligan et al., eds., *Mapping the Moral Domain,* in *The New York Times Book Review* (28 May 1989).

14. Sellner, *Mentoring*, pp. 138–39.

15. Leech, *Soul Friend*, p. 42, quoting and citing *Cistercian Studies* 3:1 (1968), p. 17.

16. Retold by Polsky and Wozner, *Everyday Miracles*, p. 394, citing Buber, *Late Masters*, p. 156.

17. Quoted by Mervyn Tower, "Without a Shadow of Compromise: The Unlovable Mystic, St. John of the Cross," in Couve de Murville, *Unsealed Fountain*, p. 78.

18. Edward C. Sellner, "Brigit of Kildare—A Study in the Liminality of Women's Spiritual Power," *CrossCurrents* 39:4 (Winter 1989–90), pp. 402–19. The perspective on Rabbi Jacob Yitzhak is taken *via* Kallistos Ware, "Symeon the New Theologian," in *Study of Spirituality*, p. 237.

19. Retold by Polsky and Wozner, *Everyday Miracles*, p. 23, citing (incorrectly) Buber, *Early Masters*, pp. 8–24; the citation should be to Buber, *Later Masters*, p. 241.

20. Buber, *Early Masters*, p. 107; also retold by Robert L. Cohn, "Sainthood on the Periphery: The Case of Judaism," in Hawley, *Saints and Virtues*, p. 101.

21. Cf. Luke 18:18–23.

22. Darrell R. Reinke, "Martin Luther: Language and Devotional Consciousness," in Elder, *Spirituality of Western Christendom*, pp. 157–58.

23. Based on a story that appears, among other places, in Newman, *Hasidic Anthology*, p. 118; and Buber, *Later Masters*, p. 157.

24. Annie Reich is cited and expanded upon by Janine Chasseguet-Smirgel, *The Ego-Ideal: A Psychoanalytic Essay on the Malady of the Ideal* (New York: W.W. Norton, 1985 [orig. French 1975]), pp. 112ff.

25. Retold by Polsky and Wozner, *Everyday Miracles*, p. 148, citing Buber, *Later Masters*, p. 284.

26. Retold by de Mello, *Heart of the Enlightened*, p. 13.

27. Gershen Kaufman, *Shame: The Power of Caring* (Cambridge, MA: Schenkman, 1980), p. 60. The paragraph preceding the indented quotation draws also on the ideas of Willard Gaylin, *Caring* (New York: Knopf, 1976), pp. 98, 109. Gaylin helps in the discovery that "moving toward the place where we fit" does not exclude efforts to shape the place toward which we are heading so that it will fit us. Spirituality is neither "conservative" nor "liberal," active nor passive, whatever those labels may connote.

28. Adapted from de Mello, *The Song of the Bird*, p. 79; another version of this story may be found in Idries Shah, *Learning How to Learn: Psychology and Spirituality in the Sufi Way* (London: The Octagon Press, 1978), p. 188.

29. Browning, *Pluralism and Personality*, p. 41.

30. "Attention means attending to, tending, a certain tender care of, as well as waiting, pausing, listening. It takes a span of time and a tension of patience." James Hillman, *A Blue Fire: Selected Writings by James Hillman* (New York: Harper & Row, 1989), pp. 18–19.

31. A useful exploration of the riches of this theme may be found in Ray Oldenburg, *The Great Good Place: Cafes, coffee shops, community centers, beauty parlors, general stores, bars, hangouts and how they get you through the day* (New York: Paragon House, 1989), especially his discussion of "third places."

    The prevalence of application of the term "self-help" to Twelve-Step groups, especially to Alcoholics Anonymous, even within apparently careful and critical academic treatments, attests to the pervasiveness of individualism as a cultural assumption. Most early members of Alcoholics Anonymous insisted, "This is not a 'self-help program'—we tried that, and it didn't work: this is a *God-help* program." As used by professionals, the term *self-help* serves the main purpose of differentiating from "help from professional helpers."

32. Leech, *Soul-Friend*, p. 43.

33. Ram Dass and Paul Gorman, *How Can I Help?: Stories and Reflections on Service* (New York: Knopf, 1988), pp. 112–13. See also Barbara Myerhoff, *Number Our Days* (New York: E.P. Dutton, 1979), for a useful discussion as well as further examples.

34. On "silence" as not necessarily the same as *listening*, see Bernard P. Dauenhauer, *Silence: The Phenomenon and Its Ontological Significance* (Bloomington, IN: Indiana University Press, 1980).

Part Two
The Discoveries of Alcoholics Anonymous

1. *The A.A. Way of Life: A Reader by Bill* (New York: Alcoholics Anonymous World Services, 1967), p. 323.

2. The then-current medical understanding is well reflected in "The Doctor's Opinion," the contribution of William Duncan Silkworth, M.D., that appears at the beginning of the book, *Alcoholics Anonymous*.

3. *Alcoholics Anonymous*, p. 83 (italics in the original).

Chapter 7 *Spirituality Is Essential . . . But Different*

1. Based on the story "Alcoholics Anonymous Number Three," as it appears in the second edition (1955) of *Alcoholics Anonymous*, pp. 182–92, supplemented by interviews as detailed in the retelling of this story in Kurtz, *Not-God*, pp. 37–39.

2. Friedman, *Dialogue With Hasidic Tales*, p. 123. On the theme of "the hidden God," see Lucien Goldmann, *Le Dieu Cache*, trans. as *The Hidden God: A Study of Tragic Vision in the Pensées of Pascal and the Tragedies of Racine* (New York: Humanities Press, 1964).

3. Newman, *Hasidic Anthology*, p. 422.

4. The story of the lost little girl is from Polsky and Wozner, *Everyday Miracles*, p. 3. Just above, C.S. Lewis is quoted by John Garvey, "When Caesar Wins: Making God a Metaphor," *Commonweal* 117:4 (23 February 1990), 106. The most pro-

found treatment of the "hidden God" theme may be found in Goldmann, *The Hidden God*; see also Abraham Josuah Heschel, *God in Search of Man: A Philosophy of Judaism* (New York: Farrar, Straus & Giroux, 1955). Specifically on "a sense of God's absence," see David J. Hassel, S.J., "Atheism in Our Prayer," *Review for Religious* 50:3 (May-June 1991), 418ff.

5. Wilson, personal correspondence.

6. Wilson, private correspondence, emphasis in the original.

7. As Wilson reminded one member in a January 1963 letter: "A.A. is not a communion of saints, it is a company of sinners. . . ." Just below, the "through the wound" quotation is from Woodman, "Worshipping Illusions," p. 64.

8. The reconstruction of this story is based on the research detailed in Kurtz, *Not-God*.

9. This correspondence has been reprinted several times in *The A.A. Grapevine*, e.g., in January of both 1963 and 1968.

10. Jung (Zurich) to Wilson, 30 January 1961.

11. This story is based on an actual experience of Ernest Kurtz.

12. R.D. Laing, *Self and Others*, 2nd ed. (London: Tavistock Publications 1969), p. 94. The Thomas Szasz quotation, just below, is from Thomas Szasz, *The Second Sin* (Garden City, NY: Doubleday-Anchor, 1973), p. 21.

   Dr. Leslie Farber, whom we shall see at a bit more length in Chapter 8, offers a brilliant description of this process in his essay, "On Jealousy," in *Lying, Despair, Jealousy, Envy, Sex, Suicide, Drugs, and the Good Life* (New York: Basic Books, 1976), see pp. 196–97. See also Laing's discussion in *The Divided Self* (London: Tavistock Publications, 1960), p. 73, of how the sense of "being an actor" reveals a cherishing of the sense of control and of mastery of one's being. This is also, of course, a large theme of existentialist insight; a good place to begin that aspect of any investigation is the treatment of Rilke by Walter Kaufmann, *Existentialism from Dostoevsky to Sartre* (New York: New American Library, 1975 [expanded ed., orig. 1950]), p. 141.

13. Nathan Ausabel, *A Treasury of Jewish Folklore* (New York: Crown Publishers, 1948), p. 321.

14. A version of this story may be found in de Mello, *Taking Flight*, pp. 46–47; de Mello follows up this story with one of his own:

   "That's a clever dog you have there," said a man when he saw his friend playing cards with his dog.
   "Not as clever as he looks," was the reply. "Every time he gets a good hand he wags his tail."

15. *Alcoholics Anonymous*, p. 570, italics in the original.

Chapter 8 *Not Magic, But Miracle*

1. The first quotation is from D.M. Dooling, "Fire Proveth Iron," *Parabola* 10:4 (November 1985), 52; the second is a comment by Friedman, *Dialogue with Hasidic Tales,* p. 126.

2. "Real Oldtimers Meet with New 'Babies' to Exchange Views on Program," *The A.A. Grapevine* 4:9 (February 1948), 5. Details on the conversation and other such discussions are supplemented by some interviews with and some tape-recorded memories of the participants.

3. Based on the retelling by Belden C. Lane, *Landscapes of the Sacred: Geography and Narrative in American Spirituality* (New York: Paulist Press, 1988), pp. 191–92, who cites but slightly varies Nikos Kazantzakis, *The Greek Passion* (New York: Simon & Schuster, 1953), p. 229. The version we offer in the text draws from both. Note also that a Sufi version of this story may be found in Shah, *Learning How to Learn,* p. 69.

    On what follows here, a useful discussion of this aspect of miracles and miracle-stories may be found in Benedicta Ward, *Miracles and the Medieval Mind* (Philadelphia: University of Pennsylvania Press, 1982), especially the first and final chapters.

4. The suggestion concerning *awe* is by Elpenor, "A Drunkard's Progress," *Harper's Magazine* (October 1986), pp. 42–48. The pen-name "Elpenor" recalls the figure in Homer's *Odyssey* who, having "drunken himself to sleep on the roof of Circe's palace [while Odysseus is dallying with her], awoke in a daze and toppled off the edge, killing himself." Afterward he appeared to Odysseus, who "denied Elpenor the least sip of the blood [of the magical ewe, which gave wisdom,] however piteously he might plead." Robert Graves, *The Greek Myths,* vol. 2 (Harmondsworth: Penguin, 1955), pp. 359–60.

5. The phrase *locating divinity in drugs* is borrowed from Dr. Leslie Farber, concerning whom, more shortly.

6. E. M. Jellinek, *The Disease Concept of Alcoholism* (New Haven: College and University Press, 1950). This quotation is from Jellinek's posthumously published article, "The Symbolism of Drinking: A Culture-Historical Approach," *Journal of Studies on Alcohol* 38:5 (1977), 849–66—edited for publication by Robert E. Popham and Carole D. Yawney.

7. al-Jerrahi, *Irshad: Wisdom of a Sufi Master,* p. 155.

8. "Openness to being changed" is also to be distinguished from the impassioned certainty of the phrase "I have been changed," a foregone conclusion best left to media hucksters.

    The substance of Bill's thoughts on the topic can already be found in the first such talk, "Basic Concepts of Alcoholics Anonymous," an address presented to the Medical Society of the State of New York, Section on Neurology and Psychiatry, May 1944; originally published in the *N.Y. State Journal of Medicine* 44 (1944), 1805–10. This presentation and the others on which we draw here may be found reprinted in *Three Talks to Medical Societies by Bill W., Co-Founder of*

Alcoholics Anonymous (New York: Alcoholics Anonymous World Services, undated [1981 reprinting]), see especially p. 23.

9. *Alcoholics Anonymous,* 1st ed., p. 399; 2nd and 3rd eds., p. 569.

10. de Mello, *Song of the Bird,* pp. 67–68.

11. Lane, "Merton as Zen Clown," pp. 260–61; see also Hyers, *Zen and the Comic Spirit,* pp.104–5, with plate illustrating "Tan-hsia burning the Buddha-image."

12. Ernest Kurtz was a participant in this project; the interchange described took place in southern Connecticut.

13. The best of Farber's essays on "will" are collected in Leslie H. Farber, *Lying, Despair, Jealousy, Envy, Sex, Suicide, Drugs, and the Good Life* (New York: Basic Books, 1976). The points developed here draw especially on "Thinking about Will," pp. 3–12, and "Our Kindly Family Physician, Chief Crazy Horse," pp. 106–19. The phrase "locating divinity in drugs" appears on p. 119.

14. A concise summary of the Midas story may be found in Herbert Spencer Robinson and Knox Wilson, *Myths and Legends of All Nations* (Savage, MD: Rowman and Littlefield, 1976 [1950]), p. 92, which reminds that unlike most alcoholics' experience of alcohol, Dionysus obligingly revoked his gift when Midas begged for that surcease; after bathing in the river Pactolus in Lydia, Midas became again ordinarily human, although the river "ever after ran gold."

15. The story is based partially on stories generously made available by former literature teachers and other English majors who have found employment in the addiction-recovery field. They are, incidentally, among the first to point out that addiction to therapies for addiction is, of course, perhaps the most subtly devious form taken by "addiction to addiction."

16. The John Gardner quotation is from *The Art of Fiction* (New York: Vintage, 1985); the third chapter of Part One, "Interest and Truth," pp. 39–81, offers a clear and cogent presentation on the topic of "free will" and that issue's relationship to storytelling. Alasdair MacIntyre explores many useful points on the nature of narrative in *After Virtue* (Notre Dame, IN: University of Notre Dame Press, 1981), especially chapter 15, "The Virtues, the Unity of a Human Life and the Concept of a Tradition" (pp. 190–209), which offers a useful discussion connecting story and quest.

17. Friedman, *Dialogue With Hasidic Tales,* p. 89.

18. Philip Rieff, *The Triumph of the Therapeutic* (New York: Harper & Row, 1966), pp. 93, 98.

19. This is not, of course, to suggest that the reader become an alcoholic. Alcoholics Anonymous holds both "closed" meetings, for members only, and "open" meetings for both members and those curious to learn more about its fellowship and program. Any meeting-book or telephone information service will direct to "open" meetings.

NOTES TO PAGES 130-138

Chapter 9 *An Open-Ended Spirituality*

1. The Wilson quotation is from his private correspondence. Martin Buber is quoted, without citation, by Donald J. Moore, "Buber's Challenge to Christian Theology," *Thought* 62:247 (December 1987), 393.

2. This story is recounted in part in the July 1962 *Grapevine* article titled "Spiritual Experiences" but is based also on Bill's expansion on that story in conversations with his wife and close friends. As it appears here, the story draws also on information from Bill's widow, Lois, 1977 interviews, and conversations with his secretary, Nell Wing, then and later.

3. On the usefulness of architecture as image, cf. Joseph Rykwert, "House and Home," *Social Research* 58:1 (Spring 1991), 54ff.

4. The comic-strip clipping in our files is undated and unattributed to any newspaper, except for the notice "Copyright 1985 Cowles Syndicate Inc." Similarly themed strips appear about once each year in the Sunday Comics section of many newspapers.

5. One penetrating, ironic, sardonic comment on such modern travel may be found in the psychiatrist's long monologue in the Peter Shaffer play *Equus* (New York: Avon Books, 1974), p. 95.

6. In *The Power of Myth* (New York: Doubleday, 1988), p. 230, Joseph Campbell attributes this formulation to Karl(fried) Graf Durckheim.

7. This quotation is Tugwell's intepretation of Macarius: *Ways of Imperfection,* p. 48.

8. The quotation is offered by Tugwell, *Ways of Imperfection,* pp. 86–87, citing the Derwas Chitty Paris edition of 1966.

9. This passage appears in that author's "Epistle on Discretion of Stirrings." Although this interpretation is inspired by Tugwell, *Ways of Imperfection,* p. 182, it draws more proximately on our reading of William Johnston, *The Mysticism of the Cloud of Unknowing* (Hertfordshire: Anthony Clarke Books, 1978).

10. Tugwell, *Ways of Imperfection,* p. 211.

11. We are grateful to Joseph Monda, professor of medieval studies at Seattle University, for his help in polishing this image and his generous making available of his classroom experience with using Alcoholics Anonymous as a way of illumining medieval practice.

It merits noting that the "she" in the text is neither anachronistic nor a fawning to feminist sensibility. Recall Chaucer: the Prioress, the Wife of Bath, the Nun's Tale. Historian and theologian Margaret Miles reminds that the very first pilgrim was a woman—even before Augustine wrote his *City of God,* which first set forth the theology of Christian life as pilgrimage, Egeria, a Christian woman from northern Europe, traveled to Jerusalem and the holy places and recorded her impressions of what she saw in letters to her "sisters" at home. Miles also suggests that the first "celebrity" pilgrim was Helena, mother of the Emperor Constantine.

12. Henry Miller is quoted by Lane, *Landscapes of the Sacred*, p. 8. The lines from "Little Gidding" appear on p. 39 of Eliot, *Four Quartets*. The Rilke is by way of Margaret Miles, *Practicing Christianity*, p. 75, who, in emphasizing the dynamic quality of Christian life, quotes "staying is nowhere." The source is Rilke's *Denn Bleiben ist nirgends.* For the Confucian quotation and Master Ummon, Winokur, *Zen to Go*, p. 95.

13. André Lacocque and Pierre-Emmanuel Lacocque, *The Jonah Complex* (Atlanta: John Knox Press, 1981), p. 54.

14. The closest thing to "official" in Alcoholics Anonymous, wherein all authority resides in the individual groups, is the annual meeting of delegates chosen regionally by the groups. These meetings are called General Service Conferences, and each issues a Final Report summarizing the matters discussed and the questions asked at the meeting. The quotation here is from the Final Report of the 8th General Service Conference of Alcoholics Anonymous, 1958, p. 20.

15. Chapter 5 of the book *Alcoholics Anonymous*, pp. 58–71 (2nd and later eds.) is titled "How It Works." Its opening paragraph describes those "unfortunates" who are "constitutionally incapable of being *honest* with themselves" as among those who could "fail" in "this simple program" because "they are naturally incapable of grasping and developing a manner of living which demands rigorous *honesty.*" Even "those who suffer from grave emotional and mental disorders," however, may "recover if they have the capacity to be *honest*" (p. 58, italics added).

16. The Wilson quotation is from his personal correspondence; the idea may be found echoed in almost these exact words by Wilson in *Alcoholics Anonymous Comes of Age*, p. 74.

17. Quoted by Beatrice Bruteau, "The Immaculate Conception, Our Original Face," *Cross Currents* 39:2 (Summer 1989), 193.

18. de Mello, *One Minute Wisdom*, p. 23.

19. Although this tale can be found in more detailed form in Jan Knappert, *Myths and Legends of the Swahili* (London: Heinemann, 1970), pp. 132–33, we offer this retelling by Marina Warner, in "That which is spoken," a review of *The Virago Book of Fairy-Tales*, ed. Angela Carter, *London Review of Books* (8 November 1990), 21–22; we prefer this source because, in a stunning example of what makes her reviews sparkle, Warner adds: "Angela Carter writes: 'Swahili storytellers believe that women are incorrigibly wicked, diabolically cunning and sexually insatiable; I hope this is true, for the sake of the women.' There can rarely have been more diverting footnotes to a volume of folklore."

Chapter 10 A Pervasive Spirituality

1. Based on conversations with participants at one of the workshops presented by Ernest Kurtz under the auspices of the Professional Development Program of the School of Applied Social Science, the University of Chicago. This particular 1990

program was offered in Oak Park, IL, and drew a number of participants from the western suburbs of Chicago.

2. This story is drawn from the personal experience of Ernest Kurtz, who was the presenter.

3. *Alcoholics Anonymous*, pp. 72–73.

4. Buber, *Later Masters*, p. 177.

5. The history alluded to here draws from details that may be found in diverse sources: Ernest Kurtz, *Not-God;* Nan Robertson, *Getting Better: Inside Alcoholics Anonymous* (New York: William Morrow, 1988); and the two more recent A.A.-published histories, *Pass It On: The Story of Bill Wilson and How the A.A. Message Reached the World* (New York: Alcoholics Anonymous World Services, 1984) and *Dr. Bob and the Good Oldtimers: A Biography, with Recollections of Early A.A. in the Midwest* (New York: Alcoholics Anonymous World Services, 1980), supplemented by many interviews and conversations in the course of researching the history of Alcoholics Anonymous. Of special help on these matters was Niles P., chief researcher of the *Dr. Bob* book.

6. Before publication, a draft of the book *Alcoholics Anonymous* was circulated in multilith form, requesting comments of some professionals as well as of members. This is the version that appears in that earliest circulated draft.

7. Sadeh, *Jewish Folktales*, p. 179.

8. O'Reilly, *Toward Rhetorical Immunity*, p. 261—although technical and complex, this is a rewarding study of some of the ways in which storytelling works in Alcoholics Anonymous.

9. The Hasidic tale is *via* Buber, *Later Masters*, p. 173; Thoreau is quoted by Hendrickson, *American Literary Anecdotes*, p. 220.

10. For the deeper spiritual resonances of this insight, beyond alcoholics, see C.S. Lewis, *Perelandra* (New York: Macmillan, 1965 [1944]), for the most direct entry to this exploration, especially pp. 47–48; this work is one of three in Lewis's "Space Trilogy."

11. The quotation used here comes proximately from Michael E. Zimmerman, *Eclipse of the Self* (Athens, OH: Ohio University Press, 1981), p. 120, who here draws on and develops Calvin Schrag's analysis of Kierkegaard's "ecstatic conception of time."

Zimmerman also credits within this quotation Hannah Arendt, *The Life of the Mind,* Vol. II, *Willing* (New York: Harcourt Brace Jovanovich, 1978), p. 178.

12. Jean-Paul Sartre, *Portrait of the Antisemite,* as reprinted in Kaufmann, *Existentialism from Dostoevsky to Sartre,* p. 333. This passage "represents a slightly abridged version of the first part of *Réflexions sur la question Juive*," according to Kaufmann, p. 280.

The William James quotation, just below, is from "The Gospel of Relaxation," in William James, *Talks to Teachers* (New York: W.W. Norton, 1958), pp. 140–41. The talks were first given in 1892, first published in 1899.

13. The precise Auden and Kierkegaard sources are lost in the mists of past reading and an (appropriately?) imperfect database; Twain is quoted by William Least Heat Moon, *Blue Highways: A Journey into America* (Boston: Little-Brown, 1982), p. 9.

14. Retold by Joseph Bruchac, as reprinted under the title: "Salish: How the Mink Stole Time," *Parabola* 15:1 (Spring 1990), p. 77.

15. Adapted from Lacocque and Lacocque, *The Jonah Complex,* p. 51, and conversations with Professor Andre Lacocque of the Chicago Theological Seminary. See Wiesel, *Souls on Fire,* p. 227: "Oblivion is at the root of exile the way memory is at the root of redemption," the Baal Shem Tov had said.

Part Three
Experiencing Spirituality

1. Huxley is quoted without citation by Laurence J. Peter, *Peter's Quotations* (New York: Wm. Morrow & Co., 1977), p. 185.

2. Retold by Joseph Gosse, "Inexhaustible Springs," *Spiritual Life* 36:1 (Spring 1990), 39.

3. On the topic of "a new universe of discourse," the interested reader may find helpful and provocative David A. Snow and Richard Machalek, "The Convert as a Social Type," in Randall Collins, ed., *Sociological Theory* (San Francisco: Jossey-Bass, 1983) pp. 259–89.

4. Retold by de Mello, *Taking Flight,* pp. 111–12.

Chapter 11 *Release*

1. Guillaume Apollinaire is quoted in Susan Hayward, *Begin It Now* (Crows Nest, NSW, Australia: In-Tune Books, 1987), unpaged; Rilke is quoted by Margaret Miles, "Pilgrimage as Metaphor in a Nuclear Age," *Theology Today* 45:2 (December 1988), 174.

2. This story is reproduced from uncitable memory—a more complicated variant may be found in Anthony de Mello, *Taking Flight,* pp. 62–63. On the relationship of such "clinging" to addiction, as explored below here, see the interview with Pauline deDampiere, "The Center of Our Need," *Parabola* 12:2 (May 1987), 24–31.

3. Some may find a kind of unconscious irony in the application of this quotation to Heidegger, as we become more exactly aware of the complexities involved in his relationship to Nazism. Along this line, see Thomas Sheehan, "Heidegger and the Nazis," *The New York Review of Books* (16 June 1988), 38–47, an extensive review of Victor Farias, *Heidegger et le nazisme;* see also Michael E. Zimmerman, "On Vallicella's Critique of Heidegger," *International Philosophical Quarterly* 30:117 (March 1990), 75–100, which offers a detailed treatment of the connections be-

tween Heidegger's thought and this aspect of his life. Despite this newer knowledge, Zimmerman's earlier study remains one of the most balanced and readable studies connecting the thought and the life of the German philosopher: Zimmerman, *Eclipse of the Self,* p. 58.

4. Caussade's most famous work is titled *Abandonment to Divine Providence*—a title that probably guarantees that he will not be read in the modern age. For a useful introduction to Caussade, a presentation that may help the serious reader decide whether to pursue his thought more deeply, we recommend the inspiration for our treatment of Caussade, which here as earlier, although based on the French Jesuit's own writings, is guided especially by Tugwell, *Ways of Imperfection.*

5. Retold by Newman, *Hasidic Anthology,* p. 375.

6. Retold by de Mello, *Taking Flight,* pp. 164–65. There are several other versions and sources, not only in the literature on the Desert Fathers, but in parallel stories told in the Sufi tradition.

7. Helpful on the topics of both "surrender" and "conversion," but especially useful on the latter, is Paul V. Robb, "Conversion as a Human Experience," *Studies in the Spirituality of Jesuits* 14:3 (May 1982), 1–58. Anyone interested in this subject as it pertains specifically to alcoholics remains well advised to begin with the classic articles by Dr. Harry M. Tiebout, "The Act of Surrender in the Therapeutic Process," originally published in the June 1949 *Quarterly Journal of Studies on Alcohol,* and "Conversion as a Psychological Phenomenon," a talk originally given before the New York Psychiatric Society, both now most easily available as reprints from the National Council on Alcoholism and Drug Dependence.

8. James, *Varieties of Religious Experience,* pp. 98–99. Although this is James's chapter on "The Religion of Healthy-Mindedness," and although James refers in this section to "mind-cure," the understanding of William James suggested here differs from that set forth by Donald Meyer, *The Positive Thinkers* (New York: Doubleday, 1965). As James makes clear, he himself was one of the "sick souls," and it is from that awareness that this passage flows. For a deeper exploration of this point in terms at once more "religious" and more Jamesian, cf. Don S. Browning, *Pluralism and Personality,* p. 251.

9. Buber, *Early Masters,* pp. 228–29.

10. The story is retold by de Mello, *Heart of the Enlightened,* pp. 30–31. The recognition here, developed just below, that "the object is not the problem," is one aspect of the fact that Alcoholics Anonymous does not agitate for Prohibition legislation. A.A.'s position, although politically pragmatic, derived from its philosophical commitment to the idea that the problem in alcoholism was not alcohol but the alcoholic. More detail on both how this insight developed and how it was implemented may be found in Kurtz, *Not-God;* for more on this point as related to the tradition of spirituality, see Margaret Miles, *Practicing Christianity,* p. 78, and Gerald May, *Addiction and Grace* (San Francisco: Harper & Row, 1988).

11. Koilpillai J. Charles, *The Power of Negative Thinking and Other Parables from India* (Madras, India: Orient-Longman, 1973), p. 63.

12. See Mark D. Hart, "Reconciliation of Body and Soul: Gregory of Nyssa's Deeper Theology of Marriage," *Theological Studies* 51: (1990), 450–78; in this era saturated with concepts of "codependency" that would label as "sick" the traditional virtues, those more interested in healing than in money-making would be well advised to begin their generous efforts by recognizing how ancient are both their concerns and the availability of wisdom that speaks to those concerns.

13. The language here draws directly on Michael D. Aeschliman, "Discovering the Fall," *This World* 23 (Fall 1988), pp. 91–98.

14. Mary Reuter, "A Second Look: Mysticism in Everyday Life," *Studies in Formative Spirituality*, 5 (1984), 81–93; Mary Reuter, "Time on Our Hands, Time in Our Hearts," *Review for Religious* 46:2 (March–April 1986), 256–65. The Rohr insight treated just below is from Richard Rohr, O.F.M., "A Spirituality for the Laity Today," *The Serran* (September 1987), 3; see also Richard Rohr, "An Amazing Gift of the Spirit," *Praying* 35 (March-April 1990), pp. 12–13.

15. From among the differing versions of this frequently retold folktale, we adapt here from Sadeh, *Jewish Folktales*, p. 183.

16. *Zen Comics*, vol. 2, compiled and drawn by Joanna Salajun (Rutland, VT: Charles E. Tuttle Co. 1982).

Chapter 12 Gratitude

1. The Zimmerman quotation is from *Eclipse of the Self*, p. 247; William Blake is quoted by Aldous Huxley, *Moksha: Writings on Psychedelics and the Visionary Experience* (Los Angeles: J.P. Tarcher, 1977), p. 130.

2. There are several versions of this story; we draw here on Gabriel Daly, "Widening Horizons," *The Tablet* 244:7811 (31 March 1990), 419–20.

3. Barrett, *Irrational Man*, p. 235.

4. This idea, and its connection with the vision of Jonathan Edwards, has been usefully explored by Michael J. Himes and Kenneth R. Himes, "The Sacrament of Creation: Toward an Environmental Theology," *Commonweal* 117:2 (26 January 1990), p. 45. For more on Edwards, the reader is unfashionably advised to begin with the writings of Perry Miller, and perhaps especially his biography of the great New England divine; then, James Carse, *Jonathan Edwards and the Visibility of God* (New York: Charles Scribner's Sons, 1967) and Sang Hyun Lee, *The Philosophical Theology of Jonathan Edwards* (Princeton: Princeton University Press, 1988).

5. Newman, *Maggadim and Hasidim*, p. 159.

6. Amy Tan, *The Joy Luck Club* (New York: G.P. Putnam's Sons, 1989), p. 70.

7. Another story that is found in several Middle Eastern traditions, this version is taken from Sadeh, *Jewish Folktales*, p. 305.

8. Hoffer is quoted without specific citation by James Hillman in Sy Safransky, "The Myth of Therapy: An Interview with James Hillman," *The Sun;* Issue 185 (April 1991), 2–19.

9. A story that can be found in many rabbinic collections, this version is taken from Twerski, *Living Each Day,* p. 176 (meditation for 26 Adar Sheni).

10. *Alcoholics Anonymous,* p. 59.

11. A challenging and thought-provoking interpretation of the experience described may be found in Gregory Bateson, "The Cybernetics of 'Self': A Theory of Alcoholism," *Psychiatry* 34:1 (1971), 1–18—perhaps more readily available in its reprinting in Bateson, *Steps to an Ecology of Mind* (San Francisco: Chandler Publishing, 1972), pp. 309–37.

12. Stanton Peele with Archie Brodsky, *Love and Addiction* (New York: Signet, 1975), p. 237. Although opinionated and a bit overreaching, this provocative early study avoids the traps of many later extensions of the concept of "addiction."

13. Newman, *Hasidic Anthology,* p. 485.

14. Ernest Kurtz participated as organizer of the workshop at which this exchange took place; Bonnie Brandel of Minneapolis was the presenter, and this story is told here with her generous permission.

15. Buber, *Later Masters,* p. 277.

16. Wiesel's Nobel Prize acceptance speech was reported in *The New York Times* for 11 December 1986, which is the version that we follow here. In the version of his addresses that appears in *From the Kingdom of Memory: Reminiscences* (New York: Summit Books, 1990), the first two paragraphs appear on pp. 235–36; the paragraph that we have placed last appears on p. 233.

Chapter 13 *Humility*

1. St. Bernard is quoted without citation by Kreeft, *Making Sense out of Suffering,* p. 58; the Mowrer is from Mowrer, "Small Groups in Historical Perspective," in Leonard D. Borman, ed., *Explorations in Self-Help and Mutual Aid* (Evanston IL: Center for Urban Studies—Northwestern University [1974]) p. 47.

2. Retold by Idries Shah, *Wisdom of the Idiots* (London: Octagon, 1979), p. 168.

3. *Gesta Romanorum,* Rev. Charles Swan translation, revised and corrected by Wynnard Hooper (New York: AMS Press, 1970 ["reprinted from the edition of 1894, London"]), p. 58.

4. The authors extend gratitude to the imaginative flavor-namers of both the Häagen-Dazs and Baskin-Robbins companies and especially the employees of the latter in Walla Walla and Ann Arbor for their enthusiastic encouragement of this aspect of our research.

5. Although this insight appears in many forms in many traditions, this most succinct statement of it is borrowed from Shah, *Learning How to Learn,* p. 121.

6. Another story told of various place-holders in diverse traditions (Roman Catholics seem to prefer the category "Monsignor"), this retelling is taken proximately from Dass and Gorman, *How Can I Help?*, pp. 28–29; another version may be found in de Mello, *Taking Flight*, p. 116.

7. Dag Hammarskjöld, *Markings* (New York: Ballantine, 1964), p. 151 (emphasis Hammarskjöld's).

8. Retold in *Yiddish Folktales*, ed. Beatrice Silverman Weinreich, trans. Leonard Wolf (New York: Pantheon, 1988), p. 306.

9. Retold by Alexander Eliot, "Astonishing Delphi," *Harvard Magazine* 92:4 (March-April 1990), 18–20.

10. The story retold here is a familiar myth found in many of the ancient Christian Fathers. A less Christological version of this story also appears in the Islamic tradition: see Charles Le Gai Eaton, *Islam and the Destiny of Man* (Albany, NY: State University of New York Press, 1985), pp. 181–82. This whole chapter of Eaton, "The Human Paradox," offers—from a generally unfamiliar perspective—useful insight into our chapter's theme.

    It also merits noting here how thoroughly this ancient mythic tale reveals the calumny of the accusation that Christian tradition demeans the human. This story was a favorite jumping-off point for the early Church Fathers to discuss the high dignity of human being: "we whom even the Cherubim and Seraphim honor."

11. Retold by Newman, *Hasidic Anthology*, p. 430; another version may be found in Fuller, *Thesaurus of Anecdotes*, p. 50.

12. On Lincoln's spiritual stature, the best introduction is Sidney Mead, "Abraham Lincoln's 'Last, Best Hope of Earth'; The American Dream of Destiny and Democracy," *Church History* 23 (March 1954), pp. 3–16, reprinted in Mead, *The Lively Experiment* (New York: Harper & Row, 1963), pp. 72–89. Mead offers a favorite quotation that might be seen as summing up Lincoln's perception of the difference between "spiritual" and "religious": "[Lincoln] once remarked that the Bible teaches us that all men are sinners, but he reckoned that we would have found that out merely by looking about us." Thérèse is quoted by Margaret Dorgan, "Thérèse of Lisieux: Mystic of the Ordinary," *Spiritual Life* 35:4 (Winter 1989), p. 201. In the following paragraph, the quotations of Thérèse are *via* Tugwell, *Ways of Imperfection*, p. 221ff., which offers an analysis of the themes being presented here.

13. Austin MacCurtain, in a review of John Updike's *Self-Consciousness* that appeared in *The* [London] *Times Literary Supplement*, as quoted by Martin Marty in *Context* 21:15 (15 August 1989), p. 3.

14. Richard R. Peabody, *The Common Sense of Drinking* (Boston: Little, Brown, 1931); the term *ex-alcoholic* appears also in the published and unpublished papers of Dr. Alexander Lambert, director of the Bellevue Hospital Clinic for most of the first third of the twentieth century, as well in the literature that derived directly or indirectly from the early twentieth-century Emmanuel Movement. See Katherine

McCarthy, "Early Alcoholism Treatment: The Emmanuel Movement and Richard Peabody," *Journal of Studies on Alcohol* 45:1 (1984), pp. 59–74.

For those interested in following this development in successive editions of the A.A. Big Book, a good place to begin is the last word on the top line of page 20 in the second and later editions, which was the sixth line on page 30 in the first edition printings. (The pagination change occurred because Dr. William Duncan Silkworth's introductory "The Doctor's Opinion," which began on page 1 in the first edition, is paginated in roman numerals in later editions.)

15. Adapted from Newman, *Hasidic Anthology*, p. 413.

16. Sa'di, *Tales from the Gulistan*, trans. Sir Richard Burton (London: Philip Allan & Co., 1928), p. 66.

Chapter 14 Tolerance

1. "Who Is a Member of Alcoholics Anonymous?" *The A.A. Grapevine* 3:3 (August 1947), reprinted in *The Language of the Heart: Bill W's Grapevine Writings* (New York: The A.A. Grapevine, 1988), p. 37.

2. There are several versions of this long-lived anecdote; for example, Fuller, *Thesaurus of Anecdotes*, p. 80.

3. The Wilson quotation that begins the paragraph: the setting was the Yale University Summer School of Alcohol Studies, 1944; the provocation, a question asked at the conclusion of Wilson's presentation on "The Fellowship of Alcoholics Anonymous." "Mr. Wilson, could you sum up for us in one sentence how Alcoholics Anonymous works?" One of those present remembered how "Bill's knuckles tightened on the lectern, as he sensed the impertinence of the question." With a tense smile Bill replied by quoting this saying, "Honesty gets us sober, but tolerance keeps us sober," which he habitually attributed to Dr. Bob Smith.

On the wider topic of the relationship between *tolerance* and *forgiveness*, see Christopher Lasch, *The True and Only Heaven: Progress and Its Critics* (New York: W.W. Norton, 1991), p. 375, which draws on the thought of Reinhold Niebuhr to point out that, "Forgiveness, not tolerance, furnished the proper corrective to the egoism and self-righteousness of groups."

4. A deeper exploration of this phrase and its meaning may be found in Kurtz, *Not-God*, pp. 214–15, 221–24.

5. There are several versions of this story, but most that we found seemed based on Buber, *Early Masters*, pp. 142–43, which we have adapted.

6. Another ancient anecdote, proximately retold by de Mello, *Song of the Bird*, p. 65. It can also be found in Fuller, *Thesaurus of Anecdotes*, pp. 408–9.

7. Buber, *Early Masters*, p. 313, which we have adapted.

8. Anonymous, "Not Eating Dates," *Parabola* 12:2 (May 1987), p. 81, which cites as "from *Tales Told by Hazrat Inayat Khan* (New Lebanon, NY: Sufi Order Publications, 1980)." A similar story—not about Mohammed and concerning sugar

rather than dates, may be found in Idries Shah, *Pleasantries of the Incredible Mulla Nasrudin* (London: Jonathan Cape, 1968), p. 107.

9. Stewart, *World of the Desert Fathers,* p. 22.

10. In Europe, this change began in August 1914, with the outbreak of World War I. For context, see Barrett, *Irrational Man.*

11. On both the way alcoholics think and contemporary medical and religious understandings, see George Vaillant, *The Natural History of Alcoholism* (Cambridge: Harvard University Press, 1983); James E. Royce, *Alcohol Problems and Alcoholism: A Comprehensive Survey* (New York: Free Press, 1988); also, for the thinking of alcoholics as limned here, the articles of Dr. Harry Tiebout, earlier cited, and perhaps most usefully his correspondence with Wilson over the question of the ratio of non-alcoholics to alcoholics among A.A.'s trustees, described by Kurtz, *Not-God,* pp. 138–42. Tiebout's thought may be most accessible in the reprinting of his article "Therapeutic Mechanisms of Alcoholics Anonymous," which originally appeared in *The American Journal of Psychiatry* (January 1944), in *Alcoholics Anonymous Comes of Age,* pp. 309–19: The "Mr. X." so carefully analyzed therein is, of course, none other than Bill Wilson. For further development of the wider theme, see not only Lasch, *True and Only Heaven,* but also Toulmin, *Cosmopolis,* and Kolakowski, *Modernity on Endless Trial.*

12. The four quotations here are from Wilson's private correspondence. The first responds to a request to offer advice to members of Recovery, Incorporated, after the death of their founder, Dr. Abraham Low. The third is from a letter of Wilson to a woman who had written Bill to complain of "goings-on" in her A.A. group, wherein what that generation termed "wolves" habitually engaged in what a slightly later generation would call "Thirteenth Stepping"—searching out amorous entanglements with vulnerable newcomers. The final quotation is from a letter of Wilson to a fairly regular correspondent. This member, who lived in California, was in the habit of finding some new, saving guru every six months or so. His correspondence with Wilson follows the pattern of breathlessly sharing his new enthusiasm and Bill rejoicing with him, but cautioning about the enthusiasm itself and pointing out especially, as here, the possible dangers lurking in too-great assuredness.

13. Unamuno, *Tragic Sense of Life,* pp. 135–36. Earlier in his study of "The Tragic Sense," (p. 17), Unamuno's insight found an expression perhaps even more precise to our understanding of Alcoholics Anonymous: "The chiefest sanctity of a temple is that it is a place to which men go to weep in common. . . . Yes, we must learn to weep! Perhaps that is the supreme wisdom."

And in the *Epistle* of the fifth-century pontiff Leo the Great, "the head of the school of the compassionate" according to Jose M. Martelli, we find the axiom: *Lavat aqua, lavant lacrimae:* "As water cleanses, so do tears."

14. Quoted and cited by Campbell, *Hero With a Thousand Faces,* p. 26, as from James Joyce, *Portrait of the Artist as a Young Man* (Modern Library: Random House), p. 239. This is also, of course, the Aristotelian sense of the term.

15. Willard Gaylin, *Caring* (New York: Knopf, 1976), p. 98; the whole of Gaylin's Chapter Six, "Identification," merits thoughtful reading in this context.

16. Buber, *Early Masters*, p. 238, adapted.

17. The "twin poles" formulation is directly from Kaufman, *Shame: The Power of Caring*, p. 64, and appears in a section well worth reading on this topic. For further depth, see Christopher Lasch, *The Minimal Self* (New York: W.W. Norton, 1984). This whole idea is best explored directly in the writings of Donald Winnicott and Margaret Mahler; for a good introduction to this line of thought, it remains difficult to do better than Harry Guntrip, *Psychoanalytic Theory, Therapy, and the Self* (New York: Basic Books, 1973). Subtitled, *A Basic Guide to the Human Personality in Freud, Erikson, Klein, Sullivan, Fairbairn, Hartmann, Jacobson, and Winnicott*, this book actually lives up to that claim!

18. Taken from the workshop presentation "Why It Works: The Intellectual Significance of Alcoholics Anonymous," presented by Ernest Kurtz and based on interviews with Lois Wilson, Nell Wing, and early New York A.A. members.

    It merits noting that, according to his biographer Anthanasius, the Desert Father Anthony made a point of emulating a variety of abbas: "He observed the graciousness of one, the eagerness for prayers in another; he took careful note of one's freedom from anger, and the human concern of another—getting attributes of each in himself, and striving to manifest in himself what was best from all." See Sellner, *Mentoring*, p. 34.

19. Kearns conducted research on recovering alcoholics, using inventories designed to measure personality changes over time. Her work, undertaken as part of a Master's program seminar project, is yet unpublished. Although not her mentor, Ernest Kurtz participated in this study as an academic adviser. The quoted comment is taken from conversation about the study's findings as they emerged.

    Recent years have seen the formation of various "Rational Recovery" and "Secular Organizations for Sobriety" or "Save Our Selves" groups by those who find Alcoholics Anonymous, at least as they have been exposed to it, to be too "religious." Given the variety of A.A. groups, it becomes both easy and difficult to see the need for such efforts. We know of no disciplined study of the newer, wary-of-religion groups, but, impressionistically, they serve an important function, making it possible for some who otherwise would find it impossible to listen at a "regular" meeting of Alcoholics Anonymous to do so in a setting often very like A.A. Also impressionistically, it appears that those who achieve anything resembling what most A.A.s refer to as "true sobriety" in R.R. or S.O.S. groups eventually find "regular" A.A. meetings that meets their needs. There remains, however, a very real need for careful study of this phenomenon and the loving, hurting people involved in it.

20. Twerski, *Living Each Day*, p. 101, meditation for 10 Teves.

21. This is taken from the conclusion of a lecture-presentation offered by Ernest Kurtz, "Why It Works: The Intellectual Significance of Alcoholics Anonymous." It and the image that precedes are developed from the conclusion of "Appendix B" to *Not-God*, pp. 305–6 of the 1991 edition.

Chapter 15 *Forgiveness*

1. The first quotation is from Dominic Maruca, "A Reflection on Guilt," *Human Development* 3:1 (Spring 1982), 42. The second quotation is from Paul J. Tillich, "To Whom Much Was Forgiven," *Parabola* 12:3 (August 1987), 38–45; sermon on text from Luke 7, the sinful woman: "her sins, which are many, are forgiven, for she loved much, but he who is forgiven little, loves little."

2. Retold by de Mello, *Heart of the Enlightened,* p. 107.

3. *Alcoholics Anonymous,* p. 64.

4. As presented and interpreted by Tugwell, *Ways of Imperfection,* p. 29; see also Ernest A. Wallis Budge, ed. and trans., *Stories of the Holy Fathers* (London: Oxford University Press, 1934), pp. 294ff. and the index listings in the same compiler's *Wit and Wisdom of the Christian Fathers of Egypt.*

5. In the words of the A.A. "Big Book": "If we were to live, we had to be free from anger. . . . Anger is the dubious luxury of normal men, but for us alcoholics it is poison." Further useful thoughts on anger may be found in Thomas Buckley, "The Vicious Inherencies: Anger," *Parabola* 10:4 (November 1985), pp. 5–6, on whom we draw here. The Sufi quotation is *via* Ehsan Motaghed, *What Says Saadi* (n.p.: n.p, 1986) p. 8.

6. Perhaps the earliest form of this game is the Japanese *janken.* See Eric Korn, "The Meaning of Mngwotngwotiki," *London Review of Books* (10 January 1991), p. 16. The idea has been used by, for example, Sheldon Kopp, *Rock, Paper, Scissors* (Minneapolis: CompCare, 1989), although our interpretation of the image here more closely parallels Buckley, "Vicious Inherencies."

7. John Patton, *Is Human Forgiveness Possible?* (Nashville: Abingdon Press, 1985), p. 179.

8. "The endpoint of human life": Wilkie Au, "Striving for Spiritual Maturity: Ideals as Obstacles," *Review for Religious* 48:4 (July-August 1989), p. 506: "Unlike the contemporary tendency to absolutize fulfillment as the basic truth and the final goal of human existence, faith reiterates the good news that forgiveness is the endpoint of human life."

   "Forgiveness belongs to the divine": D.M. Dooling, "This Word Forgiveness," *Parabola* 12:3 (August 1987), p. 6–9. Related themes, based on her own experience of having experienced physical torture, are treated simply and well by Sheila Cassidy, "Seventy Times Seven," *The Tablet* 245:7857 (2 March 1991), pp. 267–68.

9. Little of this research has yet been published, but the interested reader might see Jan O. Rowe, Steen Halling, Emily Davies, Michael Leifer, Diane Powers, Jeanne vanBronkhorst, "The Psychology of Forgiving Another: A Dialogal Research Approach," in R. Valle, R. and S. Halling, eds., *Existential-Phenomenological Perspectives in Psychology: Exploring the Breadth of Human Experience* (New York: Plenum, 1989), pp. 233–44.

   Some of what follows here draws also on Ernest Kurtz's experience with a similar research project at the Institute for Pastoral Studies at Loyola University of Chicago.

10. This is cobbled together from different interviews; the source of the interview on which this most strongly draws requested anonymity of person, place, and time.

11. Miles, *Practicing Christianity*, p. 126. Lawrence S. Cunningham, from "Old Prayers Made New," *Theology Today* 4 (October 1987), pp. 360–64; the summary of Thérèse is presented by Tugwell, *Ways of Imperfection*, p. 229. See also Margaret Dorgan, "Thérèse of Lisieux: Mystic of the Ordinary," *Spiritual Life* 35:4 (Winter 1989), pp. 201–17, and Barbara Corrado Pope, "A Heroine Without Heroics: The Little Flower of Jesus and Her Times," *Church History* 75:1 (March 1988), pp. 46–60.

12. James Brown, "Finding God in the Ordinary," review of George Dennis O'Brien, *God and the New Haven Railway, and Why Neither One Is Doing Very Well, Cross Currents* vol. 37, nos. 2–3 (Summer/Fall 1987), pp. 314–316.

13. This story is well told by Jose-Maria Martelli, *Confessions to Lay Persons in the 8th, 9th, 10th, and 11th Centuries,* author's English translation of a doctoral dissertation submitted (in Latin) to the Pontifical Institute of Liturgy, San Anselmo, Rome, 1991. Martelli's English-language citations include: Jose Ramos-Regidor, "Reconciliation in the Primitive Church and Its Lessons for Theology and Pastoral Practice Today," *Sacramental Reconciliation,* Concilium, v. 61 (New York: Herder & Herder, 1971), p. 77; Paul F. Palmer, *Sacraments and Forgiveness: Sources of Christian Theology II* (Westminster, MD: Newman Press, 1959), p. 17; O. D. Watkins, *A History of Penance* (London: Longmans, Green and Co., 1920).

14. Twerski, *Living Each Day*, p. 70—meditation for 9 Kislev.

15. Twerski, *Living Each Day*, p. 333—meditation for 5 Elul.

16. Retold by Idries Shah, *The Way of the Sufi* (New York: E.P. Dutton, 1968), p. 190.

17. The quoted words are from Au, "Striving for Spiritual Maturity."

18. Thomas Szasz, *The Second Sin* (Garden City, NY: Doubleday-Anchor, 1973), p. 51; Arthur Schopenhauer, *The Pessimist's Handbook,* trans. T. Bailey Saunders (Lincoln: University of Nebraska Press, 1964), p. 728.

19. Cf. D.M. Dooling, "This Word Forgiveness," from *Parabola,* as cited above in this chapter; also, Dominic Maruca, "A Reflection on Guilt," *Human Development,* 3:1 (Spring 1982), 40–42.

20. Many of the ideas in what follows here were first stimulated by a paper written by Mrs. Elisabeth Schanzenbach, a graduate student of Professor James E. Royce, of Seattle University, almost a decade ago.

21. Twerski, *Living Each Day*, p. 342—meditation for 14 Elul.

22. Adapted from the retelling by de Mello, *Taking Flight,* p. 64; for Islam and the divine names and the primacy of compassion, see Eaton, *Islam and the Destiny of Man.*

23. This story is drawn from one told in Dass and Gorman, *How Can I Help?,* pp. 51–54.

Chapter 16 *Being-at-Home*

1. The John Cowper Powys quotation is offered without citation by Martin E. Marty, *Context* 21:25 (15 August 1989), p. 6; Anatole France is quoted (without attribution) by J.C. Wynn, "The Hole in Our Holiness Is Other People," *Spiritual Life* (Fall 1989), p. 162.

2. This story was portrayed in the 1976 ABC television movie *The Boy in the Plastic Bubble*. Aspects of it may also be found recounted in Barry Reisman, *Jared's Story* (New York: Crown, 1984) and in Peter Kreett, *Making Sense of Suffering* (Ann Arbor, MI: Servant Books, 1986), pp. 5, 89.

3. A diffuse but challenging exploration of this theme may be followed in Helen Merrell Lynd, *On Shame and the Search for Identity* (New York: Harcourt, Brace & World, 1958); for a related perspective, see Kaufman, *Shame: The Power of Caring.*

4. Wendy Kaminer, "Chances Are You're Codependent Too," *The New York Times Book Review* (11 February 1990), 1, 26–27. The anti-woman nature of the codependecy ideology has been acutely noted and commented on by Ann Maureen Gallagher, "Book World" (reviews of books by Melody Beattie and Anne Wilson Schaef), *The Catholic World* 232:1390 (July-August 1989), 182–83; by Ellen Luff, "The Codependency Movement: The Challenge to Feminists," *Psychology of Women* (Newsletter of Division 35, American Psychological Association) 17:3 (Summer 1990), 3–4; by Carol LeMasters, "Reading Codependency," *Christianity and Crisis* (June 18, 1990), 200–203; by Ramona Asher and Dennis Brissett, "Codependency: A View from Women Married to Alcoholics," *The International Journal of Addictions* 23:4 (1988), 331–50. For a broader critique, see Tadeusz Gierymski and Terence Williams, "Codependency," *Journal of Psychoactive Drugs* 18:1 (January–March 1986), 7–13; [Anonymous], "The Culting of Codependency," *7 Days* (1 November 1989). And for perhaps the best overall perspective on this whole matter, Fred Siegel, "Blissed Out & Loving It: The Eighties & The Decline of Public Life," *Commonweal* 117:3 (9 February 1990), 75–77.

5. Garvey, *Prematurely Saved,* p. 39.

6. Some decades ago, in one of the many reflections of the spirituality of imperfection, psychiatric thinkers Donald Winnicott and Margaret Mahler urged on parents the goal of being "good enough" mothers and fathers. Humility involves not only the embrace of one's own human be-ing as "good enough"; it entails also the recognition and acceptance of others' *good-enough-ness.*

7. The question arises, "Why the tendency to ignore, to deny all this, just now?" One might almost suspect that belief in a rational universe, a belief apparently difficult to shake, leads *either* to belief in an afterlife of reward or punishment *or* to a belief that in one way or another, "the sins of the parents" are visited on their offspring. Among the ancients, a son inherited his father's moral as well as financial debts. Belief in an afterlife in which one paid one's own debts freed offspring of that burden. But now that most no longer believe in an afterlife . . . ? Does some

weird sense of justice require that "children of alcoholics" suffer in an age so enlightened that alcoholics themselves no longer need to?

Someone aware of spirituality's story might push the question further: Might at least some part of all the recent focus on *family*-as-cause signal a kind of trace hangover of some belief in a strange kind of "original sin"—an "inherited" guilt more fearsome and loathsome than any medieval beast-painter or Puritan carica-ture could conceive? Discoveries of parental influence, after all, are hardly all that new. But in treating of the worst aberrations especially in those areas now glibly labeled "addictions," most ancient thinkers attributed such inordinate attachments to the delusions to which the human condition is subject, not to specific experiences of a particular childhood. Perhaps the most helpful perspective on these questions is offered by Dodds, *The Greeks and the Irrational.*

8. Retold by, among others, Friedman, *Dialogue with Hasidic Tales*, p. 86, from whom we draw here.

9. Irmgard Schloegl, trans., *The Wisdom of the Zen Masters* (New York: New Direc-tions, 1976), p. 21.

10. This whole point is well discussed by Milton Mayeroff, *On Caring* (New York: Perennial Library, 1971), see especially pp. 67ff.

11. See Jan Rowe, et al., "Exploring Self-Forgiveness," but also the concluding words of the treatments of Steps Five and Eleven in *Twelve Steps and Twelve Traditions.*

12. The Bateson article, which appeared originally in *Psychiatry* 34:1 (1971), 1–18, can most easily be found reprinted in *Steps to an Ecology of Mind* (San Francisco: Chandler Publishing, 1972), pp. 309–37; Edward J. Khantzian, "Some Treatment Implications of the Ego and Self Disturbances in Alcoholism," in Margaret H. Bean and Norman E. Zinberg (eds.), *Dynamic Approaches to the Understanding and Treatment of Alcoholism* (New York: Free Press, 1981), pp. 163–88; Michael Balint, *The Basic Fault* (New York: Brunner/Mazel, 1979 [1968]).

13. Retold by de Mello, *Song of the Bird*, p. 129.

14. Much in this paragraph beyond the attributed quotation is drawn from Terry Eagleton, *Literary Theory: An Introduction* (Minneapolis: University of Minnesota Press, 1983), pp. 185ff.

15. Told by L. Patrick Carroll and Katherine M. Dyckman, "Lend Each Other a Hand," *Praying* 29, p. 5.

16. Fairy tales as a way of learning to deal with terror was a major theme of Bruno Bettelheim, *The Uses of Enchantment* (New York: Vintage, 1977). For an example of a story, perhaps more cherished by adults than by children, that conveys the linkage between suffering and "reality," see Margery Williams, *The Velveteen Rabbit* (New York: Avon Books, 1975), pp. 16–17.

"What is real? Does it hurt to be real?"

"Sometimes," said the Skin Horse, for he was always truthful. "When you are REAL you don't mind being hurt."

"Does it happen all at once, like being wound up, or bit by bit?"

"It doesn't happen all at once. . . . You become. It takes a long time. That's why it doesn't often happen to people who break easily, or have sharp edges, or who have to be carefully kept. Generally, by the time you are REAL, most of your hair has been loved off, and your eyes drop out and you get loose in the joints and very shabby. But those things don't matter at all, because once you are REAL you can't be ugly, except to people who don't understand."

17. This story is constructed from details that may be found in Joseph T. Shipley, *The Origins of English Words* (Baltimore: The Johns Hopkins University Press, 1984), p. 163, and Thomas Bulfinch, *The Age of Fable* (London: J.M. Dent & Sons, 1973 [1908]), pp. 266–67; for variant versions that rely more on the Germanic *heim*, see John Hollander, "It All Depends," *Social Research* 58:1 (Spring 1991), p. 37; also Joseph Rykwert, "House and Home," *ibid.*, pp. 52–53.

18. For a bit more on the topic of *boundaries* and spirituality, see Xavier John Seubert, "Weaving a Pattern of Access: The Essence of Ritual," *Worship* 63:6 (November 1989), pp. 490–503: "One of the most primitive and fundamental ways in which we condition and delimit our ability for space is through the body and its extensions. . . . A space is something cleared out, made free, namely, into a boundary, in Greek *peras*. The boundary is not that through which something ceases, but rather—as the Greeks understood it—the boundary is that from which something begins its essence. . . ." pp. 497–98.

19. Deeper discussion of the points in this paragraph can be followed, for the psychologically-inclined, in Janine Chasseguet-Smirgel, *The Ego Ideal* (New York: W.W. Norton, 1985), a translation by Paul Barrows of *L'Ideal du Moi: Essai sur la Maladie d'Idealité* (Paris: Tchou, 1975). The more culturally-inclined might prefer Christopher Lasch, *The Culture of Narcissism* (New York: W. W. Norton, 1978), or, perhaps better for the point here because more recent, Lasch's *The Minimal Self* (New York: W.W. Norton, 1984).

20. Corey Fischer, "Some Notes on Workshops," *Theaterwork* (July/August 1982), pp. 19–21.

21. Buber, *Later Masters*, p. 86.

22. Inea Bushnaq, ed. & trans., *Arab Folktales* (New York: Pantheon Books, 1986), pp. 44–45.

23. Gadamer, *Truth and Method*, pp. 419–20; the translation here is *via* Hoy, *The Critical Circle*, p. 66. Hoy's whole section on "Understanding and Language," pp. 61–68, will amply reward the thoughtful reader. This quotation of Gadamer was used earlier, in our treatment of "hearing"; here, the italics are added to emphasize the aspect of "belonging together."

24. Although he does not use this full vocabulary, Donald P. Spence, *Narrative Truth and Historical Truth* (New York: W.W. Norton, 1982), has influenced our shaping of the idea here.

25. Mary Daly, *Beyond God the Father* (Boston: Beacon Press, 1985 [1973]), p. 159; on this and also the following point, a thoughtful treatment may be found in John Navone, "Four Complementary Dimensions of Conversion," *Studies in Formative Spirituality* 10:1 (February 1989), 27–36—see especially p. 30 for the "community" and "gratitude" point and its relationship to "humility."

26. Although we have come across various versions of this story, the one that rings most truthfully is retold by John M. Staudenmaier, "Restoring the Lost Art: Storytelling, Electronic Media Public Discussion," *The Way* 28:4 (October 1988), 313, who identifies the juggler as street-entertainer Ken Feit, who was killed in a traffic accident in early 1989. It is from Staudenmaier that we borrow and adapt here.

27. Joseph Campbell, *The Power of Myth* (New York: Doubleday, 1988), p. 110.

28. Ward, *Harlots of the Desert*, p. 87; the usual citation for Hillel is *Ethics of the Fathers* 1:14; we here follow the version quoted and cited by Robert Nozick, *The Examined Life* (New York: Simon and Schuster, 1989), p. 156; cf. also the use and citation by Abraham Twerski, *Living Each Day*, p. 218. Another story of related interest, from Buber, *Later Masters*, pp. 231–32:

> The Yehudi was asked: "In the Talmud it says that the stork is called *hasida* in Hebrew, that is, the devout or the loving one, because he gives so much love to his mate and his young. Then why is he classed in the Scriptures with the unclean birds?"
> He answered: "Because he gives love only to his own."

29. *Alcoholics Anonymous,* 1st ed., p. 96; 2nd and 3rd eds., pp. 83–84.

Index

❖

Smith, Dr. Robert Holbrook, 4, 83–84, 96, 103, 105–6, 111, 206–7, 242
Sober alcoholic, 194–95, 200, 203
Sobriety
  for alcoholics, 110–11, 121, 132, 207–9
  as gift, 181–82
Socrates, 6, 32, 33, 111
Sorrow, 182, 231, 241
  vs. callousness, 183
  and spiritual love, 204
Space, 236
Spirit, 33
Spiritual directors. See Spiritual teachers.
Spirituality, 15–16, 124–25, 145
  of acceptance, 61
  and appearances, 31–32
  and being-at-home, 227–42
  beyond control, 31
  "beyond-the-ordinary," 35–40
  and compassion, 48–55
  denial of, 62
  discovering, 1–2, 13, 95
  "earthly," 18
  essential but different, 102, 105–17
  experiencing, 68–81, 160
  expressions of, 3, 46
  false assumptions about, 18
  first insight of, 199
  first step of, 19–20
  and forgiveness, 197, 213–24, 230–31
  as gift, 183
  and gratitude, 175–84
  and health, 17
  and humility, 95, 185–96, 240–41, 242
  "instant," 120, 124–25
  Irish, 89
  many forms of, 2
  message of, 120, 241
  nature of, 21–22
  not magic, but miracle, 102, 118–29
  "one day at a time," 102
  open-ended, 102, 130–43
  pervasive, 102, 144–55
  and release, 163–74, 175, 181
  vs. religion, 23–26
  simplicity of, 35–38
  and storytelling, 7–9
  vs. therapy, 26–27
  and tolerance, 195, 196, 197–212
  and twofold nature, 60
  and weakness, 45–55, 193, 197–99, 204
Spiritual love, and sorrow, 204
Spiritual teachers, 88, 142, 178, 179

Sponsors (A.A.), 207–8
Stories, 142, 182–84
Storytelling, 7–9, 17, 63–64, 130, 160
  of alcoholics, 114–16, 202
  and being-at-home, 236–39
  and community, 79–80, 239–40
  and denial, 150
  and freedom, 127–28
  and time, 151
Strength, 45
  and shared weakness, 199, 204
Submission, 221–22
Suffering, 21, 43, 231, 235, 238
Sufis, 214
  sayings of, 186–87
  stories of, 13, 58–59, 81, 93, 121, 171–72, 196, 225
Surrender, 122, 168–69, 181
Suzuki, D.T., 6
Suzuki, Shunryu, 142
Swahili tale, 142–43
Symeon the New Theologian, 89
Szasz, Thomas, 116, 223

T
"Talks to Teachers" (James), 153
Tan-hsia, 123
Technique, and limitation, 123–25
Temptation, 53
Ten Commandments, 21
Teresa, Mother, 17, 111
Thales of Miletus, 188
Thanking, 176
Theodotos, Abba, 49
Therapy, 150
  and spirituality, 27
Thérèse of Lisieux, Saint, 20, 45, 192, 220
Thinking, 132, 176
Thirst, metaphor of, 120, 121–22
Thompson, Francis, 107
Thomsen, Robert, 111
Thoreau, Henry David, 69, 152
Thoroughness, 147
Tiebout, Dr. Harry, 122
Time, 124, 151–55
  and storytelling, 151
Titans, 56
Tolerance, 195, 196, 197–212. See also Fellowship.
  and difference, 199–200, 203
Tolstoy, Leo, 208
"Torn-to-pieces-hood," 2–3, 26, 60, 73, 198, 220

Grateful acknowledgment is made for permission to reprint excerpts from the following:
A Treasury of Jewish Folklore edited by Nathan Ausubel. Copyright 1948, 1976 by Crown Publishers, Inc. Reprinted by permission of Crown Publishers, Inc.; *Irrational Man* by William Barrett. Reprinted by permission of Doubleday, a division of Bantam Doubleday Dell Publishing Group, Inc.; *Pluralism and Personality: William James and Some Contemporary Cultures of Psychology* by Don S. Browning. Reprinted by permission of Bucknell University Press; *Tales of the Hasidim: The Early Masters* by Martin Buber, translated by Olga Marx. Copyright 1947, 1948 and renewed 1975 by Schocken Books, Inc. Reprinted by permission of Schocken Books, published by Pantheon Books, a division of Random House, Inc.; *Tales of the Hasidim: The Later Masters* by Martin Buber, translated by Olga Marx. Copyright 1947, 1948 and renewed 1975 by Schocken Books, Inc. Reprinted by permission of Schocken Books, published by Pantheon Books, a division of Random House, Inc.; *Arab Folktales* by Inea Bushnaq. Copyright © 1986 by Inea Bushnaq. Reprinted by permission of Pantheon Books, a division of Random House, Inc.; Excerpts from Alcoholics Anonymous reprinted with permission of Alcoholics Anonymous World Services, Inc. Permission to use this material does not mean that AA has reviewed or approved the contents of this publication, nor that AA agrees with the views expressed herein; *The Power of Myth* by Joseph Campbell. Reprinted by permission of Doubleday, a division of Bantam Doubleday Dell Publishing Group, Inc.; "Giving Each Other a Hand" by L. Patrick Carroll and Katherine M. Dyckman, *Praying*, 29. Reprinted by permission of *Praying* magazine; *Disciple Story: Every Christian's Story* by Gregory M. Corrigan. Reprinted by permission of Ave Maria Press; "Widening Horizons" by Gabriel Daly. Reprinted by permission of *The Tablet*; *How Can I Help? Stories and Reflections on Service* by Ram Dass and Paul Gorman. Reprinted by permission of Knopf, a division of Random House, Inc.; *Heart of the Enlightened* by Anthony de Mello. Copyright © 1989 by The Center for Spiritual Exchange. Used by permission of Doubleday, a division of Bantam Doubleday Dell Publishing Group, Inc.; *One Minute Wisdom* by Anthony de Mello, S.J. Copyright © 1985 by Anthony de Mello, S.J. Used by permission of Doubleday, a division of Bantam Doubleday Dell Publishing Group, Inc.; *The Song of the Bird* by Anthony de Mello. Copyright © 1982 by Anthony de Mello, S.J. Used by permission of Doubleday, a division of Bantam Doubleday Dell Publishing Group, Inc.; *Taking Flight* by Anthony de Mello. Reprinted by permission of Doubleday, a division of Bantam Doubleday Dell Publishing Group, Inc.; "The Spirituality of the Desert Fathers" by Austin Hughes and "Without a Shadow of Compromise" by Mervyn Towers. Excerpted from *The Unsealed Fountain*, edited by Maurice Couve de Murville. Part of the Oscott Series. Published by Veritas; *Literary Theory* by Terry Eagleton. Copyright © 1983. Reprinted by permission of the University of Minnesota Press; *Four Quartets* by T.S. Eliot. Copyright 1943 by T.S. Eliot and renewed 1971 by Esme Valerie Eliot. Reprinted by permission of Harcourt Brace Jovanovich, Inc.; *A Dialogue with Hasidic Tales* by Maurice Friedman, Insight Books. Reprinted by permission of Human Sciences Press, Inc.; *The Writing of William James: A Comprehensive Edition* edited by John J. McDermott. Reprinted by permission of The University of Chicago Press; *The Varieties of Religious Experience* by William James. Published by New American Library, a division of Penguin USA; Excerpt from Carl G. Jung letter to Bill Wilson is from *Letters*, edited by Gerhard Adler and Amiela Jaffe, translated by R. F. C. Hull. Published by Princeton University Press; *Shame: The Power of Caring* by Gershen Kaufman. Reprinted by permission of Schenkman Books Inc.; *Landscapes of the Sacred* by Belden C. Lane. Reprinted by permission of Paulist Press. This excerpt is based on material that appeared in *The Greek Passion* by Nikos Kazantzakis. Reprinted by permission of Simon & Schuster, Inc.; "Morton as Zen Clown" by Belden C. Lane, *Theology Today*, 46:3. Reprinted by permission of *Theology Today*; *Soul Friend* by Kenneth Leech. Reprinted by permission of HarperCollins Publishers; *The Hasidic Anthology: Tales and Teachings of the Hasidim* and *Maggidim and Hasidim: Their Wisdom* by Louis I. Newman. Reprinted by permission of the author's estate; "Conversion of Heart" by Donald Nicholl. Reprinted by permission of *The Tablet*; "Salish: How the Mink Stole Time" by Joseph Bruchac. Reprinted from *Parabola*, The Magazine of Myth and Tradition, Vol. XV, No. 1; "The Mirrors of Mahayana" by Frederick Franck. Reprinted from *Parabola*, Vol. XI, No. 2; "Worshipping Illusions" by Marion Woodman. Reprinted from *Parabola*, Vol. XII, No. 2; "Not Eating Dates" which appeared in *Parabola*, Vol. XII, No. 2, is reprinted by permission of Omega Press; "Living in Communion" (interview with Thomas Hopko). Reprinted from *Parabola*, Vol. XII, No. 3; *Gates to the Old City: A Book of Jewish Legends* by Raphael Patai. Reprinted by permission of Wayne State University Press; *Is Human Forgiveness Possible?* by John Patton. Reprinted by permission of Abingdon Press; *Everyday Miracles: The Healing Wisdom of Hasidic Stories* by Harold W. Polsky and Yaella Wozner. Reprinted by permission of the publisher, Jason Aronson Inc., Northvale, NJ, © 1989; *Triumph of the Therapeutic* by Philip Rieff. Reprinted by permission of HarperCollins Publishers; *Jewish Folktales* by Pinhas Sadeh. Copyright © 1989 by Doubleday, a division of Bantam Doubleday Dell Publishing Group, Inc. Used by permission of Doubleday; *Mentoring: The Ministry of Spiritual Kinship* by Edward Sellner. Reprinted by permission of Ave Maria Press; *The Way of the Sufi* by Idries Shah. Copyright © 1968 by Idries Shah. Used by permission of the publisher, Dutton, an imprint of New American Library, a division of Penguin Books USA Inc.; "Blissed Out and Loving It: The Eighties and the Decline of Public Life" by Fred Siegel, *Commonweal*, 117:3. Reprinted by permission of *Commonweal*; "Restoring the Lost Art: Storytelling, Electronic Media and Fragmented Public Discussion" by John M. Staudenmaier, *The Way*, 28:4 (October 1988), page 313. Reprinted by permission of *The Way*; *The World of the Desert Fathers*, translated by Dom Columba Stewart OSB. Reprinted by permission of the publisher, SLG Press; *The Joy Luck Club* by Amy Tan. Copyright © 1989 by Amy Tan. Reprinted by permission of The Putnam Publishing Group; *Ways of Imperfection* by Simon Tugwell. Reprinted by permission of Templegate Publishers; *Living Each Day* by Rabbi Abraham J. Twerski, M.D. Reprinted by permission of Mesorah Publications, Ltd.; *The Tragic Sense of Life* by Miguel de Unamuno, translated by J. E. Crawford Flitch. Reprinted by permission of Dover Publications, Inc.; "That Which is Spoken" by Marina Warner, a review of *The Virago Book of Fairy-Tales* edited by Angela Carter, *London Review of Books* (November 8, 1990). Reprinted by permission of *London Review of Books*; *Yiddish Folktales* edited by Beatrice Silverman Weinreich, translated by Leonard Wolf. Reprinted by permission of Knopf, a division of Random House, Inc.; *Eclipse of the Self* by Michael E. Zimmerman. Reprinted by permission of Ohio University Press.